GLASGOW SCHOOL OF ART

The History

The Diploma
awarded at the beginning of this century
authorised by the Scotch Education Department
copper etching by Allan Mainds

GLASGOW SCHOOL OF ART
The History

Hugh Ferguson

THE FOULIS PRESS OF
GLASGOW SCHOOL OF ART

1 9 9 5

First published in 1995 by
The Foulis Press of Glasgow School of Art
167 Renfrew Street
Glasgow G3 6RQ

© 1995 Glasgow School of Art

ISBN 0 901904 25 2

The Publisher gratefully acknowledges financial support from

THE POST OFFICE

Trades House of Glasgow
Arvanitakis Partnership
Weightman and Bullen
The Clydesdale Bank

Designed by
James W Murray

Set in Foundry Wilson
at Glasgow School of Art
This typeface is a modern digitised version of
of one designed and cast in metal by
the Foundry of Alexander Wilson & Son Glasgow
who cast the types used by The Foulis Brothers
in printing their books in the eighteen thirties
Savage [writing in 1822] says, " The Foundry of Messrs. Wilson,
at Glasgow, has been long established,
and for many years enjoyed a monopoly
of letter founding in Scotland.
They have, however, of late experienced formidable competition
from Mr. Miller of Edinburgh,
who has derived his knowledge of the art from them,
and whose types so much resemble theirs as to require
a minute and accurate inspection to be distinguished."

Origination by Arneg Limited
Glasgow
Printed in Scotland
by
Bath Press Colourbooks

Contents

Introduction

Throughout its history Glasgow has been a city of vitality and energy, and it is hardly surprising that at the beginning of its Victorian prosperity was born the institution which is celebrated in this book, the Glasgow School of Art. At its centre, Mackintosh's brilliant conception is admired and respected the world over, as indeed are the distinguished artists, designers and architects who have walked its corridors.

Over the 150 years of its existence, the influence of Glasgow School of Art has extended far beyond the city. During the last decades of the 19th century, when the Glasgow Boys were at their zenith, and Mackintosh, McNair and the Macdonald sisters were creating the Glasgow Style, the School of Art was central to that vibrant community, and our graduates continue to make a much greater impact, at home and abroad, than their numbers might appear to warrant.

It is because of this glorious history that the Board of Governors is determined that the School's independent status, as one of the few remaining dedicated art schools, should extend far beyond its first 150 years, into the new millennium. And there can be no better time than the present, surely, to pause and reflect on our history, and to reminisce on the many talented people who have gone forth from this School to enrich our visual culture, and improve our quality of life.

David J Leslie

CHAIRMAN OF THE BOARD OF GOVERNORS

THE VISITOR: H R H THE PRINCE OF WALES

HON. PRESIDENT: MARY ARMOUR RSA RSW RGI RGI LLD

HON. VICE-PRESIDENT: DAVID A DONALDSON RSA RP RGI LLD

DIRECTOR OF THE SCHOOL: PROFESSOR DUGALD CAMERON DA FCSD FRSA

DEPUTY DIRECTOR OF THE SCHOOL; JAMES COSGROVE DA

ASSISTANT DIRECTOR (RESOURCES): MICHAEL FOLEY CA

PRESIDENT OF THE STUDENTS' REPRESENTATIVE COUNCIL: BOB GRIEVE

The 'Sit Ooteries' from the left foreground: Bob Bushnell, Bill Webster and Elsa Stevens c. 1960

Glasgow School of Art

ESTABLISHED 1844-45

GLASGOW GOVERNMENT SCHOOL OF DESIGN
(Board of Trade)

Approved for Grant 1844. Opened 6 January 1845, at Ingram Street, to 1869

Headmasters: H MacManus (1844-48)
C H Wilson (1849-52, continued to 1863)

GLASGOW SCHOOL OF ART
Ingram Street until 1869
Under Science & Art Department, South Kensington from1853
(Board of Trade & Privy Council)

Headmasters: C H Wilson (1852-1863)
1869 Move to Corporation Buildings (McLellan Galleries)
R Greenlees (1863-1881)
T C Simmonds (1881-1885)
F H Newbery (1885-1917) Director (from 1901)
School transferred to Scotch Education Department 1897.
Became Central Higher Art Institution for
Glasgow and West of Scotland.

Titled SCHOOL OF ART AND HALDANE ACADEMY, 1869-91,
as condition of Haldane Trust grant
(Under Science and Art Department, South Kensington)

THE GLASGOW SCHOOL OF ART
Registered 1892 as Charity Limited Company (Charity). Acquired Renfrew Street site in 1895.
Architectural Competition 1896. Winner announced 1897. Building first half 1897-99.
Transferred to Renfrew Street, first half Mackintosh Building 1899.
Second half completed 1907-1909.

DIRECTORS	CHAIRMEN OF GOVERNORS
F H Newbery (retired 1917)	Archibald Alison (1844-49)
J Henderson (1918-24)	Walter Crum (1849-50)
J D Revel (1925-32)	Andrew S Dalgleish (1850-54)
Sir W O Hutchison (1933-43)	James Hannan (1854-82)
A Walton (1943-45)	Robert H Leadbetter (1882-84)
H Y Alison (Interim Director 1945-46)	Sir James Watson (1884-87)
D P Bliss (1946-64)	Sir James Fleming (1887-1914)
Sir H J Barnes (1964-80)	Patrick S Dunn (1914-30)
Prof. A Jones (1980-85)	John Keppie (1930-37)
T Pannell (1985-88)	Sir John Richmond (1937-50)
W Buchanan (Acting Director 1989-90)	J Norman Cruickshank (1950-59)
J Whiteman (1991)	John D Kelly (1959-70)
Prof. D Cameron (1991 -)	Robert W Begg (1970-76)
	W Leggat Smith (1976-88)
	Henry C Abram (1988-91
	David J Leslie (1991 -)

THE GLASGOW SCHOOL OF ART

The Glasgow School of Art had a very modest beginning in 1840 in which year the Glasgow Government School of Design was founded. On its first Committee of management was the Lord Provost, the Dean of Guild, a Calico Printer, an Engineer, an Engraver, two Shawl Manufacturers, a Delaine Manufacturer, an Upholsterer, a Sewed Muslin Manufacturer, a Goldsmith and a Sheriff. In 1842 the School was recognised by the Board of Trade as a School of Design. The School was founded with a view to the improvement of our National Manufactures and in 1852 was placed under the control of the Science and Art Department of South Kensington.

To pass on to 1869 the Art School was transferred from Ingram Street to the Corporation Buildings, Sauchiehall Street. At that time there were nearly 1200 students. In the same year the Art School benefited from a bequest made by James Haldane, an Engraver, and the School was known as the Glasgow School of Art and Haldane Academy. At this time early morning classes were held from seven until nine and it was in these classes that Sir John Lavery studied. In 1882 under the South Kensington scheme, the School took the greatest number of awards in Scotland and won the largest Government Grant of any Art School in Britain. In 1897 the School took the largest number of medals of any British School.

A HISTORY OF THE ART SCHOOL WOULD BE INCOMPLETE WITHOUT MENTION OF

Charles Rennie Mackintosh

He was born in Glasgow on June 7th, 1869, and was educated at Allan Glen's School. In 1885 at the age of sixteen, he entered the old Glasgow School of Art, for which he was afterwards to build such a celebrated home. Mackintosh won many awards for his designs while still a pupil at the Glasgow School of Art but it was not until 1894 when he was only 25, that his great opportunity came. His design for a new School of Art was accepted from amongst those of half-a-dozen Glasgow competitors. This building has since become part of architectural history, and it is therefore enough to say here that it is brilliantly planned, exactly suited to its purpose and distinguished by a restrained originality. When Mackintosh died in 1928 the Times stated—"It is indeed, hardly too much to say that the whole modernist movement in European architecture looks to him —as one of its chief originators.

On 25th May, 1898, the Foundation Stone of the new School was laid by Sir Rennie Watson, Chairman of the Bellahouston Trustees who had provided a free site for the School. In the following year the control of the School was placed under the Scottish Education Department and on 20th December of the same year, the first portion of the new building was formally opened by Sir James King. In 1901 Article Old Classes for Day School Teachers commenced which later became known as Article 55 Classes. In the same year the School was recognised as the Central Institution for Glasgow and the West of Scotland and authorised to issue Diplomas and Certificates. The official opening of the Art School took place on 15th December 1909.

In looking over the list of distinguished students we find amongst the early records, David Allan and James Tassie. There seems some doubt as to whether Orchardson, Pettie and McWhirter studied here, but it is certain that Joseph Henderson, James Docherty, Colin Hunter, Sir David Murray, Sir D. Y. Cameron, Sir John Lavery, George Henry, Sir John Burnet, Sir W. Reid Dick, Charles Mackintosh, Alex. Roche, Muirhead Bone and Francis Dodd were students at the Glasgow School of Art.

Allan McInnes 1954

Lettering panel from foyer of 'Mackintosh Building. Subsequent investigation has proved that the dates shown are wrong

I

Art and Industry

GLASGOW'S INDUSTRIAL DEVELOPMENT

AT THE TIME OF THE ACT OF UNION, Glasgow had no industry, and such economic life as there was revolved around weaving and fishing, particularly salmon fishing. With the Union, the door was opened for Glasgow merchants to trade with the tobacco-exporting colony of Virginia, and this

was the launch-pad for Glasgow's subsequent prosperity, until the tobacco trade was broken off by the American War of Independence.

Although the Virginia merchants lost a great deal of money, the West India merchants, who had been importing cotton for some time, now began to flourish, and the rapid growth of the cotton industry in Scotland, especially in the area around Glasgow, is the most spectacular development in the last twenty years of the eighteenth century in Scotland.

The need to supply outward cargoes for the tobacco ships had earlier stimulated the growth of a wide variety of local industries in the West of Scotland, linen goods chiefly, and it was the legacy of the fine linen industry which made the transition to cotton feasible. Also, the wealth generated by the big tobacco firms helped to expand industrial activity and played a key role in supplying funds for the development of the Glasgow banks.

Thus, the economic development which provided the springboard for Glasgow's 19th century commerce and industry derived directly from the Act of Union, and the importance of that American and West Indian colonial trade is marked in the names of its streets: Union Street, Virginia Street, Jamaica Street and Glassford Street. Glassford, e.g., is recorded as a financial supporter of the Foulis Academy, and Tobias Smollett tells us in HUMPHREY CLINKER that John Glassford alone owned twenty-five ships and traded for above half a million sterling a year.

In the mid-18th century the River Clyde below Glasgow was much wider than now, and full of sandbanks, to the extent that it was fordable at several points, and ocean-going vessels were loaded and unloaded at Port Glasgow and Greenock, with such goods as had to come up to Glasgow brought up by river

Old Glasgow Bridge c 1820
John Knox.
Panorama of Clyde River front.
Surviving landmarks are
St. Andrew's Cathedral and
Merchant's House Steeple

craft or pack-horse. However, by 1805 the Clyde had been deepened sufficiently to allow the first square-rigged vessel up-river, the SWALLOW OF BELFAST, which caused great excitement at the Broomielaw, drawing crowds to the harbour. And in 1839, Swan, in the commentary to his VIEWS OF THE CITY, could write:

> *The Broomielaw, with its enlivening bustle, and its crowded shipping, presents a foreground of peculiar interest: the bridges, the sweep of the river, its green banks slightly wooded, and the rows of chaste and elegant houses on either side forming Clyde Street and Carlton Place...*

Glasgow was thus fortunate that just when the new cotton industry was being born, she had both the capital and the skilled labour resources necessary to develop it. Also, the fact that the fine linen areas of Lancashire had made the transition to cotton a few years ahead of Glasgow and Paisley meant that the Scots could draw on that experience and technology, without having to pay the heavy development costs of innovation. Most of the machinery for Glasgow's weaving shops and early textile mills was brought from England or the Continent, and it was through maintaining such imported machinery that the city's first mechanics learned their craft. They proved able apprentices, and soon showed an aptitude for improving the inventions of others.

The first cotton mills were dependent on water power, and the countryside around Glasgow had many fast-flowing streams. One of the largest of the new factories was built near the Falls of Clyde at Lanark, by David Dale, and the New Lanark Mill became famous through Robert Owen, Dale's son-in-law, who established a remarkable model village for his work-people there, which has since been restored. Owen and his friends called their utopian ideas "socialism"and the term first appeared in the CO-OPERATIVE MAGAZINE, in 1827.

After 1800 or so, steam-powered looms became general, which meant that new cotton mills could locate in the city, where Glasgow's damp climate proved a positive asset. However, the application of steam power to weaving also marked the beginning of the end for the hand-loom operators, and the first real threat to their livelihoods came as early as 1801, when John Monteith installed two hundred power-looms in his factory in Pollokshaws. By 1818, James Watt's invention had given Glasgow 18 steam-powered weaving factories, 52 cotton mills and 18 calico printing works, and factory chimneys soon began to darken the sky, as their smoke settled in a pall over the city.

In the same year as Monteith installed his power looms, Charles Tennant launched Glasgow's chemical industry by establishing his works at St. Rollox for the manufacture of the bleaching powder he had invented (chloride of lime), soda, vitriol and other substances. This developed into the largest chemical works in Europe, and according to a German observer, its 450-ft high factory chimney, known locally as Tennant's Stalk, "rose over the city and its fog like the Minster over Strasburg."

This, then, was the Glasgow for which a Government School of Design was proposed in 1841, by the Board of Trade, and in which the West of Scotland Academy had just formed itself.

*Foulis Academy
Interior.
Engraving
after painting
by student
David Allan
at age 16.
The Academy
was just a large
Art Room with
a dozen or so
students*

*Engraving of
one-day open-air
Exhibition
in Glasgow College
(University)
by Foulis Academy
in connection with
Royal Anniversary
Holiday 1761
(Details in
Appendix A)*

*New University Library building
of 1745.
Upper floor was given over to
Foulis Academy.
Note correspondence of windows
in interior perspective.*

EARLY ARTISTIC LIFE IN GLASGOW

The history of pictorial art in Glasgow really begins with the Foulis Academy.
The name is preserved in the Glasgow School of Art's Foulis Archive Press and
its Foulis Building, but there is no direct line of descent to the present School.
The Foulis Academy, founded in 1753 and housed in the University buildings,
was the first art school in Britain which set out to train professional artists.
Whereas the Royal Academy disdained trade, the Foulis Academy was created
in the expectation that it would benefit local manufactures and effect a general improvement of taste.

With the encouragement of the University, the brothers Robert and
Andrew Foulis set up their Academy on the upper floor of the New Library, an
Adam building of 1745. A painting of the interior by David Allan shows stu-
dents at work, and Allan himself went on to be Headmaster of the Trustees'
Academy in Edinburgh, which was the earliest state-assisted Art and Design
school in Britain. David Allan also functioned as an industrial designer for the
Carron Ironworks Company, as did Robert Adam, whose designs included
large cast-iron fireplaces with classical decoration.

Robert Brydall, sometime master at the Glasgow School of Art, gives an
account of the Foulis Academy in Art in Scotland (1889), reproduced in part in
Appendix A, and it is noteworthy that the Academy appears to have been the
first art school in the UK to award travelling scholarships - three senior students were sent to Gavin Hamilton's studio in Italy - before the Royal
Academy was established in 1768.

However, the Foulis brothers' venture was undertaken against the advice of
their friends, as Brydall notes, and their pessimism seems to have been justified. In 1764, James Boswell visited Voltaire at Ferney, where the conversation
naturally turned to books:

> *We talked of Scotland. He said the Glasgow editions (by Foulis) were*
> très belles. *I said an Academy of Painting was also introduced there,
> but it did not succeed. Our Scotland is no country for that. He replied
> with a keen archness, "No, to paint well it is necessary to have warm
> feet. It is hard to paint when your feet are cold"...*

As distinct from a private academy, however, the first public institution in Glasgow to offer instruction in the Fine Arts was Anderson's University. Thomas Gilfillan, who was Professor of Drawing & Painting there, taught very large classes, indicating that amateurs were catered for, although aspiring professionals may also have used the classes for access to a model for life drawing. In 1841, Gilfillan emigrated to New Zealand, where his wife and two daughters were murdered in an incident which began the Maori Wars.

Gilfillan moved on to Australia and worked as a topographical artist, sending reports on the Australian gold-rush, with sketches of the goldfields to the Illustrated London News, but returned to Scotland by 1865, when he exhibited at the Glasgow Fine Arts Institute. Gilfillan was thus Glasgow's first full-time professor of Fine Art subjects, holding his post at Anderson's University, which was founded under the will of Professor John Anderson of Glasgow University.

Anderson was rather litigious in his time and fell out with practically everyone, decreeing that no drunkards or anyone associated with Glasgow University was to be employed in his university. Unfortunately, the funds he left for the prosecution of his aims were wholly inadequate, sufficient only to employ one professor, and since the idea of a university with one professor was absurd, the trustees called it Anderson's Institution, at least to begin with.

The first Andersonian Professor, appointed in 1796, was Professor Garnett, who is said to have lent his name to Garnethill, on which today's Art School sits. Garnett's house was reputedly the first building erected on the hill, and he kept the Glasgow Astronomical Society telescope in his garden. In the fullness of time the Andersonian University was merged with other institutes to create the Glasgow and West of Scotland Technical College, and this in turn became the Royal Technical College, the Royal College of Science and Technology, and finally the University of Strathclyde, in 1964.

Tassie medallion of Robert Foulis, Co-Founder of Academy. James Tassie was former student of Foulis Academy. Eminent portrait medallionist.

Lithograph view of Gorbals by
William Simpson Student at School of Design from 1845
Simpson was later early war artist in Crimea and special artist for Illustrated London News.

Military Scene in Crimea. Simpson became known as "Crimean" Simpson
and was regularly invited to Balmoral by Queen Victoria.

II

The Glasgow School of Art

INSTRUMENTS OF GOVERNMENT

ACCORDING to the THIRD STATISTICAL ACCOUNT, the Glasgow School of Art was the progeny of the West of Scotland Academy, founded in 1840, a date almost universally cited, though the original seal of the Glasgow School of Art Company, formed in 1892, has the date 1842 embossed on it. However, amid the general excitement of the building of the new School in 1895-96, the former Janitor wrote to a newspaper pointing out that 1840 was wrong, and that the correct date was 1845, but no attention was paid to this.

At any rate, the history of the Glasgow School of Art falls into three main periods, according to the government departments which controlled it. Originally it was a Government School of Design, under the Board of Trade 1845-52, then a Government School of Art, under the Science and Art Department, later transferred to the Committee of Council on Education in 1858, and this second period lasted until 1897, when the Glasgow School of Art was transferred to the Scotch Education Department (Scottish from 1918) Thus, the modern period effectively begins in 1897, though the School became academically independent only after 1901, when it was free to develop its own curriculum and its own Diplomas, subject to the approval of the Scottish Education Department.

The coincidence of dates will be observed in relation to the new School building designed by Mackintosh at the turn of the century. The first half of the building was commenced in 1897, the year of transfer to the Scotch Education Department, and completed in 1899. The second half was built in 1907-09, and was thus finished just as the Scotch Education Department opened its Edinburgh branch, mainly to deal with business arising from the Education (Scotland) Act of 1908. It was at this time that art teaching in schools, and associated teacher training was put on a proper footing and the building of Jordanhill Teacher Training College was commenced. Up until this time the School of Art was directly responsible for the training of teachers.

It follows from these dates that if the first full intake of students to the new building was in session 1909-10, then this cohort of students would finish their four-year Diploma course in session 1912-13. Since there were no grants at that time the number of full-time students was small, but in any case there was just one more final year, 1913-14, when all was nipped in the bud. The Diploma of Architecture had been introduced in 1904-05, but only seventeen students had taken the Diploma by 1914, and as W NW Ramsay put it:

> *The Glasgow School of Architecture was just on the point of going places when the War came...*

Worse still, the Professor of Architecture, Eugène Bourdon, a diminutive but charismatic Frenchman, was killed on the Somme in 1916. Bourdon was one of a number of Professors brought in by the Governors of the School after its

William Simpson in Indian dress (with Boundary Commission). Hon. Vice Presisdent of Glasgow Institute of Architects and RIBA (gave important papers on Indian Architecture).

transfer to the Scottish Education Department, which approved the appointment of eminent artists who did not hold the Art Masters' Certificate of the Science and Art Department. At the same time a number of women were appointed to teach crafts with no paper qualifications, since there were no official examinations in practical work under the South Kensington system.

The Glasgow School of Art was thus fortunate in getting off the mark with its plans for development around 1896, so that it was to have a clear decade or more of complete freedom from interference by external bodies. The Scottish Education Department queried only financial matters and routinely approved other proposals from the Governors.

The Secretary of the Scottish Education Department at the time, Sir John Struthers, is credited as the man responsible for raising the School of Art from a predominantly evening-class Government School, to the Higher Art Institution for Glasgow and the West of Scotland, and for obtaining special permission from the Treasury to appoint Professors, something only hitherto permitted at the Royal College.

Thus the notion that Francis Newbery was single-handedly responsible for the development of the Glasgow School of Art into a major institution is far from the truth. He was very much a servant of his Governors, who were eminent in the world of art and business and were not men who would be instructed by anyone, least of all a paid official.

However, there is no doubt that Newbery put the School on the map artistically, such that it was regarded as one of the art centres of Europe, and art journalists from France and elsewhere came to Glasgow to write up the phenomenon for their readers. Newbery was adept at what would now be called public relations, and he seems also to have been a good talent spotter, and brought on those students who had the 'gift', which Newbery knew was not a product of the syllabus, or teaching methods. He himself wrote: "Art cannot be taught, but anyone can teach a craft".

Perhaps the most remarkable thing about the four-year Diploma courses introduced by Newbery and his Professors was that they lasted so long (1901-1979. Almost equally remarkable is that the Art and Architecture Diplomas operated throughout this time without detailed regulations, and no doubt a factor in this was that the majority of teachers appointed were former students of the School, understood the system, and as Diploma-holders themselves, had no wish to see it superseded.

The Diploma in Art dates from 1901 when the School became the Central Institution for Higher Art Education in the West of Scotland. The term in effect means 'centre for advanced work', and the regional intention in the first Central Institutions can be seen in their titles: Glasgow and West of Scotland Technical College; Glasgow and West of Scotland College of Domestic Science; Glasgow and West of Scotland Commercial College.

The geography of Scotland divides itself conveniently into regions centred on the major cities, and higher education and technical instruction was planned accordingly. The country already had the four ancient universities, to which were added the four great technical colleges, Glasgow, Edinburgh (Heriot-Watt), Dundee and Aberdeen (Robert Gordon's); likewise four art schools of varying size and scope: Glasgow, Edinburgh, Aberdeen and Dundee. The training of teachers was similarly organised on a provincial basis parallelling the universities. Thus it can be said that in Scotland from the turn

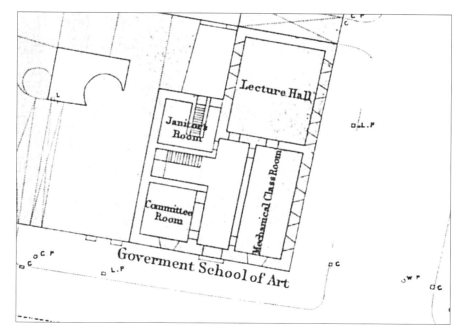

Portion of first ordnance survey showing details of Government School of Art Building in Ingram Street.

View West along Ingram Street c 1840 In middle distance on right hand side of Street is Hamilton Building of 1805 housing School of Design from 1844.

of the century there was a planned provision of higher education institutions under which umbrella the further education service would develop.

When the Scottish Central Institutions were created in 1901 the official statement equated them with "universities of industry', a concept dating from the mid-Victorian period, when Prince Albert planned a German-style Technical University at South Kensington. The drive towards 1900 was for technical education, and art schools at that time were seen as important providers.

The School of Art thus awarded its own Diplomas from 1901-1979 and thereafter degrees of the CNAA (Council for National Academic Awards). As a result of closer affiliation to the University, the Glasgow School of Architecture was eventually replaced by the Mackintosh School of Architecture, initially a joint Department of the University of Glasgow and the School of Art.

Discussions with the University on the question of joint teaching and regulation of courses had been entered into as early as 1910, though inconclusively. The question of a University link for the School of Art was revived in 1916, but the Director Newbery retired the following year, and nothing further was done until 1924 when the Ordinance for the BSc in Architecture was approved, under which the School of Art was approved as a teaching Institution for the University. These arrangements ceased in 1964-65, and the last BSc candidate graduated in 1966. The Glasgow degree of B.Arch, taught wholly at the School of Art in the Mackintosh School of Architecture , produced its first graduate in 1973.

The first degrees of Glasgow University awarded in Fine Art and Design subjects were conferred in 1993, more or less concurrently with the Government funding of the School being transferred from the Scottish Education Department to a new funding Council, SHEFC (Scottish Higher Education Funding Council), and this marks the beginning of a fourth chapter in the history of the School.

CHANGES OF ADDRESS

During its 150 years of existence, the Glasgow Government School of Design/Glasgow School of Art has occupied buildings on three different sites, which correspond, very roughly, to the three main administrative periods already described - Board of Trade, Committee of Council, SED. These are: Ingram Street at the corner of Montrose Street; Corporation Buildings, Sauchiehall Street (now known as the McLellan Galleries); Renfrew Street between Dalhousie Street and Scott Street.

The first home of the Glasgow Government School of Design was at No.16, Ingram Street, in a building erected around 1805 for commercial use, designed by the architect David Hamilton. The School opened on 6th January 1845, was almost immediately over-subscribed and the accommodation was deemed inadequate. An extension was put in hand, by the purchase of an adjacent property in Montrose Street, and the various alterations meant that 1846-47 was the first full teaching session. The School left the Ingram Street premises in 1869, when it moved to Sauchiehall Street.

Remarkably, the Ingram Street building itself survived until 1982, in a much altered state, shop-windows having been inserted at street level. Fortunately, the Listed Buildings Section of the City Council made a photographic record shortly before demolition, so that some idea may be had of the size and scale of the Art School. A schedule of accommodation also survives in an official report of 1864, and apart from the usual classrooms, mentions a large hall which was used for lectures and exhibitions of student work.

Records are scant from the School of Design period, and the only students known are those mentioned in reports of prize-winnings, while the names of several who achieved distinction in their professional lives can be found in reference works. Former students occasionally published autobiographical accounts, but very few from this time. No examples of student work from the early School of Design survive either, as far as is known.

In 1869 the School of Art moved to Corporation Buildings, Sauchiehall Street. There are no plans extant of the School of Art accommodation on the upper floor, with ground floor access from Rose Street, via the doorway which still exists. Since the School of Art moved out of the premises in 1899 (when the first half of the Mackintosh building was complete) the Sauchiehall Street building has been extensively refurbished twice, once in 1911 when the McLellan Galleries were constructed, and again after a major fire in1986

The building was originally designed with the upper floors as domestic houses, and presumably these were knocked together to provide sizeable class-rooms or studios. As the greater part of the work of the School in those early days was in night classes, daylight could not have been a primary considera-tion. At night the building was gas lit, and the combination of gas jets and overcrowded classrooms must have produced an oppressive atmosphere. Thomas Simmonds, Headmaster, refers in three consecutive annual reports (1882-84) to the unsatisfactory nature of the accommodation.

The building was fitted out as an Art School at the expense of the Corporation, and a rent was charged, which was defrayed by a grant from the Haldane Academy Trust. In effect, the School enjoyed its premises rent free, but without tenure. That is, notice to quit could be given at any time. This was not considered a viable proposition by the Governors of the School, and they resolved at that time to make their own arrangements for a new building.

The history of the building of the new Glasgow School of Art has been thor-oughly described by members of the School's teaching and library staff, in MACKINTOSH'S MASTERWORK, edited by Bill Buchanan, and published in 1989. The evolution of Mackintosh's design was extremely complicated, particu-larly in relation to the second phase of the building, 1907-09. This is basically the West Wing, (containing the Library) and the new Boardroom conversion, and it will be seen from the dates that these developments belong to the period after the Science and Art Department had ceased to exist and financial control had passed to the Scottish Education Department. The Science and Art Department had worked within stringent cost limits per square foot, and the early scheme for the School is quite rudimentary. Thus, as the School had departed from the curricular control of the South Kensington Department, so it also escaped from its building control, when the Department disappeared in 1900.

In the period up until 1908 the School received part of its funds from the Scottish Education Department, and the balance from the Corporation of Glasgow, under the provisions of the Customs and Excise (Residue) Act, 1890, which allowed the equivalent of a penny rate to be spent on Technical Education. Thereafter, the School was funded from a number of sources, but mainly by the Scottish Education Department, which also contributed to the Building Fund (second phase) as one among several subscribers.

The Schools of Design

THE SELECT COMMITTEE ON ARTS AND MANUFACTURES

THE SCHOOL OF DESIGN IN LONDON, with branch schools in the provinces, came into existence as a direct result of evidence given to the House of Commons Select Committee on Arts and Manufactures of 1835-36. The Select Committee can be seen as an attempt to grapple with problems posed by the Industrial Revolution, specifically factory production methods, and with the threat posed by foreign competition. British pattern-designers were clearly ill-equipped to compete with French imports, and many manufacturers even had design-buyers based in Paris. That this was a matter of widespread concern is confirmed by the letter (see Appendix B) sent in 1837 by William Dyce and Charles Heath Wilson, later Headmaster at the Glasgow Government School, to the Committee of the Trustees' Academy in Edinburgh, proposing major changes to the curriculum.

Why exactly British designs were so poor exercised considerable thought at the time of the Select Committee inquiries, and the lack of organised training for designers was an obvious factor. The period of the Regency had been one of fads and fancies, such that designers of carpets and textiles were left behind as tastes changed rapidly in favour of Greek, Gothic, Chinese or Egyptian styles. Machine production also created an insatiable appetite for new 'lines', which all added up to a destabilising effect in the area of taste and design.

The first Government grant had been made to assist elementary schooling in 1833, and many manufacturers voiced the opinion that the State should likewise provide funding for the training of designers to improve industrial products, and hence the country's trading position. Up until this point state intervention had not been entertained, as the idea ran contrary to the prevailing socio-economic doctrines of self-help and laissez-faire. However, the superiority of French designs was attributed to the existence of art schools throughout France, and the Select Committee also heard evidence on German Trade Schools. As far as France was concerned, the arts and crafts had been supported as a matter of State policy since the time of Louis XIV, and good design and craftsmanship actively fostered. Somewhat surprisingly, the French art school system in the post-Napoleonic period was not centralised, nor did it set out to train designers for specific industries. The French art schools provided a general artistic training, and the student developed design skills specific to a particular industry at a later stage.

By contrast, the eventual British solution was a centralised system of Design Schools, following the German example, which deliberately did not provide a full artistic education, but a limited type of training for students in the skills deemed necessary for the ornamental designer. The British approach was to try to train a new animal, intermediate between artist and artisan, called an 'ornamentist'. The Schools of Design took in students already employed in the manufactures, and there was no entry test; only at the Head School of Design in London was elementary drawing ability insisted on, and the prevailing philosophy in the provincial Branch Schools was that the necessary drawing skills could be acquired by anyone, given instruction. Artistic talent was not considered a prerequisite for the designer, as it was in France.

However, after a decade or so in which the Schools of Design amounted to little more than drawing schools, with hardly any students proceeding to original design, it was realised that designers had to be able to draw well, and that there was such a thing as natural design ability. Thus, in the reorganised Schools of the Science and Art Department which replaced the Schools of Design, an intensive system of drawing instruction was introduced together with a national competition and awards scheme, to identify and encourage the talented.

At any rate, around the same time as the Government was establishing its central or Head School of Design in the metropolis, a number of schools of design in the provinces had come into existence as a result of private initiatives, and these began to request assistance. In 1841 the Government voted £10,000 to the Board of Trade to assist in the establishment of Schools of Design in the industrial districts in the provinces, and between 1841 and 1852 seventeen of these Branch Schools were established.

THE GLASGOW GOVERNMENT SCHOOL OF DESIGN 1842-52

Preliminary to the formation of Branch Schools of Design in the provinces and in Scotland, the Council of the School of Design in London sent a circular to various civic authorities, including Glasgow:

> *Sir, – A Parliamentary grant has recently been made for the encour-*
> *agement of Branch Schools in connection with the School of Design*
> *already established in London, for the purpose of teaching Ornamental*
> *Design as applicable to manufactures, both to those employees as*
> *Pattern Designers and to artisans generally, and also for the formation*
> *of collections of casts of works of Art, for the purpose of instruction in*
> *such Branch Schools; such collections to be gratuitously accessible*
> *under certain regulations to the inhabitants of towns in which they*
> *shall be placed... The Council of the School of Design request, that if*
> *there be any School or Institution now existing in Glasgow, in which*
> *Design is taught with a view to its application to manufactures, you*
> *will acquaint them with this fact at your earliest convenience, as in*
> *that case they would be desirous of procuring from you additional*
> *particulars in reference to such School...*

The Schools of Design were thus the first direct state intervention in the provision of training, and were regarded initially as very much an experiment. The circular letter to civic authorities would have been received at the Ingram Street office of the Sheriff of Lanarkshire, Archibald Alison, and in his memoirs, Alison records that he was responsible for getting together a committee of manufacturers and others to subscribe towards a School of Design. This Committee seems to have formulated its proposals to the point of public

Marble Bust of Sheriff Archibald Alison, First Chairman of Governors of School of Design 1844-49.
Formed original Glasgow Committee of 1842-43.

announcement by 1843, when a celebratory dinner was held to mark the launch of the project, at which Alison emphasised the urgency of the situation:

We see foreigners daily flocking from all parts of the world to the shores of the Clyde or the Mersey, to study our railways, and our canals; to copy our machinery, to take models of our steam-vessels - but we see none coming to imitate our designs. On the contrary, we, who take the lead of all the world in mechanical invention, in the powers of art, are obliged to follow them in the designs to which these powers are to be applied. Gentlemen, this should not be. We have now arrived at that period of manufacturing progress, when we must take the lead in design, or we shall cease to have orders for performance - we must be the first in conception, or we will be the last in execution...

In reports of Alison's speeches at later School of Art prizegivings he is always referred to as Sheriff Alison the historian, and his ten-volume HISTORY OF EUROPE became a standard work. Alison duly became Chairman of the Local Committee of Management of the Glasgow School of Design, which opened on January 6th, 1845, once the Ingram Street building had been fitted out, and the first Headmaster was sent up from London. He was Henry MacManus, an Irishman, and previously a teacher in the Head School at Somerset House.

MacManus started off on a high note, winning the confidence of the Governors, who recommended him for a salary increase the next year. This followed a favourable notice in May 1846, by Charles Heath Wilson, Director of the Head School, in his monthly report to Council:

Henry MacManus in old age in Robes of Royal Hibernian Academician. First Head Master of Glasgow School of Design 1844-48.

In no place is there greater promise of success in the ultimate object of the Schools than at Glasgow. With an active, intelligent and influential Committee (for the principal manufacturers and magistrates of the town have shown the greatest interest in the undertaking) and an able Master, who devotes himself seriously to his duties, the pupils already exhibit much proficiency in their pursuits, and the advantages of the School are eagerly sought by the manufacturing population. The additional buildings which have been some time in progress are not yet completed, but when these rooms are all opened there will be accommodation for 500 pupils, and the number, it is not doubted, will be immediately filled up...

However, difficulties arose later between MacManus and the local Committee of Management, and although the Glasgow students got up a petition to have him retained, the end result was that MacManus was transferred to Dublin to head the new School of Design there.

Of MacManus himself, little is known except that he was an indefatigable exhibitor at the Royal Hibernian Academy, which eventually appointed him Honorary Professor of Painting. At his best, MacManus seems to have been an indifferent painter, and according to Strickland's DICTIONARY OF IRISH ARTISTS, although his early works display some merit, "his pictures, as a whole, were poor in colour, and in his latter years became puerile and even ludicrous".

The Development of the Curriculum

BY THE TIME the Glasgow Government School of Design opened, the pattern of courses in the Head and Provincial Branch Schools had already been standardised as follows:

Class		
	I	Design
	II	Modelling
	III	Perspective
	IV	Geometrical Drawing
	V	Painting the Figure
	VI	Figure Drawing from the Round
	VII	Figure Drawing from the Flat
	VIII	Colouring
	IX	Chiaroscuro Painting
	X	Shading from Casts
	XI	Shading from the Flat
	XII	Elementary Drawing

The Design Class was in fact the apex of the system, which began with Elementary Drawing, and this was extended to some twenty-six stages after 1853, to create the National Curriculum. At this point, however, enrolment figures for the various classes show that no pupils arrived at the Design class in Glasgow, and the picture in the Branch Schools nationally was the same - no pupils or students graduated to Design, and in consequence no designers had been produced. Only at the Head School was there any enrolment in the evening Design class.

In Class VII, Drawing from the Flat is referred to, which means learning to draw by copying a specimen drawing, and in a period when all reproduction was by engraving or lithography the ability to copy accurately was of economic value. Usually the student was set to copying the figure larger or smaller than the original so that sizes could not be taken off by measurement, and the drawing masters generally prepared their own copy sheets for their students.

Class XI, Shading from the Flat, involved copying specimen drawings of geometrical solids, and in this class they probably drew out the Greek orders - Doric, Ionic and Corinthian. This was a standard exercise for junior art and architecture students until about 1960, and no doubt one reason why such exercises remained popular so long is that they were time-consuming and could occupy very large classes with only one master in charge.

Class IV, Geometrical Drawing, was originally called Architectural Drawing, but the class attracted many architects' apprentices who were interested in furthering their professional studies. The authorities in London at the Head School viewed this development with disfavour and had the title changed to Geometrical Drawing, with flower drawing in the summer. The School of Design did not exist to provide a 'cheap architectural academy".

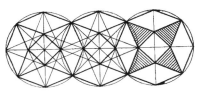

Figure showing pattern geometry from student textbook on Ornamental Design c 1900.

Class III, Perspective, was considered a very important subject throughout the 19th century, and especially before the advent of commercial photography. Perspective geometry involves constructing a picture of an object or view, identical to the geometry of that same picture from the standpoint of a camera. Thus, before photography, perspective was the key to accurate representation in topographical drawings, and artists, architects and engineers all had to be expert in its use. One 18th century directory on furniture design, for example, devotes the first third of the book to detailed instruction on perspective drawing.directed to illustration of catalogues.

Class VIII, Colouring: The first book with coloured illustrations printed from the stone rather than hand-coloured, UNDERSTANDING CHROMOLITHOGRAPHY, appeared in 1835, and thereafter coloured books came forward in increasing numbers, including works on colour decoration in historical architecture. Many of these books were very expensive and were issued as part-works, and loose plates sold. The School of Design was thus supplied with more authentic copies of ornament for study.

Class II, Modelling in Clay, requires little explanation, but again, students began by copying casts. The object was not to produce sculpture, but to comprehend form, and to acquire the ability to make models of designs for manufacture.

Class I, Design: As previously mentioned, no-one actually graduated to this level, and since the teaching of original design never became operational, the problems of developing a systematic curriculum were never faced up to in practice. Wallis, the Headmaster of Birmingham, however, did produce a worked-out course and sent it to the Head School of Design, whose Council thought sufficiently highly of his effort to send it out as an official circular.

When the term 'Design' is used, we have to be careful. The Schools of Design were not Fine Art Schools, and were created with the purely utilitarian function of assisting in the production of improved manufactures with a view to their sale. That is, they were concerned with commercial art or art-manufactures, and basically, the first Schools of Design set out to train better designers of applied ornamental and printed patterns, in the making of which the fundamental activity was drawing; hence, School of Design, in the ambivalent sense of 'design as drawing', like French dessin, or Italian disegno.

THE MOVEMENT FOR REFORM

Eventually, the Schools of Design and their direction from Somerset House came to be seen as a failure. Reform of the Schools had been discussed with Prince Albert by Henry Cole as early as 1848, and Cole was commissioned to prepare a report on the Schools with proposals for their rehabilitation. Cole was however seconded from the Record Office to help plan the Great Exhibition of 1851, and the question of reform was deferred. That the Schools of Design had failed, there was no doubt, since they had proved incapable of training any original designers. They had made some contribution to training the workforce, but at the level of pattern-drawing - basically for copyists or draughtsmen. Ambrose Poynter, Inspector of the Provincial Schools, told the Committee of Enquiry of 1847:

> *The Provincial Schools are, in fact, mere Drawing Schools, and have
> no pretension to be called Schools of Design. No element of art whatev-
> er beyond the imitation of form and colour has ever been introduced
> into their system...*

Nor can Charles Heath Wilson's contribution to the debate have endeared him
to the authorities. He told the Committee:

> *We cannot make original designers. Nature makes them, by bountifully
> bestowing the necessary aptitude to be such. We can only educate them...
> to teach invention is utterly impossible...*

As an officer of the Board of Trade, Heath Wilson was perhaps too forthright
for his own good. He was, in effect, declaring that the enterprise on which the
Board had embarked was doomed from the outset, and that, in consequence,
public money had been wasted. A year or so later, Heath Wilson was informed
that his Inspectorship was to be abolished and he was offered the now vacant
post of Glasgow Headmaster.

Henry Cole was appointed Secretary of the School of Design in October 1851,
and soon afterwards wrote to the President of the Board of Trade, Henry
Labouchère, recommending that the School of Design should be retitled the
Department of Practical Art. This recommendation was accepted, and in
February 1852 the Department of Practical Art came into being, with Cole as its
full-time superintendent, assisted by Richard Redgrave, RA, as Art Director.

The following year, a Science Division was added to the Department of
Practical Art, and the Department of Science and Art thus came into existence, under the Board of Trade, with Cole and Lyon Playfair as joint
Secretaries. This was eventually located in South Kensington, and during its
lifetime, a national curriculum for Art instruction was in operation.

The Science and Art Department later incorporated the Government
School of Mines and Science, the Museum of Practical Geology, the
Geological Survey, Museum of Irish Industry and the Royal Dublin Society,
and this remarkable portfolio of interests was regarded by some as a subject for
mockery. Thus, W S Gilbert's comic song, in THE PIRATES OF PENZANCE:

> *I am the very pattern of a modern Major-Gineral;
> I've information vegetable, animal and mineral...
> I'm very well acquainted too with matters mathematical;*
>
> *I understand equations, both the simple and quadratical;
> I'm very good at integral and differential calculus;
> I know the scientific names of beings animalculous...*

refers directly to Major-General Sir John Donnelly, who was Director of the
Science Division and Chief Executive Officer at South Kensington. Donnelly
had risen from the rank of Captain, RE, to Major-General, spending all his
service at the Science and Art Department, in a lounge suit, not uniform. At
any rate, the Schools of Art were satellites of this amazing rag-bag of institutions which was not broken up until the end of the century.

Art Certificate of the Science and Art Department issued to John Young, later art master Glasgow High School and Glasgow School of Art (Teachers' classes).

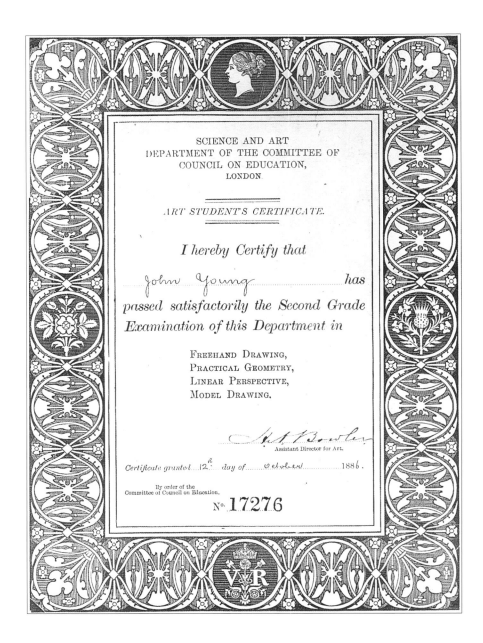

SCIENCE AND ART
DEPARTMENT OF THE COMMITTEE OF
COUNCIL ON EDUCATION,
LONDON.

ART STUDENT'S CERTIFICATE.

I hereby Certify that

John Young *has*

passed satisfactorily the Second Grade
Examination of this Department in

FREEHAND DRAWING,
PRACTICAL GEOMETRY,
LINEAR PERSPECTIVE,
MODEL DRAWING.

Assistant Director for Art.

Certificate granted 12 *day of* October 1886.

By order of the
Committee of Council on Education.

Nᵒ. 17276

IN NATURE'S INFINITE BOOK
OF SECRECY
A LITTLE CAN I READ

THE COMMITTEE OF HER MAJESTY'S MOST HONOURABLE PRIVY COUNCIL ON EDUCATION,
DEPARTMENT OF SCIENCE AND ART,
LONDON.

IT is hereby Certified that *John Young*

obtained a First Class in the Elementary Stage of Practical, Plane and

Solid Geometry at the Examination held on the 14th May 1887.

BY ORDER,

Colonel R.E., Secretary.

N.B.—At this Examination 5,949 Candidates presented themselves. Of these 201 came up in Honours, 879 in the Advanced Stage, and 4,869 in the Elementary Stage. The results were as follows :—In Honours, 17 obtained a First Class, 63 a Second Class, and 121 failed. In the Advanced Stage, 120 obtained a First Class, 341 a Second Class, and 418 failed. In the Elementary Stage, 828 obtained a First Class, 2,029 a Second Class, and 2,012 failed.

The Design of the Certificates represents applied science with a cornucopia of gear wheels and machine parts. Machine drawing was taken by art masters as an extra subject.

THE SOUTH KENSINGTON SYSTEM

The South Kensington system was designed to cater for the art-workman, not to produce easel painters, although intending artists did frequent the schools, since there was nowhere else to go in most cases. According to one source on Lavery's career, his training at the Glasgow School of Art was like all schools in Britain at that time, frankly bad. Ruskin said something similar about the teaching of drawing in England, that there were two methods, the correct method, and that adopted by the Government Schools of Art. It may be added that although Ruskin was a Socialist, he set up his School of Drawing at Oxford University specifically for the middle classes, declaring that, for the artisan class, the Science and Art system at the Oxford School of Art was quite good enough.

The officially recommended style of drawing in the Schools was outline drawing, with a hard pencil, then modelling of the form by tinting and shading, the tones built up laboriously to a highly finished state. As a liberalising move, a 'fuzzy' line came in as a new fashion, and later the use of the stump, a wedge of folded paper, basically, to build up tones. A great deal of time was spent on the finishing of drawings, with little room for improving basic skills in observation of form.

Examination Board
assessing submitted works.

When Redgrave retired from the Department in 1876, his successor Sir Edward Poynter, PRA, said of him that he was "the author of the most perfect system of national art instruction ever devised", but Poynter was merely being kind to Redgrave at his last prizegiving. Earlier, in an address at the opening of the Slade School of Fine Art, Poynter had said:

> *Look at the drawings sent up by the Government Schools of Art to the central competition at South Kensington; are any of them executed under six weeks of painful stippling with chalk and bread? How much knowledge of the figure is it to be supposed that the student has acquired during the process?... Is it a wonder that when our national prizes are given for such work as this, we are behind the rest of Europe in our knowledge of drawing; and that those who have aspirations towards a higher kind of work than the market-produce which over-whelms our exhibitions, have either to seek for a better form of study on the Continent, or to keep up a life-long struggle against difficulties, which they have never been taught to overcome, but which are the ABC of art education abroad?*

Sir Edward Poynter succeeded Redgrave as Art Director at South Kensington and did attempt some liberalisation of the system. Poynter had been an art student himself under the South Kensington regime, and knew the whole sorry story. Redgrave, for his part, seems to have been a thoroughly decent individual, and back in 1852, when his appointment as Art Director was announced, one of the art journals expressed astonishment that someone like Redgrave could team up with Cole, "a malevolent dwarf".

By the 1880s, the South Kensington system was falling into disrepute. Very few students ever managed to ascend the ladder of Redgrave's course to the point of producing original designs to a professional standard, i.e. capable of execution in materials, and this same failing had been identified as early as 1847: design consisted of paper or drawing-board studies, and students had only the vaguest idea how the things they designed might be made. Indeed, they were often in unrelated employment and their knowledge of materials and processes was non-existent.

This lasted more or less unchanged until the early 1890s and was the system in operation in the Glasgow School of Art until 1900, although the Glasgow School had been transferred to the Scottish Education Department three years earlier. In 1900, the Science and Art Department was replaced by the Board of Education whose examinations were taken by Glasgow students for one year only, 1900-1901; thereafter, the Glasgow Diploma courses began and Newbery's prospectus announced, "There is now no connection between this School and the English Board of Education."

There are some intriguing aspects of the Science and Art Department regime, not least the fact that its Schools were primarily intended for the artisan class, through whom the quality of manufactures was to be improved, by better design. The Department thus went to some lengths to define the artisan class, and only paid grant aid in respect of evening-class artisan students and teacher-training students. Middle-class students, e.g., were not eligible for Department prizes, an interesting early example of what would now be called positive discrimination. Under Cole, however, the Art Schools were opened to all, and a general pattern developed that day classes tended to be populated by middle-class amateurs, who were charged a higher fee than ordinary students and in consequence were good business. The evening schools, as they were called after 1890, were crowded out with students of the artisan class and others in trade employment. ('Artisan' class students were renamed 'Industrial' in the 1890s).

By 1900 considerable changes had already taken place in the world of design. Designers increasingly became self-employed freelances or worked collectively in "shops" of their own, as opposed to being factory employees. They were now part of a service sector, removed from the category of industrial worker, and made up a new professional group.

Meanwhile, design allied to the crafts had become largely the domain of the middle-class female art student, with practical craftwork and art-needlework "all the rage". Previously, design had been associated with "trade", which led to the kind of attitudes made explicit by a contributor to ART UNION in 1847:

> *The great end in becoming a designer or ornamentist is to* gain a living. *This class of Art does not offer the stimulus of fame, nor does it all involve the notion of constituting a gentleman, nor give the* entrée *into society as such. In devoting a child to this pursuit, the parent has only to view the acquisition of a talent that will procure a tolerable means of existence; the student will come from a calculating industrious class, and not from the rich and wealthy among the middle classes who allow their sons to study the Arts for the gentility of the thing, and can afford to keep them at their studies for a sufficient number of years, without any effort being required for their self-sustenance...*

In exactly the same way, science and technical subjects were regarded as the province of Mechanics' Institutes and artisans' night schools. Glasgow University, for example, did not organise its Faculty of Science until 1893, and Oxford did not offer an Engineering degree until 1908. Thus, the low status of technology in our own century can be traced to its position in the 19th century as exclusively a night-school subject, an image reinforced by the fact that many modern colleges and polytechnics were the direct descendants of Mechanics' Institutes, in the same industrial towns as the original Schools of Design.

By the converse argument, it can be seen that through its increasing commitment to the Fine Arts, and the studio crafts, involving artist-designer-craftsmen, the status of the School of Art was enhanced. At the same time it phased out the teaching of elementary and purely technical or mechanical arts, which were eventually transferred to other training centres.

At the Glasgow School of Art, the proportion of students training in Industrial Design, decorative trades, and other design-related employment, was much higher than the national average, and it was also, at one point, the largest School of Art in the South Kensington system, no doubt reflecting Glasgow's position as a major industrial centre. In a conference speech in 1889 the Glasgow School Headmaster gave the Glasgow statistics as 25% of students engaged in Fine Art (Painting), with 75% vocational students engaged in handicraft work and design subjects. However, these figures are slightly suspect insofar as they appear to be based on a comparison of register totals for day, and evening classes, and up until Newbery's time, the work of the School was predominantly evening-class teaching.

Charles Heath Wilson ARSA second Head Master of Glasgow School of Art. Designed some ship interiors. and undertook architectural work for Duke of Hamilton.

Italian Antique Cast. At first casts of ancient mediaeval and later ornament had to be imported to Britain but in time firms of Italian modellers set up in Britain to supply Schools and Museums. (Guisti Bros. Glasgow until 1960s).

In the 1890s, the universities were not open to women, and the art schools were one of the few alternatives. Under pressure from the Arts and Crafts movement, craft workshops were progressively introduced into art schools, and these new facilities attracted numbers of middle class women eager to work in materials. There were, of course, no student grants or bursaries at that time, so only those who either had a source of income, or did not require to work could attend the schools in the day time. They were also free to experiment, since they took no examinations, and the South Kensington Department did not examine in crafts in any case.

Another interesting feature of the Science and Art Department regime was the system of 'payment on results'. This was first applied in the Science Division, and later taken up by the Education Department, where it was imposed on the elementary school system, with adverse effects in the long term. Payment by examination or test results was made only in respect of the 'three Rs', with the consequence that schools concentrated on little else, and the expansion of the curriculum to include other subjects was delayed by decades.

In the art schools, payment on results lasted until 1896, when a new funding system was introduced, and the Glasgow School of Art prospectus after 1900 is careful to point out that "the system of payment on results is at an end." Up until 1863, teachers in the Schools of Art were paid according to their qualifications, and student numbers. The payments on results system removed fixed-point salaries and replaced them with what is today called performance-related pay. This was eventually seen to be baleful in its effects: "the entire system was an engine driven by money", a teacher explained to a Departmental Committee of 1911. We may note in passing that, almost a century after its abolition, that same principle is being re-introduced in all branches of the education service. Concentration on the "three Rs" is being touted as a return to some kind of Victorian virtue; in fact this narrow emphasis in schooling was thoroughly discredited by the end of last century, in Victoria's lifetime.

An additional aspect of Cole's system for schools of art, was his intention that they should eventually be self-supporting, on the assumption that their fee income would progressively increase, and support from the Treasury reduce, till it was nil, and the schools would in effect become 'privatised'. For most of his life, Cole saw "the height of a school's ambition as the ability to decline any pecuniary assistance from the Government", and further believed that "schools could not succeed if their funds were independent of their own exertions." Needless to say, this met with Treasury approval, and Cole did succeed in reducing the average cost to the taxpayer of training an art and design student.

However, Cole's idea that the nation's technical education programme could be funded largely from the nominal fees charged to artisan students became increasingly absurd in the 1870s, at a time when Germany, newly unified, was consolidating its technical education provision and developing elite institutions. The need for increased state investment in technical training in Britain became increasingly obvious, and over the decade 1890-1900, there was a continuous review of these questions, resulting in a massive programme of investment in new art schools, technical colleges and university buildings.

Early Headmasters

CHARLES HEATH WILSON 1849-63

CHARLES HEATH WILSON was the second Head of the Glasgow School of Design, and took over in January 1849. Before his appointment, Heath Wilson had been Inspector of the Provincial Schools, and in that capacity had visited Glasgow to report on the difficulties between the Local Committee of Management and the then Master, MacManus. At the time of his report, Heath Wilson had no idea that his roving Inspectorship was to be abolished, but when the news leaked out that MacManus was to be sent to Dublin, and Heath Wilson was to take his place, having penned the very report that caused the vacancy, the art and architectural journals had a field day. The ART JOURNAL affected to believe that Heath Wilson had connived to get MacManus's post, while THE BUILDER thought that sending a man of Heath Wilson's standing to be Branch School Head in Glasgow was "a degradation".

Italian Antique Cast

Charles Heath Wilson was an artist and architect and had spent his boyhood in Italy, so when the Head School of Design decided to send an agent to Italy to acquire architectural and decorative casts, he was the obvious choice, and made so many purchases that the Secretary's office at the School was crammed with them. This first collection of casts furnished the beginnings of the South Kensington Museum, later the Victoria and Albert. Similarly, there was a large cupboard at Somerset House containing a variety of books for the use of students. Heath Wilson took charge of this collection and developed it into a library, making regular purchases and producing a catalogue, and this eventually developed into the National Art Library of the V & A. After his arrival in Glasgow, Heath Wilson also started a lending library in the School of Art, and undertook to find books for it on the secondhand market.

Heath Wilson would have been instructed in drawing and painting from an early age by his father, who had taught drawing in several military academies. His own work in many ways resembles the topographical watercolour of the 18th century, which is, of course, what he grew up with. It is perhaps a little too photographic in effect to be of interest today, but literal depiction of buildings and landscape was then much in demand. Certainly, Heath Wilson had no difficulty selling his work at the RSA, a fact he pointed out to a Committee of Inquiry at the School of Design, when his record as an artist was referred to as inconsequential.

Charles Heath Wilson took over as Headmaster at Glasgow at the beginning of 1849, and at the end of that year the Inspector, Ambrose Poynter, made a very favourable report:

> *Since the appointment of Mr Wilson to the School at Glasgow, that gentleman has applied himself with great zeal to its general organisation, and to the classification of the students. The number on the books amounts for the present month of November to 362, an increase of 28*

over the corresponding period of 1848... and an additional evening class has been opened three times a week for mechanical and architectural drawing, numbering 48, which is as many as the room appropriated to it will accommodate. This class is under Mr Bruce Bell... and is independent of a lecture which Mr Wilson gives to the whole School once a week on practical geometry, and its applications to the forms of mouldings, etc... The same lecture is repeated to the female class. The life class (self supporting) is at this time attended by 11 students, but these are not all regular pupils of the School...

Thus, in 1849-50, a life class was in existence, and the students at this class probably included some professional artists, as the fact that artists were making use of the School at Glasgow was later referred to by Henry Cole. It will be noted that Heath Wilson's practical geometry lecture was repeated separately for the female students. This shows that the School was not fully co-educational, and indeed according to Mary Armour, male and female studio classes in the School of Art were conducted separately as late as 1925-26.

The appointment of Bruce Bell to teach Mechanical and Architectural Drawing in November 1849 is the first mention of an architectural subject in the School curriculum, and by 1863, the last year of Heath Wilson's Headship, the Mechanical class had grown to be the largest in the School. The demand for instruction in engineering drawing reflects the level of industrial development by that date, but the 'Cotton Famine' resulting from the American Civil War of 1861-64 badly affected Glasgow textile manufacture, which ceased to be a major employer. Many of the early schools of design were in textile industry districts, e.g., Leeds, Bradford, Manchester, Coventry, and Glasgow.

The Inspector's Report on Glasgow in 1847 found 54 pupils working as pattern drawers and another 15 studying for the same employment, while a further Report of 1850 notes that:

There continues to be a considerable number of established designers attached to the School, but, as happens generally with this class of students, a press of business is apt to draw them all off for a time. During the past year, nine pupils have found employment with manufacturers, of whom three are with calico printers, and four in the sewed muslin trade. In the drawing of patterns for the latter branch of business, it is undoubted that the School has produced a considerable effect...

Heath Wilson superintended the advanced classes and the courses of study were modified to retain established designers and pattern drawers in the School, through exercises which made their work more adaptable to the process of block printing then in vogue. More interestingly, the Inspector reports:

For the use of the advanced classes a supply of natural plants is kept up, and a small greenhouse has been made for their better preservation, and by an arrangement worthy to be noted, the cuttings of the palms and other exotics in the Botanical Gardens, which would otherwise be thrown away as useless, are secured for the School...

Thus, the little cantilevered conservatory in Mackintosh's Art School building is not a piece of whimsy by the architect, but the building-in to the design of a authentic function which had existed since the 1840s.

In 1850, the Glasgow Local Committee resolved that:

> *With a view to the desirable object of retaining the advanced pupils, the freedom of the School and a Diploma should be granted to the successful competitor for the most important prizes...*

This is the first mention of the award of a Diploma in a School of Art, albeit in a restricted sense; however, there is no evidence that the Diploma was ever awarded, since in 1852 the Department of Practical Art introduced a new regime in the Schools. A completely new Local Committee appears to have been nominated then, following an inspection by Captain Owen, RE. The use of Engineer Officers as Inspectors in the Henry Cole period arose from Cole's admiration for engineers, as opposed to architects, whom he thought over concerned with aesthetics and matters of style.

Army engineers were among the few people with an adequate technical education; they knew about structures, building construction, and could draw and watercolour. Additionally, they were of a social class able to deal with the School managers and Local Committees, in many cases composed of local gentry and magistrates and the like. Drawing masters were generally of low status, and it was a sore point that promotion to Inspector was closed to them.

At any rate, Captain Owen, RE came up to Glasgow to inspect, but although he might cast an eye over students' work, his task was primarily to go over the School's books to see that fees and the expenditure of the grant were properly accounted for; that the School's casts and other equipment were being looked after; and that registers of attendance were properly kept and not falsified. He could also report on the state of buildings and make recommendations on grants. Engineer Officers were still at the Department of Science and Art in the 1890s. Indeed, Mackintosh's plans for the new Art School were sent down to South Kensington for approval by the Building Grants Officer, one Captain Festing RE.

In 1853, with the creation of the Science and Art Department, the Glasgow School of Design became the Glasgow School of Art. The national curriculum for art schools then established, continued virtually unchanged until 1890 or so, and in 1863, as earlier noted, payment on results was introduced to the schools of art, to be calculated on examination pass rates (as an index of teaching efficiency). Cole's proposal, announced as a fait accompli, caused a near revolt, and the ensuing row was used by political factions who were gunning for Cole. The outcome was a Commons Select Committee to enquire into the affairs of the art schools and Charles Heath Wilson was one of those who gave evidence in 1864.

Heath Wilson reported that in 1863 he had received a letter from the Department giving notice of the termination of his Headmastership, which had been a Board of Trade appointment. In effect, he was to be dismissed, since the Department was no longer willing to pay the fixed salaries of Heads of Schools appointed under the old regime. Heath Wilson might apply to be re-appointed, and accept the payment on results scheme, but he in fact tendered his resignation before the Department had time to abolish his post, and Robert Greenlees, a former student and teacher at the School, succeeded him as Headmaster.

Thus ends the account of Heath Wilson's Headmastership. Although he was eased out by Cole and the Department, he was presented with a testimonial of

£700 by subscribers, equivalent to about £32,000 today. In his valedictory speech, Heath Wilson spoke of his hopes for the School of Art, and also that before long a Chair of Fine Art would be established at the University. This seems to have been a particular hobby-horse of his, since he entered into correspondence with the Senate of Edinburgh University when the question of a Chair became a live issue in the 1880s. Edinburgh did in fact create the first Chair of Fine Art in Britain, though they disregarded Heath Wilson's advice that any Professor of Fine Art should be a practising artist.

After his resignation, Heath Wilson is listed as Honorary Director of the School, and he was also one of the Haldane Academy Trustees. Thus, he remained a power behind the scenes, and his successor, Robert Greenlees, was left to function simply as a teacher, unencumbered by political in-fighting of the type that cast a shadow over Heath Wilson's departure.

Heath Wilson was very well connected, and had given evidence to several Select Committees, as well as preparing a report for a Commission on the Design of the National Gallery. Thus he was not a typical provincial school head, totally in awe of the functionaries of the Science and Art Department, and this was doubtless another reason why Cole felt uncomfortable about his continuing appointment.

ROBERT GREENLEES 1863-81

Robert Greenlees had been a pupil teacher in the Glasgow School, a position which required the winning of a bronze medal. A small stipend was offered and the pupil divided his week between his own work, and teaching drawing in the elementary schools. Greenlees had progressed through the various grades of attainment on the national curriculum and was awarded an Art Master's certificate on the basis of his accumulated subject passes.

It was also possible to leave one district and settle in another, taking accumulated passes to a new Art School, so that there was the element of credit transfer present in the system. Moreover, students could take as long as they wished to accumulate their passes, and there was no restriction on entry, nor entrance test, i.e., 'total access'. By the end of the century, however, this was all swept away and the notion of 'courses' of prescribed subjects, taken within a limited time period, was introduced, and entrance tests of general education were required for all full-time courses after 1900.

In the days of the Science and Art Department, all and sundry were admitted, subjects could be taken piecemeal, attendance could not be required, and some Art Masters took twenty years to gain all the available certificates. Pass rates were so low that there was actually a Department regulation requiring the closure of any Science School with an 80% failure rate. The efficiency of the Art Schools seems to have been measured by the numbers of medals gained in national competition, and where schools did particularly well, their Headmasters received a performance bonus.

When Greenlees became Headmaster of the School of Art in 1863, Engineering Drawing was the largest class in the School. Engineering Drawing was among the first of the Science subjects taught in Art Schools, and other Science subjects were later added. To the Victorian mind this twinning of art and science seemed obvious, and indeed up until 1896 the Glasgow School of Art was listed in the Art Directory as a School of Art and Science. In addition to Engineering Drawing, Science subjects taught in Greenlees' time included Plane and Solid Geometry, Machine Drawing, Ship Drawing, Building Construction, and even a class on the Steam Engine. The common element among these Science subjects was geometrical drawing, or Science Drawing, as it was known, to distinguish it from Geometry and Perspective for Art students.

The design and manufacture of any product starts with a drawing, and in the case of buildings, ships, engines, railway curves and gradients, cuttings and tunnels, complex and advanced geometry is involved. The Victorians believed that research in geometry would lead to genuine discoveries, though by 1880 or so the subject had been pronounced a dead end. At the inception of the Science and Art Department in 1852, however, Cole could confidently assert that the basis of all design was geometry, and that applied geometry would be one of the foundations of Art education in the Schools of Art. (One might liken this to a similar indiscriminate enthusiasm for computer studies at the present day, regardless of the student's subject area).

Architectural drawing was a distinct branch of geometrical drawing, mainly concerned with the accurate setting out of the classical orders and other details to a large scale, and problems typically involving complicated roof surfaces. The modern name for this subject area is Descriptive Geometry, and the Glasgow School of Art was probably the last institution in the country to maintain both Descriptive Geometry and Perspective as examinable subjects for Architecture students, until 1964.

Ship drawing also appeared in the School of Art during the period of Robert Greenlees' service and an article in THE BAILIE refers to most of the designers in the Clyde shipyards having been his pupils. This may have had something to do with the fact that the Institute of Engineers and Shipbuilders were neighbours of the School of Art in Corporation Buildings. Also Robert Napier, a shipbuilder, was a Governor of the School. In passing, it is worth noting that James Howden, the founder of the Glasgow engineering firm, taught at the School in the 1850s.

Early ships' curves were drawn by eye, using flexible rulers ('splines'), but by the 1880's the old approximate methods were giving way to a more mathematical approach to design, using equations for curves, and involving resistance of hull profiles, buoyancy and stability. In 1882 the Mechanics' Institute appointed its first lecturer in Naval Architecture, and in 1883 the University of Glasgow established the David Elder Chair in the same subject. However, while these events mark the beginning of the two University Naval Architecture Departments at Glasgow and Strathclyde, it can be argued that the foundations were laid in the School of Art.

As far as Engineering Drawing was concerned, a related category of employment in this field was tracing, and it is likely that trainee women tracers were sent to the School of Art by the locomotive builder Henry Dubs, a German immigrant, whose firm was eventually absorbed by the North British Locomotive Company. Dubs was the first employer in Glasgow to employ women tracers, and significantly he was a member of the Local Committee of Management of the School of Art. By 1914, Dubs' original works were the Southern Division of NB Loco, and interestingly also the location of a secret War Office project to produce a new weapon. When the prototype emerged from the old tank engineworks *The Tank* entered the language.

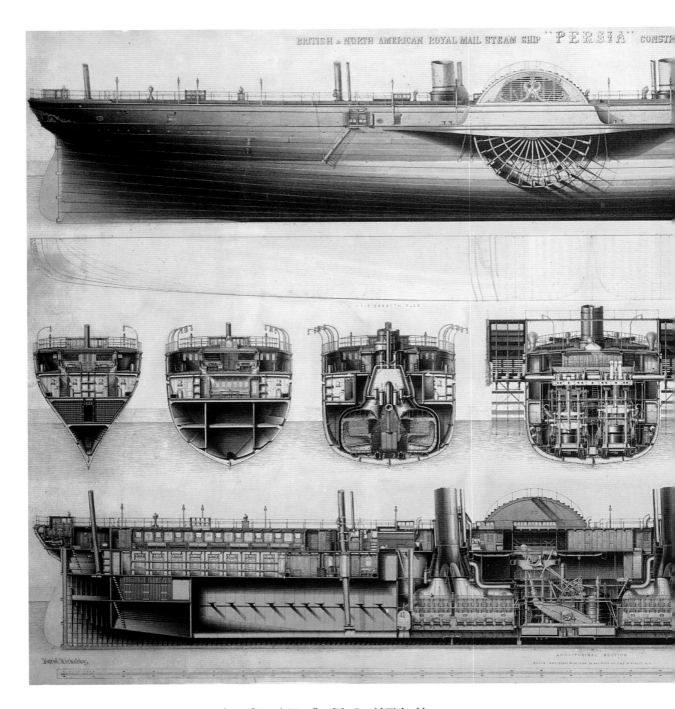

Drawings of "Persia" 'as fitted' by David Kirkcaldy,
exhibited Royal Academy 1861.
Only engineering drawings ever accepted by Royal Academy

David Kirkcaldy in later life.
Was student at Glasgow School of Art
around 1850.
Clearly studied shadow projection
and water colour rendering
in an architectural style.

"Persia" under construction on stocks in Robert Napier's Yard in 1855. One of the last ocean going paddle steamers to be built.

P.S.Persia at Sea.
Cunard mailship for Alantic run won Blue Riband for Eastward crossing.

Machine Drawing was originally a branch of Engineering Drawing concerned with mechanisms and the design of moving parts Machine Drawing in
the South Kensington system was a species of measured drawing, where scale
drawings in plan, elevation and section of ships, steam yachts, locomotives,
etc., were often nicely tinted up in watercolour. It is interesting to note at a
fairly late date the incorporation of architectural elements on machines, such
as dwarf Doric columns in the Greek style with fluting, and there was obviously an effort made to create engineered objects which performed efficiently,
and were at the same time pleasing to the eye.

Greenlees was at first overshadowed by Heath Wilson, who carried on as
unpaid Head as far as policy was concerned. Greenlees was however responsible for organising the transfer of the School from Ingram Street to
Sauchiehall Street at the end of 1868-69, the same session in which the
Glasgow Art Club was founded. According to a pamphlet on the history of the
Club, some of the local artists were in the habit of dining at the old School in
Ingram Street, and the group formed sketching parties in the summer. Out of
this group emerged the Glasgow Art Club in 1868, and Greenlees was a
founder member. Greenlees was also a founding member of what later became
the Royal Society of Watercolour Painters in Scotland, and in his own work he
specialised in West Highland subjects, typically woodland scenes with birch
trees growing out of a carpet of ferns. His technical skill is impressive, and he
ranks as a very competent landscape painter.

Greenlees' daughter Georgina was one of the first women teachers in the
School of Art, and she and some of her friends founded the Lady Artists' Club,
which later had premises in Blythswood Square, with a doorway by
Mackintosh. Georgina Greenlees was also a prizewinner in a competition for
the design of fans, now in the Prints and Drawings Collection at the V & A,
and this is one of the few examples of student work from the early period of
the Art School.

THOMAS C. SIMMONDS 1881-85

Thomas C Simmonds.
Head Master
Glasgow School of Art
prior to Newbery.
Portrait shows him after 1900
in Academic dress
of Honorary A.R.C.A.
(conferred on long serving
provincial Headmasters).

Robert Greenlees was succeeded as Headmaster in 1881 by Thomas Simmonds, formerly at Derby School of Art, where he was listed as a teacher of both Science and Art subjects, and whether he returned as Headmaster four years later. From available records, Simmonds seems to have been on the staff at Cheltenham School of Art early on his career, and in evidence to the Educational Endowments Commissioners in Glasgow he seemed very knowledgeable about the teaching of Drawing in the Birmingham Schools, which suggests he may also have had a spell there.

Simmonds was very businesslike and and his subsequent career suggests he was a good Headmaster in a managerial sense. Of his artistic abilities almost nothing is known, and it has not been possible to trace any of his work in a public collection. While Simmonds was Headmaster at Glasgow he tried to promote links between the School of Art and the Woollen College, a small independent textiles college concerned with training weavers. Nothing came of this but the Woollen College was later absorbed into the Technical College, and a co-operative liaison eventually led to a joint Diploma in Textiles shortly before the First War.

Simmonds was Headmaster at Glasgow for only four years, 1881-1885, and it is unlikely that he made much difference in that time, considering that practically all the students were part-time or evening, and a great many were in elementary stages. As already noted, Simmonds regularly complained to the Committee of Management about the School's unsatisfactory accommodation. and just as Simmonds left there were serious proposals for the building of a new central School.

Simmonds was succeeded by Francis Newbery who took up his duties as Headmaster in 1885. Newbery thus arrived on the scene when the School was very busy, when a new building was being mooted, and when Technical Education had become a live issue, precipitating a drastic revision of the South Kensington system.

McLellan Galleries Block
(Old Corporation Buildings)
c.1952.
Glasgow School of Art
was housed in East End
facing Rose Street, on right.
Small side door
old School entrance.

The Haldane Academy Trust

THE GLASGOW SCHOOL OF ART was probably unique among the Government Schools of Art in that it also received grants-in-aid from a private charity to develop the study of the fine arts, namely, the Haldane Academy Trust, set up by James Haldane, an engraver in Glasgow. As a condition of financial assistance, the Trustees required that the name be incorporated in the School's title, and the Glasgow School of Art and Haldane Academy was the form agreed on. However, for Science and Art Department purposes it was officially the Government School of Art, and indeed the School was advertised as such. Eventually, in 1891, the Trust itself asked the School of Art to drop 'Haldane Academy' from its title, as it was being confused with the Trust.

James Haldane created his Trust in 1833, and its provisions were that on his death, a capital sum would be realised from his estate, the interest from which would accrue to his wife during her lifetime. Following her death, the Trust would be activated for the purposes Haldane set out, i.e., to create a School of Art in Glasgow, teaching Drawing, Painting, Sculpture, Architecture and Garden Design. However, when Mrs Haldane died in 1868, the Trustees came to the conclusion that the School of Art by this time was providing an extent of art instruction which complied with most of Haldane's expressed wishes, and ruled that the object of the Trust funds could best be met by supporting the School of Art, rather than by duplicating its efforts.

The principal benefit which the School of Art enjoyed from the Haldane's Academy Trust was that the Trustees negotiated with the Corporation for accommodation to be made available for the School of Art. A rent was to be paid to the Corporation by the School, and the Trustees undertook to make an annual grant to the School equal to the amount, so that the School of Art enjoyed its tenancy in Corporation Buildings effectively rent-free.

The School of Art thus moved from Ingram Street to Corporation Buildings, Sauchiehall Street in 1869, at which time the name of the School was modified. The Trustees also introduced various prizes and awards, and in connection with these, appointed their own examiners of student work at the School of Art. From the phraseology used in the old records, it is clear that they regarded the School of Art as embodying the Haldane Academy as an entity, quite separate from the Government School of Art under the direction of the South Kensington regime. Thus, in a sense there was a School within a School, dedicated to the pursuit of Fine Art, free of the restrictions of the Government curriculum, allied to the needs of art manufacture.

The Trustees also arranged special lectures on art and architecture, for example, concerned particularly with the history and theory of fine art, and this was probably unique at that time, since the Government Schools of Art were almost wholly concerned with instruction in practical skills. The lecture series were known as the Haldane Lectures, but the only ones now remembered were those given by the architect Alexander 'Greek' Thomson. The Trustees experienced difficulty in persuading suitably eminent lecturers to visit – Ruskin was invited but declined – and it was possibly for this reason that they fell back on local resources and invited Thomson to give his Haldane Lectures on Architecture. These were subsequently published and reprinted as a pamphlet.

Alexander Thomson was one of the Haldane Trustees, and acted as a kind of 'shadow' Governor of the School of Art. To illustrate his lectures, Thomson recruited students from the Art School to prepare large diagrams of historic buildings, but only one of these diagrams has survived into modern times – a large plan and section of the Pantheon, Rome. A list of the others exists, but curiously, none of the buildings he chose was Greek.

The content of Thomson's lectures is uninspiring, and consists of very generalised observations. It is possible that they were tedious even to Victorian ears, and we can picture Thomson holding forth in his broad accent, in the manner of a Sunday School Superintendent, referring to his diagrams with a pointer, while the gas jets hiss and flare.

Thomson was referred to as a genius in his own lifetime, and described as such in the memorial set up after his death as the Alexander Thomson Studentship. This was to be awarded every three years on the basis of a design competition, and the successful student was to travel in the Mediterranean area to study ancient classical architecture. All those who have written about 'Greek' Thomson remark on the 'fact' that he never travelled abroad, and in particular had not visited Greece. However, there were no passports required in Thomson's day, and it was possible to sail from the Clyde to the Piraeus in little over a week, so that there is no reason why Thomson could not have visited Greece, or why any such visit should have been recorded.

The Haldane Academy Trustees included some prominent Glasgow figures, and Charles Heath Wilson became a Trustee when he resigned from the Headmastership of the School of Art. Other members were Blackie the publisher (father of the Blackie who commissioned Mackintosh), and Annan the photographer. Several of the Trustees were Professors at Glasgow University, and among them J Macquorn Rankine, Professor of Civil Engineering, whose name lives on as the deviser of Rankine's Formula (which relates to the bending or deflection of short columns). This connection of the School of Art and the Haldane's Academy Trust brought Professors of the University into contact with Trustees from the world of architecture, business, and industry, and was one of the few forums where town and gown came into direct contact.

By coincidence, the year in which the School of Art moved to Corporation Buildings, 1869, was the same year as the foundations were laid of the University of Glasgow's new buildings at Gilmorehill. Also, the Glasgow Institute of Architects was established in 1868, as was the Glasgow Art Club. Thus, 1868–69 is an important time in the artistic and educational history of Glasgow.

The activities of the Haldane's Academy Trust in bringing on the fine art side of the School from 1870 onwards, independent of Government grants, enabled a base to be established on which Francis Newbery could build, when he arrived as Headmaster in 1885. Of the engraver James Haldane, who left his estate to set up the Trust, little is known, and no likeness of him exists apart from an idealised portrait on a Haldane Medal. The only reference to him in

Alexander 'Greek' Thomson,
Architect.
Marble Bust by
John Mossman.
Mossman Governor GSA
and Teacher of modelling.

T. Craigie Annan, photographer
by Fra Newbery.
One of Mackintosh circle.
His father knew 'Greek' Thomson well.

print seems to be in an account of a trial involving anonymous letters, in which Haldane gave evidence as an expert witness on handwriting.

Haldane was a founder member of the Glasgow Philosophical Society, and engraved their Diploma of Membership. Haldane also had a sizeable library, auctioned off after his death, with sections on landscape, architecture, and art - subjects in which he had a strong interest - as witness the provisions of his Trust. A box of his engraving tools was recorded as being in the School Library of the Mackintosh building around 1910, but what became of them is not known.

Fra Newbery

FRANCIS H NEWBERY   1885-1914

Bram Stoker endowed an annual Medal at GSA in 1903. Stoker was a friend of Newbery before he wrote Dracula (1897)

IN 1886 the Glasgow and West of Scotland Technical College was formed, the first of the major rationalisations arising from the work of the Educational Endowments Commissioners. Two years later, in 1888, the Glasgow Exhibition took place, the proceeds from which paid for the new Kelvingrove Art Gallery and Museum, and in Lavery's large group painting of the exhibition opening, Francis Newbery is depicted, presumably as a member of the Art Section committee. Clearly, Newbery had established himself on the local scene, and had taken over as Headmaster of the School of Art just as a rolling programme of educational and training reform was gaining momentum.

Newbery is arguably the most important Director the Glasgow School of Art has had. It was during his Headship that Mackintosh's new School was built, and also that the School became completely independent of the Science and Art Department in London, with authority to issue its own Diplomas in Art, Design, and Architecture, and the departmental structure of the School created under Newbery's direction lasted virtually intact until 1964.

Newbery's active career at the School divides into two more or less equal parts. The first, 1885-1900, runs from his appointment to the end of the Science and Art Department, during which period the School operated under the South Kensington system, and the students took examinations set and marked in London. Crafts and the execution of designs in materials had been progressively introduced from 1894, beginning with Art Needlework, and after 1899, when the first half of the School's new building was finished, purpose-built workshops became available.

The second phase of Newbery's active Headship may be considered as running from 1900-1914, and in 1901, the Glasgow School of Art was designated the Central Institution for Higher Art Education in Glasgow and the West of Scotland, and given powers to award its own Diplomas, subject to inspection from time to time by the Scotch Education Department. That the Glasgow School of Art was highly regarded by the SED and the Treasury is clear from the authority granted to its Governors to appoint Professors in Sculpture, Painting, Architecture, and Design. Indeed, the only other School of Art permitted by the Treasury to have Professors was the Royal College of Art.

At the time, the Glasgow School of Art was moving into its new building and entering what Professor Christopher Frayling termed its 'golden age', while the Royal College of Art was without a decent building, had no workshops, and taught no crafts, other than etching. Also, black and white illustration (an expanding field with the growth of illustrated magazines using line blocks), was not taught there, although often the only employment for ex-College students in London was in illustration. Glasgow, on the other hand, seems to have been particularly strong in this area, particularly the women artists, and their work was much featured in the art journals of the time, such as THE YELLOW BOOK.

Fra Newbery and female students late eighteen-nineties.

Thus, with the move into the first half of the Mackintosh building, the Glasgow School of Art was 'up and running' at exactly the right time for maximum impact. Perceptively, one writer has described Newbery as being like an impresario, with his stable of high-fliers, stage-managing their appearances in exhibitions, and in print. Locally, he was nicknamed "The Ringmaster", no doubt because he cracked the whip over his protégés, and also because he habitually wore a top hat. Newbery was noted for his energy, and was a familiar figure bustling about the town. He was also a prolific correspondent, writing up to six letters a day, and became an effective fund-raiser.

It was through the Newberys that Mackintosh met Patrick Geddes, who was their occasional dinner guest. Newbery's daughter, Mrs Mary Sturrock, recalled Geddes standing at the fireplace after dinner, holding forth to the assembled company for about forty minutes non-stop: "It was marvellous - but it was a pity no-one took it all down. Of course, he was quite mad". Another eccentric guest of the Newberys was Bram Stoker. Mrs Sturrock recalled first meeting him at the age of eight, when she was with her father outside the Royal Academy, in Piccadilly. Desmond Chapman Huston may have been the link to figures from the literary and theatrical worlds who mixed in the Newbery circle. Bram Stoker, the author of Dracula, endowed a prize at the School of Art in 1903, which is still awarded annually for "the most imaginative work of the session in any branch of effort in the School".

Newbery exhibited a very modern profile, akin to a hustling empire-building University Vice-Chancellor - a roving ambassador for his institution, well known in the corridors of power, and constantly promoting plans to keep his charge in the public eye. A certain degree of myth-making, however, has resulted in Newbery being presented as the man who made everything happen,

Fra Newbery.
Caricature from Quiz 1894.
Newbery was an effective
publicist and was frequently
featured in gossip columns
of local magazines.

but his success would have been impossible without the support of both his Governors, and the then Secretary of the Scottish Education Department, Sir John Struthers.

Newbery himself always deferred to the Governors, whose decisions had to be communicated to the SED, and could not be authorised until Department approval had been given. This even extended to the appointment of part-time teachers on hourly rates of pay, and the wording of the School prospectus, for example, had to be sent through in draft to Edinburgh for vetting before it was printed. There was thus a very distinct chain of command and Newbery was conscious of his position as a servant of the Governors.

Once the new building was complete, the Governors mainly concerned themselves with financial management and staffing matters, and can be compared in some ways to a University Court. In curricular and teaching matters, however, Newbery and his staff enjoyed complete freedom. In this respect, Glasgow may be contrasted with the typical municipal art school in England, which was managed by the Corporation Education Committees that ran the ordinary schools, and not allowed to handle its own finances. Centrally funded by the Treasury, and constituted along the lines of a University College, the Glasgow School of Art had by 1914 achieved a position of independence not

The half-completed building.

reached by colleges in England for another 75 years or so, when the local authority polytechnics were transferred to the Department of Education and Science.

The School of Art moved up to a half-completed building in Renfrew Street in 1899, and this was finally completed in 1909. The School thus reached its full physical size at the end of a decade of transition, and Newbery only had a couple of years before the War put an end to his grand design. Women students volunteered for war work - Newbery's daughter Mary went into munitions - and the men went off to the services. The new School was depopulated and student numbers dropped back to the level they had been in Corporation Buildings, before 1899.

In THE THREE MARYS (1930) by Frederick Niven, a former student at the School, Newbery makes a thinly-disguised appearance as 'Francis Raeburn', who opens an Art School on the island of Arran:

> *Raeburn had a name, if not as a great painter, as a great art master. He provoked enthusiasms. He could bring out of his pupils what capacity was in them. In appearance he was as if out of Italian opera. One expected him to clear his throat, touch his lips with a finger, and break forth in song, basso profondo. But instead he painted, and taught. He had intended to call his School of Art the Fra. Raeburn Atelier, and had all the copy at the printer's for the prospectus, when a photographer opened what he called an Atelier in the same street. And though to call a school of art an atelier (outside of France) is not as pretentious as calling a photograph-establishment so, Raeburn was not annoyed, save momentarily. He felt that the photographer had rescued him from what, outside of France, might smack of affectation. School of Art, he decided, was better, better even than Academy of Art which, as a substitute for atelier, had occurred to him next, prone as he was to a little flaunt in life, a gesture. That egregious photographer decided it. He was all for directness, simplicity: The Raeburn School of Art. But he kept the Francis as Fra. on the prospectus: "Headmaster, Fra. Raeburn, RI, RBA"...*

Newbery and male students - 1890

As a teacher, Newbery also seems to have been fond of military analogies, and an example of his style, taken from a lecture to the Royal Philosophical Society in Glasgow in 1887, is given in Appendix C.

Newbery had his first serious illness in 1914, and although he had been overworking for some time, according to Mrs Newbery, the outbreak of war seemed to have been the last straw. Eventually he went back to the School, but in 1916, the news of Professor Bourdon's death came as a great shock, and Newbery suffered a relapse the following year, and did not return.

In 1917 he was granted early retirement on medical grounds, diagnosed by his doctor as "acute neurasthenia". This is now an obsolete term, but several recent papers in medical journals argue that the modern diagnosis of ME (Myalgic encephalomyelitis) is the old neurasthenia in new guise. In Newbery's day, the only treatment was complete rest, and he eventually did recover, to resume his painting activities, and indeed lived on in retirement at Corfe Castle in Dorset, until 1946, when he died at the age of 92.

*Outing of the staff of the
Glasgow School of Art,
Tarbet Hotel, Loch Lomond 1890.
This includes Fra Newbery
(standing centre),
Sir James Fleming,
Sandy McGibbon,
J Arnold Fleming,
Sir James Guthrie and
D.Mitchell
(janitor, standing top right).*

Newbery painting: 'Accord'

VIII

Margaret Macdonald Mackintosh

THE CIRCLE OF WOMEN ARTISTS, ILLUSTRATORS, and designers associated with the School of Art around 1900 has been christened "The Glasgow Girls", presumably meant as the counterpart to "The Glasgow Boys", though the common factor among the latter was Paris experience, not the School of Art, and they actively disliked the name, said to have been coined by Whistler, and taken up by the newspapers.

Margaret Macdonald and her sister Frances, along with their future husbands, Charles Mackintosh and Herbert McNair, were reputedly known as "The Four", though there is scarcely any contemporary evidence of that. In modern times, of course, the fame of The Four has spread, and indeed a recent review article in THE TIMES referred throughout to "The Glasgow Four", a term which will no doubt enter the cuttings files along with the Guildford Four and the Birmingham Six.

The first craft subject to be taught at the School of Art was Art Needlework, introduced in 1894. This commended itself to the School partly because no special facilities were required, and properly equipped workshops could not be provided in Corporation Buildings - one reason why the School badly needed new premises. Over the period 1891-93, the Technical Instruction Committees in England proposed schemes for instruction in various subjects, and in 1894, the Science and Art Department permitted designs worked in materials to accompany drawings sent to South Kensington for examination.

Though this is the first official recognition of craftwork within the Government examination system, practical crafts, often to a very high standard, had long been an approved activity for middle-class young women. THE STUDIO, founded in 1893, even had a competition section for amateurs, in which their work would be published alongside that of noted professionals, and a few years later THE ART JOURNAL noted a number of young artist-craftswomen exhibiting their own jewellery designs, and observed that women were now attempting work previously done only by tradesmen.

The same phenomenon is noted by Muthesius, in his THE DILETTANTE CRAFTWORK MOVEMENT IN ENGLAND, and the momentum for this home handicraft activity obviously derives from the Arts and Crafts Movement. Workshop space was often necessary, and in the case of metal-bashing pursuits this meant relegation to an outbuilding, coach-house or disused stable. Clearly, such work could not be carried on in a tenement, and only those young ladies who lived in big houses and had no other occupation were likely to be active metalworkers. Once the Schools of Art were equipped for craftwork, towards 1900, there was a considerable middle-class influx, mostly to the day classes. Amateurs were already well represented in the drawing and painting classes, and the social mix in the day-classes was becoming more like that of the Universities, and much less like that of the technical schools, which catered primarily for those in industrial employment, and taught mainly at night.

Margaret Macdonald Mackintosh

To return to Margaret Macdonald, the chronology of her life shows that she spent most of it in England, variously in Staffordshire, London and Suffolk. Indeed, the only decade she was more or less continuously in Glasgow was in the 1890s, and even then the summer months would be spent away from the city. It could thus be argued that the term "Glasgow Girl" is inappropriate, and given the social milieu in which a number of them moved, "Glasgow Gels" might have been more apt. Nora Neilson Gray's father, for example, was a shipowner, and Agnes De Courcy Lewthwaite Dewar lists forestry as a hobby, suggesting a landed background (her father was a tea-planter in Ceylon)..

Neil Munro, the author of PARA HANDY, elsewhere describes a visit by one 'Erchie', and his friend Duffy the coalman, to the Sauchiehall Street gallery of the Royal Glasgow Institute of the Fine Arts in 1904:

> *"By Jove!" said Duffy, suddenly, "here's a corker!" and he indicated a rather peculiar drawing with a lady artist's name attached to it.*
>
> *Erchie himself was staggered. "It's ca'd 'The Sleeper' in the catalogue," said he. "It's a wumman, and her dozin'. The leddy that pented it wasna ower lavish wi' her pent. That's whit they ca' New Art, Duffy; it just shows ye whit weemen can dae if ye let them."*
>
> *"And dae ye tell me there's weemen penters?" asked Duffy in astonishment.*
>
> *"Of course there's weemen penters."*
>
> *"And hoo dae they get up and doon lethers?" asked Duffy.*
>
> *"I'm tellin' ye Art pentin's a brench by itsel," said Erchie. "The lady art penters dinna pent windows and rhones and hooses; they bash brass, and hack wud, and draw pictures."*
>
> *"And can they mak a living at that?"*
>
> *"Whiles. And whiles their paw helps."*

"The Sleeper", incidentally, was a painting by Margaret Macdonald Mackintosh, and the mention of bashing brass and hacking wood of course refers to the Arts and Crafts activities already noted as a middle-class female preoccupation of the time. The suggestion that Daddy sometimes helps out financially also tends to confirm the fact that few of the Glasgow women artists needed to earn a living wholly from their art work and teaching.

Margaret Macdonald Mackintosh is stated as having a private income from investments of £250-£300 a year, before the First World War, suggesting a capitalised value of almost £7000 - at today's values, somewhere in the order of a quarter of a million. Putting her income in context, it is perhaps worth noting that Professors Bourdon and Gourlay, e.g., were on £450 p.a., an Assistant Keeper of the National Gallery of Scotland was on £250, and a lecturer at the Technical College, £150.

Margaret Macdonald and Mackintosh were married in 1900, and in the same year she appears in the GPO Directory as the owner or occupier of a flat in North Kensington, then a very fashionable newly-developed area. Quite possibly she used this as a studio, and for the decade 1900-1910, the Mackintoshes had a pied-à-terre in London; it can be assumed she was up and down to the city a good deal, keeping up with her smart friends, some of

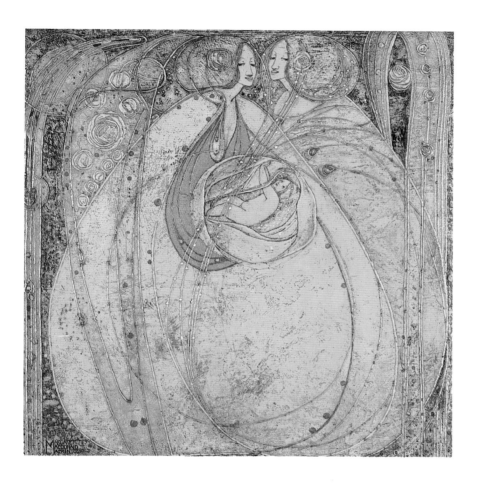

'The Heart of the Rose'
gesso panel by Margaret

whom ranked high on the social scale. Lady Alix Egerton, for example, often visited the Mackintoshes in Glasgow, and "loved waking up in that attic bedroom" in their house in South park Avenue, with the chorus of the University clock in the distance. Most likely visits were reciprocated and the Mackintoshes would be received at Lady Alix's home, Bridgewater House, the town house of Lord Ellesmere, her father, which faced on to Green Park at the rear of St. James' Palace. However, judging from the vehemence of one of his letters to Margaret on the subject, it is clear that Mackintosh had encountered a few offensive snobs among the upper classes.

In a sense it was the Mackintoshes' misfortune that their stock was highest in those European centres of café society - Vienna, Budapest, Munich, Brussels - which would be engulfed by the war, and whose regimes would not long survive. Also, it is probably true to say that pre-war Art Nouveau, Jugendstil, Secession, etc., were cosmopolitan, urban styles for bourgeois sophisticates, and of little interest to the aristocracy, who tended to inherit their homes and furniture. For example, it is unlikely that any great country house had an Art

Dunglass Castle, Dunbartonshire, parental home of Margaret Macdonald until her marriage to Mackintosh (photo c. 1890; now demolished)

Nouveau Room in the way that, say, Chinese Rooms were common in 18th century stately homes in England.

The Mackintoshes occupied the Southpark Avenue house in Glasgow from 1906-1914, when they left for England and rented the house out to a friend of Sir Walter and Lady Raleigh. Raleigh had been Professor of English Literature at Glasgow University, and then Oxford, and clearly Margaret Mackintosh had kept up their acquaintance. Another friend, Desmond Chapman Huston, who had introduced Margaret to Lady Alix Egerton, later acted on Mackintosh's behalf on the occasion of the "spy business" in 1915, and was well enough connected to prevail on Lord Curzon, then out of office, to write to the Home Secretary, asking him to give his personal attention to Mackintosh's petition to clear his name.

Margaret Macdonald Mackintosh was herself on the point of appearing in WHO'S WHO in 1933 when she died, and the entry was cancelled. A printer's proof of her entry survives, the contents of which are unremarkable except for the entry against education, where she listed Germany, as well as schools in Britain. This suggests that she may have spent some time there, perhaps with a family, to improve her proficiency in the language, and there is a letter in fairly good German from the Mackintoshes in a Vienna archive, a reply to some invitation which they had to decline. Margaret Macdonald also studied music, and according to a retired teacher from her old school, the Orme School for Girls in Staffordshire, there are newspaper notices of her success in open examinations in music, with a high placing.

Considerable effort has gone into portraying Mackintosh's life as tragic, but in the view of Lady Barnes, the real tragedy was the curtailment of Margaret's own artistic career, when she more or less gave up her art in order to look after her husband. Whether she had the potential for continuing development can never be known, but once they left Glasgow, her artistic work fell away. Around that time, 1926, her own health was not good, and she was receiving treatment, probably for some arthritic condition. In fact, to outward appearance, she seems to have been in worse shape than he was, for just a few weeks before Mackintosh noticed the first symptoms of his final illness, a German tourist told him he was the "healthiest looking man he had ever seen".

Margaret Macdonald died at the age of sixty-eight, well beyond the average life expectancy of her time. When she entered the Glasgow School of Art in 1890, she was already twenty-five, what would be termed today a "mature student", and her artistic development was such that it must be presumed she had had some prior art training in England. The Macdonald sisters are referred to in a STUDIO article as two Glasgow artists "who were until recently denizens of the Metropolis", and this suggests that Margaret might have been a student at one of the London Art Schools, perhaps St John's Wood, or Heatherley's.

According to THE DICTIONARY OF BRITISH ARTISTS 1880-1940, the earliest date traced in an exhibition catalogue for her was 1880. If this entry is correct, it means that Margaret Macdonald exhibited work somewhere at the age of 15. Unfortunately, however, the publishers have not retained the research papers of the compilers. In 1880, Margaret Macdonald would still have been at school in North Staffordshire, and there was a Government School of Art at Newcastle-under-Lyme, though no records survive from that date. Perhaps she had a good teacher from the Newcastle Art School, or attended a private school. At any rate, a reasonable case can be made for Margaret Macdonald having had ten years of art activity of some kind before she enrolled at the Glasgow School of Art.

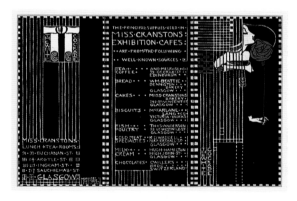

Menu Cover from
Miss Cranston's restaurant/tearoom.
Designed by Margaret Macdonald Mackintosh.

C H A P T E R *IX*

Charles Rennie Mackintosh

CHARLES RENNIE MACKINTOSH was born in 1868, the son of a police Lieutenant, and grew up among eight brothers and sisters. His father latterly attained the rank of Superintendent, and spent almost his entire police service in the Chief Constable's Office, engaged in administrative work. Much of his spare time was spent on his allotment, and he was a regular prizewinner at flower shows. Mackintosh often helped his father, and was presumably familiar with the botanical names of the species.

Mackintosh may have begun flower drawing in connection with an Art School class, and by 1893 he was collecting pressed flowers for drawing purposes, as evidenced by a drawing in Glasgow Art Club: "Anemone: Found Lamlash, Arran, May 1893: Drawn, May 1896". The title reveals that the drawing was made from the pressed flower ('copying from the flat').

It is generally assumed that Mackintosh's art training began when he left school and became an architect's apprentice, thereafter joining evening classes at the School of Art. Mackintosh attended Allan Glen's Institution, and while the general education was more or less standard for the time, there was a rule that "Greek shall not be taught in the School" - most probably to make room for modern languages, rather than from any anti-classical bias, since Latin was compulsory. Of particular interest, though, is the existence of a Technical Department, offering instruction in workshop practice in wood and metal, fully a decade before such subjects were introduced in English schools.

The official classification of Allan Glen's at that time was as an "Organised Science School", as defined by the Science and Art Department at South Kensington. This meant that subjects were studied systematically in "courses", then a new idea, and boys followed the syllabus for some Art and Science subjects as pursued at the Art School. There is no record of the grades achieved at school by Mackintosh in Perspective and Practical Plane and Solid Geometry, but he later re-took these at the School of Art and gained an "Excellent" rating.

Drawing was a compulsory subject at Allan Glen's, following the orthodox approach of the time, and Mackintosh very possibly also did some Engineering Drawing in the school's Technical Department. Projects undertaken in the workshops progressed to a high level of craftsmanship. The main exercises in Woodwork, for example, were the making of sectional and reduced-scale models of machines with moving parts for demonstration in the Engineering classes. It may be assumed that Mackintosh left school with the woodworking skills to make a piece of furniture, and if metalwork was taught to the same standard, some decorative wrought iron may even have been made. Mackintosh's own metalwork skills are well demonstrated in the repoussé brass box he made for Jessie Keppie.

In a report on the Scottish Art Schools in 1905 Pittendreigh McGillivray, RSA, lamenting the lack of workshop training for architects, observed that:

Photograph of C R Mackintosh by Annan, Glasgow, c 1900.

The architect... ought not to rest as what the engineer styles in his profession, an office clerk...

Mackintosh's exposure to workshop instruction, and to a fairly high level, was thus unusual for the period. Also, in following the Science and Art syllabus at Allan Glen's, it can be seen that Mackintosh had already taken some Art School subjects, before leaving school to begin his apprenticeship, at the age of 15.

Mackintosh's name first appears in Art School registers in 1883, and for the last time in 1894. In the prize lists he appears from 1884 onwards, and won the Alexander Thomson Studentship in 1890, which enabled him to travel in Italy.in 1891.. This could be considered a kind of postgraduate award, as he had completed his professional training by 1890. The spread of Architecture and Art subjects which Mackintosh had studied virtually constituted a full course in Architecture, of the type familiar until the early 1960s.

It seems likely that Mackintosh also took some structural subjects – mechanics and steelwork design perhaps – possibly at the Technical College, although there is no listing for him on surviving registers. He may have taken Engineering Science classes at the University, which a few of the architects did, since he seems to have calculated his own steelwork for the School of Art building.

What is evident from Mackintosh's record as an evening student at the School of Art, over the period 1883-94, is that he took far more subjects than any other architectural trainee of the period. His success rate in competitions is very good, though not exceptional, and according to Chapman Huston, Mackintosh had been especially noted for his life drawing. He also studied Modelling, and in 1889 was awarded a local prize for modelling ornament from the cast, the adjudicator being the sculptor John Mossman. This indicates Mackintosh's competence, and a decade later, in 1899, he modelled the ornamental keystone for the front doorway of the Art School in plaster, full size, in his office.

Thus, in addition to being gifted with pencil and brush, Mackintosh could confidently turn his hand to woodwork, metalwork and modelling, and had been steadily refining these skills over a period of ten years or so, at evening school, after the daily grind of the drawing office.

Among the more curious subjects Mackintosh studied after his apprenticeship was Sciography (shadow casting), which he took in 1889-90. Sciography was usually pursued as a branch of Descriptive Geometry, and got out of the way early on. However, Newbery no doubt encouraged as many students as possible to enter for the Government examinations, since a success at 1st Class would bring the School a payment, although in the case of middle-class students, no payments were made. Eventually, of course, the 'carrot and stick' South Kensington system was swept away and replaced by the block grant, but during his career as a student, Mackintosh won several design prizes and medals. His last examination pass at the School of Art was in 1892-93, in Design 23c, 1st Class, and fellow students listed include Frances Macdonald, Herbert McNair and John Quinton Pringle.

The subject of Design 23c was previously called Design Ornament, and was one not often taken by architects. It included pattern geometry, historical study, textile and wallpaper design (what would now be called two-dimensional design) and this would have given Mackintosh the opportunity to experiment with repeat patterns and other devices in textile design, which he was later to exploit during his sojourn in London, after 1914.

Mackintosh joined Honeyman and Keppie in 1889, the year before he won the Alexander Thomson Scholarship, and was made a partner in the firm in 1901, when it became Honeyman, Keppie and Mackintosh. Mackintosh did not become a member of the RIBA until 1906, when he was elected a Fellow, on the basis of his record as architect and designer, and a glowing tribute from Keppie, extolling the qualities of the recently completed Scotland Street School.

Contrary to Professor Howarth's 1952 chronology of the architect's life, Mackintosh did not become a Fellow of the RIAS in 1908, since that body was not founded until 1918. It should also be noted that Mackintosh became a FRIBA without first having been an Associate, and in fact completed his training before the RIBA Examinations in their modern form were introduced.

Under the South Kensington system, all art subjects were examined by drawings, designs and modelled work, and it can thus be stated with confidence that, after he left Allan Glen's, Mackintosh probably never sat a written examination again.

The South Kensington system ended in 1900, and from 1901 full-time Diploma courses were introduced, and formally recognised by the Scotch Education Department as proof of 'professional ability', rather than academic qualifications. Indeed, when a Degree in Architecture was mooted at Glasgow University in 1923, the SED officers were not enthusiastic about the proposal, since it might appear to devalue the Diploma, which was a different, and if anything, superior qualification, in so far as its holder was fit to enter professional practice in a position of responsibility, and was not simply a graduate trainee.

The SED officers were also insistent on practising architects and designers being appointed as external assessors for the new Diploma courses, and took the same line with the Technical College. When the College Director wanted to appoint two University Professors from England to examine in engineering subjects he was told "these are men of theory only" and was advised to reappoint assessors from local industries. When Diploma courses were introduced at the School of Art in the several sections, each section also had a panel of Examiners for the award of bursaries and studentships, and Mackintosh served for a time as a local examiner in the Design and Decorative Art section.

Mackintosh was a member of the Glasgow Institute of Architects and was elected to its Council, rising to be one of the three Vice-Presidents in the years before 1914, and if the war had not intervened he would no doubt have become President. In 1892, membership of the Board of Governors of the School of Art had been widened to increase local representation, and the Glasgow Institute of Architects was granted a seat on the Board. Mackintosh was nominated as a Governor between 1910 and 1914, hence his addition to Newbery's well-known group portrait of the Governors of the School.

While Mackintosh served on the GIA Council, he was a member of its Town Planning Committee. This does not necessarily indicate interest in urban design, and it was in fact was a watchdog committee concerned about the effects of the first Town Planning Act of 1909, and its encroachment on the powers and functions of the architect. Fortuitously perhaps, Mackintosh had completed his masterwork, the School of Art, just before the era of statutory planning commenced.

Mackintosh left Glasgow in 1914, and although he returned to the city a few times during the war, doing work for Miss Cranston, the date of his last appearance in the Art School is unknown. Certainly, he wrote to a friend after the war, asking who the new people were at the School, and said that probably the only one he would know was Grieffenhagen.

Mackintosh died in December 1928, and a number of obituaries were published. However, the School of Art Annual Report, issued in the summer of 1929, did not note his death, no doubt because there had been very full appreciations in the press earlier in the year. The next reference to Mackintosh in the text of a School of Art prospectus does not occur until session 1938-39, thirty years after the building was completed, and it observes that:

*Group portrait by Newbery
presented to Governors in 1914.
Mackintosh was added to the
group as he had become
a Governor of the School
representing The Architects
Institute.*

*This building is of historic interest and was designed by Charles
Rennie Mackintosh, who is regarded by many as the pioneer of modern
architecture...*

In April 1947 the Mackintosh Room was opened in the School of Art, as a
museum of furniture, designs and watercolours by the architect, and later that
year, Douglas Percy Bliss wrote an appreciation of Mackintosh for SCOTTISH
FIELD which admirably sums up his significance in a national and international context (see Appendix D).

As regards Mackintosh and the School of Art building, there was a very
considerable increase in the number of publications coming forward during
the Directorship of H Jefferson Barnes. In 1961, D P Bliss produced an attractive little brochure for visitors, titled CHARLES RENNIE MACKINTOSH AND
THE SCHOOL OF ART, and Barnes produced two companion volumes on
Mackintosh's Furniture and Metalwork. In the same year, Barnes organised
loans of Mackintosh items to the Council of Europe Exhibition in Paris, entitled "Sources of the XXth Century", which was held at the Musee d'Art
Nationale Moderne. When these items were returned to Glasgow, Barnes
arranged a large exhibition in the School's Museum area, and in a lengthy
article in ART AND ARTISTS, in 1968, Mario Amaya observed that:

Total recognition of Mackintosh was complete in April, 1961, when the Glasgow School of Art …. held a large retrospective of his work that included everything from watercolours to doorways and knives and forks".

This contrasts strangely with a passage in Grigor and Murphy's THE ARCHITECTS' ARCHITECT, published in 1995, which claims that:

It is hard to imagine now that in the Glasgow of the 1960's Mackintosh was a nearly forgotten figure.

In fact, the 1961 Mackintosh Exhibition at the School of Art was well attended by the public and excited great interest locally. And in 1964, when the RIBA held its Conference in Glasgow, three or four hundred architects from England attended, bringing in their wake the architectural press. A reception was held in the School Museum, and the visitors were suitably impressed. Most of them had not been to Glasgow before, and a number of articles on the School of Art appeared in trade papers, and were picked up by the Sundays.

Mackintosh's centenary fell in 1968, and plans were laid for a 'blockbuster' exhibition, at the Royal Museum of Scotland in Edinburgh. This was designed by Henry Hellier, Head of Interior Design at the School of Art, and it caused a great stir, moving on to the V&A, and then to venues in Europe, generating articles in several languages. The evidence thus does not really bear out the notion that Mackintosh was neglected in the 1960's, and Mackintosh scholarship has continued unabated up to the present day.

Charles Rennie Mackintosh Knives and Forks.
One of the few architects who designed cutlery.
From Miss Cranston's tearooms.

On the following two pages:
Original 1896 competition design drawings for School of Art discovered Scottish Records Office 1994 (previously thought not to exist). Found by the author.

They were redated 1897 and sent directly to South Kensington for a building grant (see dept. stamp).

THE GLASGOW SCHOOL of ART
COMPETITION DESIGN FOR NEW SCHOOL

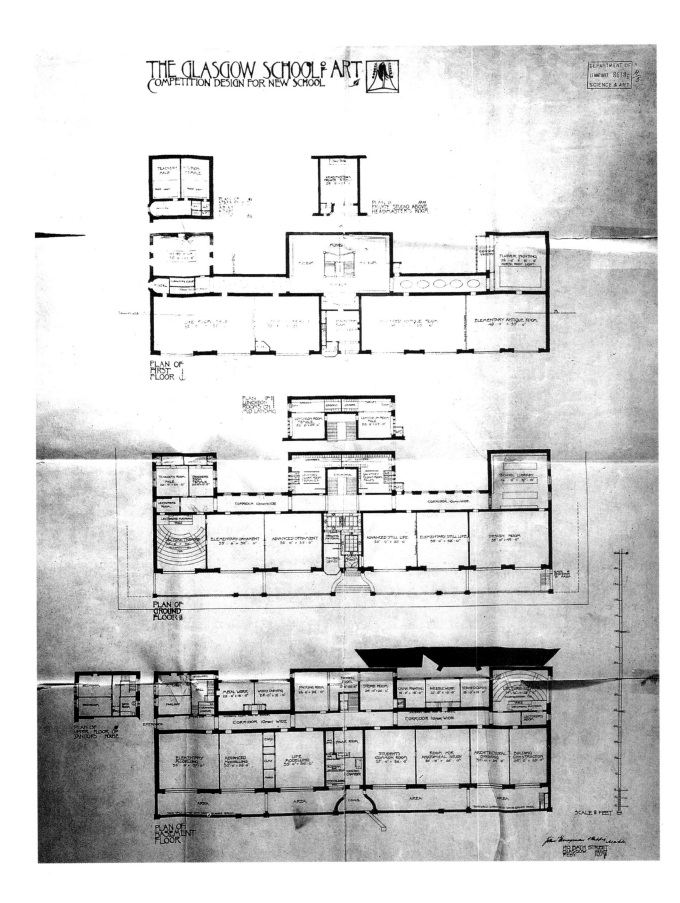

PLAN OF
FIRST
FLOOR

PLAN OF
GROUND
FLOOR

PLAN OF
BASEMENT
FLOOR

PLAN OF
UPPER FLOOR OF
JANITORS HOUSE

SCALE 8 FEET

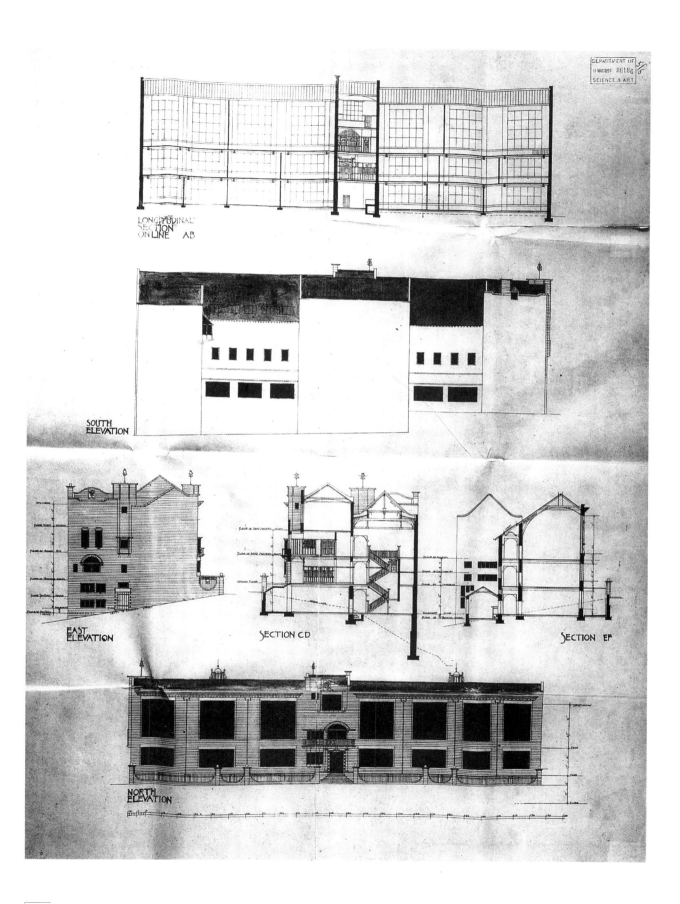

LONGITUDINAL
SECTION
ON LINE AB

SOUTH
ELEVATION

EAST
ELEVATION

SECTION CD

SECTION EF

NORTH
ELEVATION

The Glasgow School of Art Building

A DETAILED STUDY of the School of Art building, MACKINTOSH'S MASTERWORK, was published in 1989. In it, Bill Buchanan explains the complicated sequence of events which led to the first state of the design. Most interestingly, he was able to locate the original conditions of the Architectural Competition of 1896, which had eluded Howarth. Howarth also declared that Mackintosh's original drawings no longer existed, and the statement has been followed by all subsequent commentators. In fact, the Competition drawings do exist, though Howarth could not know that, since they were discovered only in the summer of 1994, in the Scottish Record Office, where they have now been added to the Register House Plans series, reference no. RHP 93854/5.

Mackintosh's plans, elevations and sections were found in an envelope in a General Administrative File which contained building grant correspondence with the Science and Art Department. These papers were transferred to the Scottish Education Department shortly after 1900, when the South Kensington Building Grants section was absorbed into the Board of Education. And when the Scottish Education Department moved to St. Andrews House in 1938, the papers were sent to the Scottish Record Office.

Without going into too much technical detail, it will be seen that the plans are identical to the floor plans illustrated in the School Prospectus for 1907-1908 in connection with the Building Fund Appeal and the Scottish Record Office plans should be read in conjunction with the Architectural Competition conditions reproduced in MACKINTOSH'S MASTERWORK, pp. 205-209.

The most important of the stipulated conditions is No. 8:

> *The south elevation may not have any lights in its walls, in a line with the building line, except perhaps in the upper floor...*

That is, the lower portion of the walls running along the site boundary to the south must be free of windows. The reason for this is that in Scotland there are no rights to light from outwith a building plot - all benefits must accrue from within a proprietor's own boundaries. Thus, it was conceivable that at some future date the adjacent proprietor to the south of the School of Art could build up along his northern boundary, and account had to be taken of the fact that another building might legally blot out any windows on the School's southern boundary wall.

Interestingly, the south front of the School as designed and built has two rectangular recesses, at the bottom of which lantern lights provide top light to classrooms. In the event of another building going up, these two recesses would become light wells, and the small windows on the south front walls along the boundary would be lost. However, the rooms contained in those parts of the façade which break forward to the south have extra windows on their flanks, looking east and west into the light wells. Thus, the entire modelling of the southern front of the School takes as its point of departure the functional requirements of Condition No. 8.

Also recently located in the School of Art records is a copy of a handwritten report which accompanied the first designs of Honeyman and Keppie, presumably by Mackintosh. The argument in favour of the design is entirely framed in terms of its technical merits, and the functional efficiency of the plan, with no reference whatever to its external appearance or architectural character. The main concern was simplicity of construction, value for money, and the provision of the requisite square footage of space. This is what the Building Grants inspectors were interested in at the Science and Art Department. They were Royal Engineers officers, who inspected plans against the official book of rules, and questions of appearance were not part of their remit.

The grant received from South Kensington was £500, the maximum allowed under the Building Grant Regulations. The Scotch Education Department appears to have played no direct part in the building of the second half of the School, except for financial assistance, no doubt treating it as already approved when the entire design was vetted by the Science and Art Department and passed for grant. It is therefore probably fair to say that the first half of the School was built under fairly strict conditions, but that by the time the second half came to be built the Governors had almost complete autonomy.

The familiar and oft-repeated story is that Mackintosh was constantly at loggerheads with the Governors, and this version of events seems to have derived from Desmond Chapman Huston who claims that Mackintosh was exhausted by "constant battles with the Corporation". However, the Corporation had nothing to do with the School of Art, except as landlord until 1899 (Corporation Buildings). George Rawson, Assistant Librarian in the School is currently engaged on a major study of the Newbery period and can find no evidence of any discord between the Committee and Mackintosh, merely routine minuting of the monthly meetings at which the architect made his progress reports, although tight guidelines were laid down at the outset.

Chapman Huston also makes the absurd claim that Glasgow treated Mackintosh badly by giving him such a poor site for his School of Art. Of course the sequence of events was site acquired first, competition for design second, and winner picked third, architect identified last of all.

The design competition, promoted in 1896, was not advertised, and half of the competitors already had a connection with the School. Those who were Governors resigned from the Board for the duration of the competition, and in all, eleven firms competed.

Mackintosh's winning entry, submitted in his firm's name, was accompanied by a written report which concerned itself almost entirely with the technical and functional merits of the design - heating, lighting, ventilation, drainage, construction, cost. These were all aspects of design mentioned in the Building Grant Regulations of the Science and Art Department, and it is clear that the competition conditions were drafted with those in mind.

Among the regulations, it was required that "the windows should be large, and in Art Schools, free from mullions or small panes", and Regulation 14(b) stipulated:

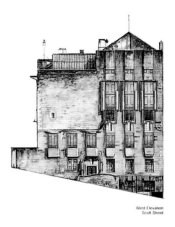

West Elevation
Scott Street

*Half-building line drawing
by McGibbon c. 1900.
First half of School building
completed 1899.*

*A room for study from life or life-size casts, not less than 20ft x 24ft.
This room should be lighted from the North side by a single large
window, the top of which (carried up in a dormer if necessary)
should be at a height above the floor equal to 3/4 the depth of the
room, or if the pitch of the roof be steeper than 60°, a skylight should
be made in continuation of the windows, so as to give the same effect
in lighting...*

This formula was applied by Mackintosh to achieve the window height of 26ft
on a room depth of 35ft for the first floor studios facing Renfrew Street. Thus,
the leading dimension of the tall studio windows is the direct result of apply-
ing an arithmetical rule in a building regulation, and not any architectural
"expression of function" by the designer. However, rather than a dormer solution for supplementary top light, Mackintosh does show originality in
providing strips of horizontal glazing in the School's flat roof, set back from
the window walls. Geometrically quite different from the recommended solutions, it achieves the desired effect.

Once the Treasury grant was confirmed, work on the building started, but
only on that portion which could be completed in 18 months, in the first
instance, so that the grant could be claimed. Payment was conditional on com-
pletion within the time limit, and this partly explains the drive to complete
the first half by 1899. At the end of that year, the Board of Education took over
the functions of the Science and Art Department, which ceased to exist. The
School of Art transferred to its new premises, and began collecting funds to
pay for the second half of the building, constructed in 1907-09.

The competition conditions of 1896 did not ask for a West elevation, only
North, South and East. Thus the West elevation remained undesigned until
1906, ten years after the preparation of the winning entry. Since then,
Mackintosh had had a further decade of personal development, and it is no
surprise that the Library wing should be so different from the earlier building. It is certainly the case that the most interesting interiors belong to the
second phase: the Secretary's Office (doubling as the new Board Room), the
Library and Life Modelling Room.

*Front elevation of
Glasgow School of Art
plus two end views
by Dugald Cameron 1981.*

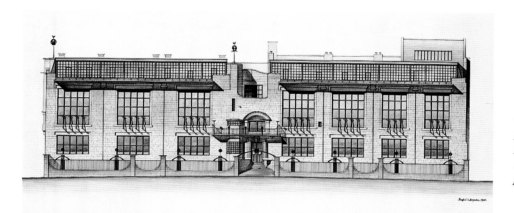

*Glasgow School of Art :
North front.
Hugh C S Ferguson
measured drawing;
pen ink, watercolour, 1962.*

*Lorraine Gilmour's
painting of
Glasgow School of Art,
student work 1989.*

The third drawing in the set showing cross sections of the proposed building.

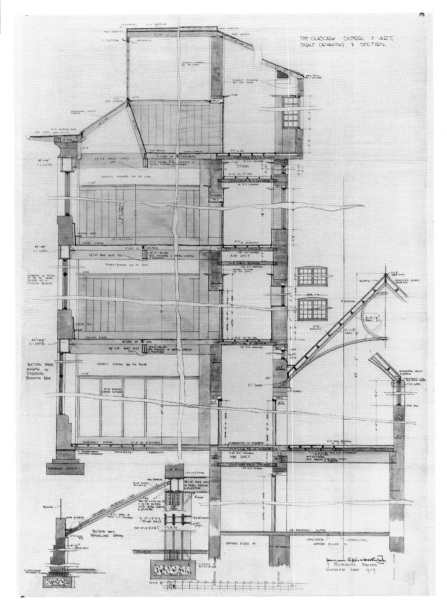

In summary, three main sets of drawings show the development of Mackintosh's designs for the School of Art, and these are: the Competition Drawings, 1896, used as Building Grant Application drawings, and now housed in the Scottish Record Office; the Dean of Guild Court Drawings, 1907, application for building permission, now in Strathclyde Regional Archives, with copies in the School of Art Collection; and the Record Drawings of the School of Art as built, 1910, a set of ten in the School of Art Collections.

Close study of the Dean of Guild Court drawings of 1907 suggests that Mackintosh submitted his drawings for permission to commence building, then progressively redesigned each room in turn to a large scale. Surprisingly, no large-scale detailed drawings of the Library survive, or any perspective views of the exterior or interiors before execution. As Mary Sturrock later observed, "The Governors didn't really know what they were going to get", but Mackintosh clearly enjoyed the confidence of the Building Committee.

The lack of surviving drawings probably arises from a rather scrappy hand-to-mouth way of working as he redesigned internal spaces, keeping one or two rooms ahead of the tradesmen who were fitting them out. He would not have time to keep accurate copies of all drawings issued, and this probably explains the necessity for the 1910 set of revised plans and elevations made after the building was complete.

Only after the building was completed did Mackintosh make the fully comprehensive set of Record Drawings, which should be regarded as akin to measured drawings after the event. These have been widely reproduced, and regarded as evidence of a premeditated, unified design, but many features were fact additions, adaptations or afterthoughts. For example, the attic storey along the Renfrew Street front, which was built to house the Professors' studios, was added in 1909, and extended east over the first half of the building. On the south façade, the two side staircases were later additions, which were taken up to the top of the building and a bridge constructed to link them, the Loggia and 'Hen-Run'. And the lean-to arrangement behind the front railings, extending the basement rooms and Sculpture Department was similarly an afterthought, since the sunken basement area had been originally proposed as open, and lined with white reflecting brick.

Thus it can be seen from this brief list of improvised solutions that there were never any premeditated designs, showing the north and south fronts entire as they were to be built. Indeed, it is arguable that the success of the south front of the School in evoking the character of Scottish baronial architecture may be in part due to the building process being adaptive, akin to the way the builders of castles worked, adding on a wing, or a turret, or dormer windows as required.

In the RIAS Quarterly, in 1933, J J Waddell wrote a lengthy appreciation of Mackintosh in which he refers to the architect's wife having collaborated with him "in the decoration of many of his buildings". Mackintosh himself confirms this, writing to her from France, on more than one occasion, that her contribution to his architectural projects had been of the greatest importance.

This leads one to wonder just how much of the decorative elements in the School of Art, small stained glass panels in doors, and so on, may in fact be the work of Margaret Macdonald? It seems quite likely that an architect under pressure to provide builders with detailed construction drawings would have had little time to devote to intricate designs for stained glass panels. At any rate, the completed building was opened in 1909, and as part of the celebrations a Masque was staged, "The Birth and Growth of Art", written by Newbery. The programme interestingly credits Charles R Mackintosh for the design of the stage sets, but no record of these has survived.

In 1933 Allan Mainds, former teacher at the School and Professor of Fine Art at Durham University, wrote in THE LISTENER:

> *To those of us who worked within its walls as students, and later as members of staff, the Glasgow School of Art is a landmark in the history of architecture, and Mackintosh is recognised as a pioneer. That his work has been misunderstood by many and derided by not a few is not to be wondered at; had it been universally understood and accepted at its inception it would not have been worthy to take its place in the new world order that it foreshadowed...*

School Reports

GLASGOW SCHOOL OF ART IN 1901

FROM 1901 ONWARDS, there are good contemporary accounts of the School of Art in various journals, and the following notes are taken from a compilation by Newbery himself, prepared for the conference HANDBOOK, published for delegates to the meeting of the British Association for the Advancement of Science, in Glasgow in 1901. For the benefit of delegates from England, Newbery begins by stressing that the School is not a municipal school, and describes the composition of its Board of Governors, twenty-two in all, including the Lord Provost and the Chairman of the School Board ex-officio with three more Governors representing the town council, and the remainder appointed by the University, the Haldane Trustees, and the other artistic, educational, legal, medical, and commercial bodies of the city.

The income of the School, Newbery observes, is derived from fees paid by the students; grants from the Scotch Office; subscriptions and donations; subsidies. The teaching staff number 38 in all, with 840 registered students, and work is organised under four heads: life painting and drawing; architecture; modelling; design and decorative art. The session is of 40 weeks, and local artists and architects act as visitors to the classes and as examiners under the local prize scheme.

Newbery further notes that life classes for both male and female students are held daily, and the arrangements are similar to those obtaining in the art schools and ateliers of London and Paris. The architectural tuition of the School aims at both preparing students for a professional career, or supplementing office training, and imparting a knowledge of architectural form to painters, sculptors and decorative artists. Students in the Technical Art studios learn design in and through the use of material, and the instructors are artist-craftsmen in their subjects, namely - textiles, wallpapers, metalwork, pottery, stained glass, wood and stone carving, embroidery, mosaics and enamels, bookbinding, colour printing, poster design, wood engraving, drawing for the press, etc. On materials for study, Newbery notes a large and varied collection of casts, and the existence of reference and lending libraries, as well as a reading-room for periodicals.

Newbery also gives details of the local prize scheme, which permitted artisan students free admission to evening classes by means of bursaries - ninety provided by the Haldane Trust alone, for example, and various studentships granted by the Scotch Office. The Haldane Trustees also grant an annual travelling scholarship of £50, as well as the Alexander Thomson Travelling Scholarship of £60, and all such bursaries, scholarships, and studentships are awarded on examination results. Especially interesting is the School's record of success in national competition, and Newbery points out that since 1885, the School had taken a total of 513 awards, including 15 gold, 62 silver, 158 bronze medals, and 259 Queen's Prizes. Indeed, the School won a Gold Medal award at

THE GLASGOW
SCHOOL OF ART
167 RENFREW
STREET :
GLASGOW
HEADMASTER :

LOCAL PRIZE
AWARDED TO

FOR EXCELLENCE
IN

SESSION :

SECRETARY :

*Certificate designed by Jessie M King,
awarded as a local prize
by Fra Newbery.*

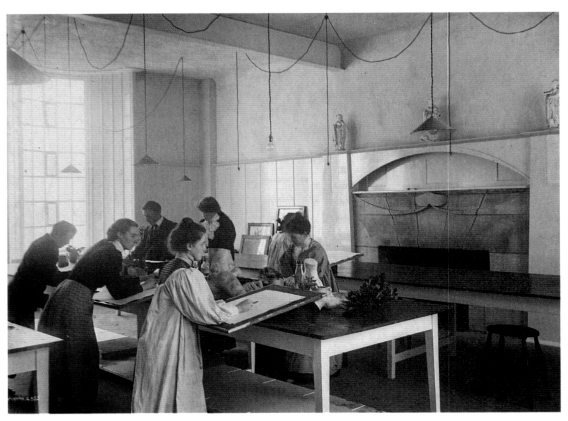

*Drawing in the
Mackintosh Room
c . 1900*

*Drawing in the
Museum c.1900*

Daisy McGlashan dress c. 1910.

*Jessie M King in costume for a Glasgow
School of Art masque as St. Margaret.*

*Jessie M King and friends in the hallway of the old Lady Artists' Club,
Blythswood Square, Glasgow, wearing batique dresses designed by her.*

Garnethill, Muirhead Bone, 1911

GSA Artists Football Club 1910.

the Paris International 1900 Exhibition. In relation to finance, Newbery also notes that the School has no endowment, receives no aid from the rates, and is practically self-supporting.

GLASGOW SCHOOL OF ART IN 1907

In 1907, the work of the School of Art was described by a French visitor, M P Verneuil, an art-journalist and decorative designer. Verneuil published an article on the School in ART ET DECORATION five years after first being impressed by the work of the Glasgow designers exhibited at Turin in 1902. Significantly, Verneuil emphasises that the School is no longer connected with the South Kensington system (continued in England by the Board of Education), and assigns a key role to Newbery.

Ann Macbeth's Embroidery

Newbery's idea, according to Verneuil, is to satisfy every artistic aspiration through teaching all methods of expression:

> *His programme is enormous; one might even ask if it is not too much, considering the many and varied techniques which artists might wish to learn. Is it necessary, therefore, to create as many workshops as there are different techniques? And, if one wants to do so in a practical way, what material and personnel must one provide for?*

Here we have a beautiful dream, says Verneuil, which one must believe can be in part realised, but unfortunately only in part.

Verneuil then goes on to describe the School's workshops, e.g., embroidery, jointly directed by Jessie Newbery and Ann Macbeth, and book decoration, by Jessie M King and John Macbeth. Other workshops included those mentioned earlier in Newbery's account, as well as gold and silversmithing, repoussé work, and ceramic decoration. Verneuil also draws attention to the healthy enrolment figures, which by 1907-1908 had reached a total of 1,254 registered students.

Christmas Ball Ticket , 1903.

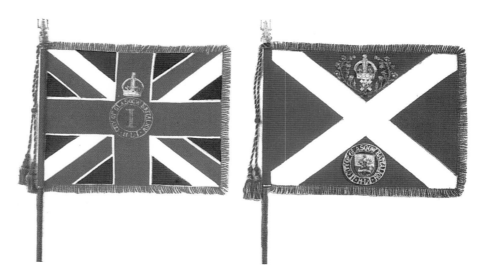

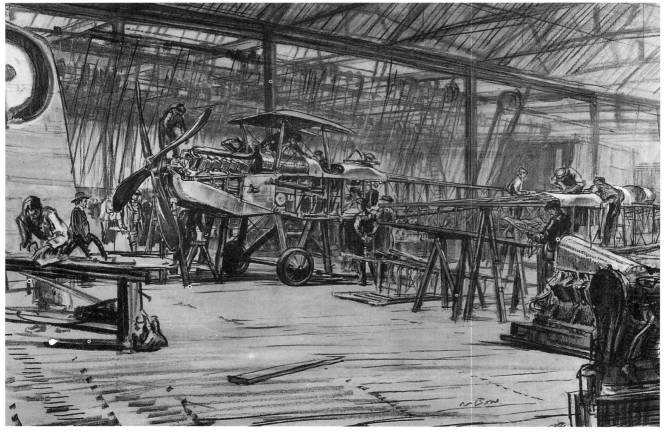

*An aircraft under construction,
Farnborough. Muirhead Bone ,
war artist 1914-18.*

GLASGOW SCHOOL OF ART IN 1916

In a review of the work of students in the leading art schools of Britain and
Ireland, published in 1916, and edited by Charles Holme, there is a very full
description of the various branches of art, design and crafts taught in the
School towards the end of Newbery's Directorship, summarised thus:

... The Glasgow School of Art became early identified with that which was best in the new decorative movement; it became the established centre of rational and individualistic art training and execution, and so earnest has been the pursuit of the new idea there, that there is hardly a craft within the scope of its influence that has not long ago shed the blighting effect of the Victorian era.

Furniture is now utilitarian, and of excellent design; decoration is rational and inspiring; needlework is sensible, and brings a new joy in the beautifying of apparel and domestic articles; metal-work is promoted to an important place in decorative schemes; fabrics, by reason of their choice colouring and skillful pattern, are an endless delight; posters are arresting; pottery has a fresh individuality; while printing, lettering, and illumination have advanced with the general order of things.

The school has led, public opinion has followed, and even the discouragement of the manufacturer, with his rigid standard of £ s. d. has been powerless to arrest the onward march of the arts and crafts in Glasgow. The secret of the success of the school, reduced to a single word, is practicability... At the same time, individuality is allowed free play...

And in the same article, the author singles out the teaching of embroidery at the School of Art for particular mention:

> *Of all the crafts taught there, are none more interesting, utilitarian, or more enthusiastically indulged in than needlecraft and embroidery. This is due in great measure to the strong personality of the director, Miss Ann Macbeth, who has a genius for adapting means to ends, for getting much out of little, and for producing art with the meanest accessories. "Economic embroidery," the inception of Miss Macbeth, will prove perhaps a greater medium for carrying the joy of art into the homes and hearts of the people than any other method or practice ever thought of or adopted...*

GLASGOW SCHOOL OF ART IN 1928

Newbery was succeeded as Director of the School by John Henderson, who served from 1918 to 1924. The years immediately after the War were very unsettled, but by 1928 the affairs of the School had returned to normal, and the state of course development was recorded by the then Director, John D Revel.

In that year, the British Association once again held their annual conference in Glasgow, and Revel provided their conference HANDBOOK with an account of the organisation and teaching arrangements at the School of Art. In his report, Revel pays tribute to Newbery's thirty-two years of notable service and records that he directed the activities of the School with great wisdom:

> *... Mr Newbery realised that while art may be national in character, it was in language international, and by the introduction of foreign professors and interchange of work with Continental cities, the School was in touch with all movements of importance in Europe and America. Under Mr Newbery's direction the School attained a world-wide reputation...*

Revel goes on to describe the structure of the School, in four main areas, Architecture, Painting, Sculpture, and Design, and notes that its Governors are authorised to grant Diplomas in each group, bearing the seal of the Scottish Education Department. Students who wish to qualify for teaching at that point, undergo a further year of professional training at Jordanhill College, and this endorsed Diploma is also accepted by the Scottish Education Department as proof of practical attainment for teachers of special Art subjects.

The School of Architecture, Revel notes, is superintended by a Joint Committee, representative of the Royal Technical College and School of Art, and for the purposes of the Degree of B.Sc. in Architecture, the curriculum is recognised by the University of Glasgow, to which the Royal Technical College is affiliated.

Revel observes that the School of Painting has long been noted as one of the premier training centres in Europe, with Composition and Figure Painting its most highly developed subjects, though the School also recognises the new movements of the day, regarding freedom of individual expression as a first principle. The School of Sculpture at this time was relatively small, but the subject was required as a general qualification in all Diploma groups.

Newbery Medal awarded traditionally across all disciplines to the student who is voted by Academic Council as having achieved the highest standard in their year

The School of Design, as Revel describes it, is concerned with the training of artist-craftsmen, and in the application of aesthetics to industry. It has three main groups: Pictorial, Industrial, and Crafts. The Pictorial group deals with printing crafts, such as lithography and etching, etc. The Industrial offers training in the design of fabrics woven and printed, carpets, stained glass, silversmithing, metal crafts, carving in wood and stone, etc., while the Craft group gives specialised instruction to intending artist-craftsmen, in such departments as Illumination, Stained Glass, Pottery, etc.

Revel goes on to commend the Governors for their wise counsel in the difficult business of adjusting the balance between the aesthetic and utilitarian sides of the curriculum, and offers a brief resumé of the School's distinguished former students, including most of those now celebrated worldwide as the 'Glasgow School'.

'Clive' (of India) on the steps of Foreign Office, London by John Tweed former Glasgow School of Art student.

Drucilla' by John Tweed (known in his own day as the English Rodin - he had studied under Rodin). There is a Tweed archive, Reading Art Gallery.

Architecture, Painting & Design

THE SCHOOL OF ARCHITECTURE

AN ACCOUNT OF ARCHITECTURE at the School of Art is not included in the foregoing reports, and the Glasgow School of Architecture was seen as something slightly aside from the main body of the School, since part of it was housed in the Technical College. Its history is recorded in a separate chapter, but a brief summary may be appropriate at this point.

A professional School of Architecture was constituted in 1903-04 with the appointment of Professor Bourdon and the establishment of the Glasgow School of Architecture. The four-year Diploma Course was extended to five in 1919-20, and the Diploma in Architecture was recognised by the RIBA as granting exemption from the Institute's Final Examination. The four-year BSc Degree was introduced in 1924, the year of John Henderson's sudden death, and as noted elsewhere, the Professor and Head J B Fulton had died the previous year after only a short time in the post.

The period of Henderson's Directorship was a difficult one, and while Professor Bourdon was the only member of staff killed in the War, some forty students and former students lost their lives - their names are listed on the School's Roll of Honour. The numbers from the School killed in action, however, were relatively few compared with those from the Royal Technical College, where 411 students, former students and staff were killed. As a concession to ex-service students, a special three-year route to the Diploma in Art was temporarily introduced, involving a longer session and some evening attendance.

The modern structure of the School thus provided for Departments of the three Fine Arts: Painting, Sculpture, and Architecture, and Architecture was traditionally regarded as the mistress Art, with Painting and Sculpture her handmaidens. The various branches of design and the crafts were collectively grouped in the Design School, though its composition has changed considerably since the sections were first listed in Newbery's prospectuses of the early 1900's.

DRAWING AND PAINTING

The history of the Drawing and Painting Department does not go back much before the restructuring of 1901, when the modern pattern was introduced, consequent on the ending of the South Kensington connection. The South Kensington system had as its original aim "the application of Fine Art to Industry", and was not conceived to train easel painters. Paradoxically, with the opening of the Schools of Art to all, they were used as a training ground for artists, who treated the Government Schools as a kind of foundation course facility in such subjects as Geometry, Perspective, Flower Painting, Figure

Drawing, etc., usually before going on to more specialised instruction else-where. London students tried for places in the Royal Academy Schools, in Edinburgh there was a Life School at the Royal Scottish Academy, and of course the better-off might go to Paris - the Ecole des Beaux Arts for architects and private academies for painters, such as the Académie Julian, which attracted an appreciable number of Glasgow artists.

In Glasgow, senior painters often helped the younger ones by criticism of their works, and to a large extent the artists taught each other. It was partly out of this habit of regular group criticism that the more permanent forum of the Glasgow Art Club emerged in the late 1860s, with sketching parties in the sum-mer, and regular exhibitions and 'crits'. The Art Club also organised its own Life Class, which suggests that drawing from the nude model was only inter-mittently available at the School of Art. A Life class (male model) was introduced in the School of Design in session 1849-50, and an Inspector's report observes that not all the students were registered pupils, which confirms a later report referring to local artists making use of the School at that early date.

Such classes may be seen as the beginnings of Fine Art instruction not specifically utilitarian, and where a class was in effect privately run by the School, instructors could be appointed without Science and Art Department certificates, so that the amateurs and intending professionals serious often had very good painters as teachers. Indeed, it was the 1897 relaxation of the requirement that appointees must hold South Kensington teachers' certificates that enabled the School of Art to appoint eminent foreign artists as Professors, and it is with such appointments that a professional School of Drawing and Painting is properly established.

Glasgow Cathedral.
Muirhead Bone
View from East at twilight

THE SCHOOL OF DESIGN

In Revel's report of 1928, the School of Design is described as being composed of three main groups: Pictorial, Industrial, and Crafts. However, in the School Calendar for the following year, Industrial Design is listed as embracing Mural Decoration, Needlework and Embroidery, Lettering and Illumination, and it is clear that the notion of what constituted industrial design was very limited. This was still the case when Conrad McKenna (later a teacher in the School) entered as a student in 1940, and he recalls Campbell Mackie, then Head of Design, teaching along these same lines. "Design meant decorative panels and borders." Historic ornament was an examinable subject, and most of the Industrial Design lectures were on styles. Indeed, up until the Second World War, Schools of Art generally were still under the influence of the Arts and Crafts movement, concerned with the one-off bespoke artefact, and not at all industrially minded.

It was only after the War that the Design School was put on a proper footing and given adequate workshops and equipment and financial support. This was entirely due to the policies of Douglas Percy Bliss, Director from 1946-64, who realised that continued investment of public funds in the School of Art would depend on it being seen as a productive asset to the country, and that there was economic benefit in the training of designers for industry. Bliss was shrewdly aware that in the period of post-war reconstruction, with many claims on the taxpayer's purse, a purely Fine Art School might be seen as an expensive luxury. As he observed in a foreword to the Prospectus:

> *Ours has been called the Machine Age, and certainly the importance of Design in every aspect of contemporary life cannot be over-stressed. This School, founded to teach Design, is more than ever required to teach Design. The Fine Arts have lost none of their prestige and amenities.*

New Annexe built 1929-30. Assembly Hall Building designed by Graham Henderson of Keppie Henderson, completed 1930, now Student Union.

The suite of Painting Studios at Glasgow School of Art has no equal in Britain. But of recent years much has been done and will be done to equip and further develop the power and influence of the numerous sections of the School which deal with Design subjects...

By the end of Bliss's term, the Glasgow course in Industrial Design could be described as the only one of its kind in Scotland, dealing as it did with design for modern factory production. This new post-war approach left behind the limitations of the dilute Arts and Crafts philosophy, which had been a liberating force in its heyday, but by the 1930's was a negative influence, engendering an anti-industry bias in many Art Schools, particularly in England.

In Newbery's time design was very much allied to the crafts, although there were some forward-looking writers who sought to encourage a true union of art and industry. One of these was Henry Dyer, a Governor of the Glasgow School of Art and also of the Technical College. Dyer had been Principal of the Imperial College of Engineering in Tokyo, and in his book THE EVOLUTION OF INDUSTRY, he predicts that:

Probably the most important department of technical education in the future will be that in which the students are trained to apply art to industry...

Dyer also sounds a cautionary note, however, on the teaching of such students, which has particular relevance now, at a time when inspectors of quality, teaching performance, and research proliferate in higher education. They must, according to Dyer:

Be kept free from all unnecessary officialism and routine, which crush out originality, and convert the students into hod-workers quite as much as the worst forms of the factory system...

Christmas Ball 1940's

The Inter -War Years

JOHN HENDERSON 1918-24

JOHN HENDERSON HAD STEPPED into the breach and acted as Director when Newbery had his first illness in 1914. When Newbery took early retirement in 1917, Henderson again took over, initially on a temporary basis. Henderson, a landscape and portrait painter, was seen as "a safe pair of hands", and had served as a Governor. His father Joseph Henderson, described by THE STUDIO in 1900 as the doyen of the Glasgow artistic community, had also been a Governor of the School of Art and had been privy to all the business surrounding the building of the new School. Between them, the two Hendersons knew everything there was to know about the School and its personnel in this formative period, but unfortunately none of it was ever recorded in memoirs. A third Henderson, Joseph junior, was also an artist, and interestingly, all three had taken the MA Degree at the University before commencing professional art studies at the School of Art.

Glasgow School of Art was in fact unusual among the Government Schools in having a fair number of university graduates among its male students. This is not surprising, since in England, for the greater part of the nineteenth century, there were only four universities, and three of these were in the south. The Royal College of Art did attract a few graduates, though, something that came as a surprise to the Chairman of an Inquiry in 1911. "Do you mean Varsity men?" he asked, puzzled as to why the young gentlemen should be found in such a place. That rather Bertie Woosterish attitude did not exist in Scotland, since practically everyone's forebears had 'come up the hard way' or 'stuck in at the night school', and the rest depended on industry for their living, one way or another.

At any rate, there is little doubt that the School of Art commended itself to the University as a collaborator through its having a well-educated student body, and also a Governing Board on which there was a fair number of Glasgow University graduates. Rather than the School knocking at the gates of the University, it was in fact Professor Phillimore who first publicly expressed hopes that ere long there would be a formal link between the School and the University. This paved the way to serious discussions in 1910, and the cementing of formal teaching links was eventually achieved with the introduction of the Architecture degree course in 1924, the year of John Henderson's sudden death.

With the Architecture link, the School of Art became a university teaching institution alongside the Royal Technical College, which had been recognised as a University College in 1917. Thus by the end of Henderson's period as Director, Glasgow had the largest technical education institution in the world, in the Royal Technical College, and one of the premier Schools of Art in Europe, housed in a building reckoned to be the finest of its type. This was a considerable achievement, given that it was largely due to local initiative, and the Governors of the Technical College and the School of Art were truly building for a new century. Newbery himself believed that:

> *Some day Glasgow might be remembered like other commercial cities, like Bruges and even Venice, for her Art as much as for her wealth...*

Following Henderson, the next three Directors were J D Revel, W O Hutchison, and Allan Walton. They had much in common. Firstly, they all knew each other in Chelsea in the 1920's, and all knew Mackintosh when he lived in London. Revel, Hutchinson and Walton were members of the Chelsea Arts Club, where Mackintosh was a regular guest, and old hands at the Club recall that Mackintosh's boon companions were the illustrators Nicholson and Pryde, who traded under the name "Beggarstaff Brothers" for their poster work in the 1890's.

Hutchison and Walton regularly lunched at the "Blue Cockatoo" restaurant in Cheyne Walk, as did the Mackintoshes and the Schwabes (parents of Lady , formerly Mrs H. Jefferson Barnes). Thus almost all the Directors of the School of Art from Revel down to Sir Harry Barnes had some connection with Mackintosh in his London period. One might also include D P Bliss, who followed Walton as Director in 1946, and was a close friend of the Sturrock family. Mrs Alex. Sturrock was the former Mary Newbery, the daughter of Francis, and had very clear recollections of both Mackintosh and Margaret Macdonald, and of the opening of the completed School building in 1909.

J D REVEL 1925-32

John D Revel, who succeeded Henderson as Director in 1925, was formerly Principal of the Chelsea School of Art, then mostly involved with evening school students. Revel had been a prize-winning student at Dundee and won a scholarship to the Royal College, where he gained the ARCA in Painting and Architecture. The Glasgow School of Art holds some of Revel's architectural drawings from that period, which are quite remarkable as the work of an art student.

During the First World War, Revel served in the Indian Army and was attached to the British Expeditionary Force in Mesopotamia, where he was later given a roving commission as a war artist. Some of his drawings are in the Imperial War Museum, and are rather uneven in quality, but as Revel himself explained, they had been executed in very difficult conditions, not least extreme heat and humidity.. After he left Glasgow in 1932, Revel painted a number of portraits and showed work regularly in major exhibitions in England.

Revel left Glasgow School of Art in somewhat unhappy circumstances, and while the precise circumstances surrounding his departure are not clear, gossip at the time suggested that some kind of 'dirty work at the crossroads' was involved. Dr David Donaldson, who was a student towards the end of the Revel period, recalls that long after the events, Henry Y Alison was moved to tears in recounting the circumstances of Revel's going. Henry Y, as he was known, was an extremely tough character who had been a German prisoner of war and had been shot in the eye. As David Donaldson puts it:

"Henry Y normally only cried with one eye, but when telling the story of Revel's undoing he cried with both."

According to another source, Revel had had a bad time in the war, having lost many of his friends. And it is said that he blotted his copybook at some public function. However, there is no documentary evidence for the precise circumstances leading to his departure, and it is more likely that Revel made enemies on the Board of Governors by controverting their opinions and policies. In the matter of the Glasgow School of Architecture, Revel appeared to side with the Technical College, which wanted to train architects alongside builders and engineers, rather than painters and sculptors, and he seems to have been rather naively impressed with futuristic visions of ferro-concrete, steel and glass. Governors of that era did not put up with any nonsense, and perhaps Revel had not been sufficiently diplomatic, or 'politically aware'. At any rate, Revel departed from Glasgow in 1932, to settle eventually in a village near Didcot.

Revel's period at the School of Art was not particularly eventful, but Dr Emilio Coia, who was a student then, remembered him as "the best Director the School ever had." Another former student recalls that Revel took the occasional architects' drawing class, and to this extent he was still in the tradition of the teacher-Headmaster and Director. On occasion Revel even played badminton with students in the new Assembly Hall, built in 1929-30, and designed by Graham Henderson of Keppie Henderson. The Assembly Hall became the venue for balls and dances, a role which it still fulfils.

*Jack Coia. Bronze bust
by Benno Schotz
Royal Incorporation of
Architects in Scotland*

The Assembly Hall was built on the site of a former Catholic nursing home, and before this, the site had been occupied by the family home of the writer Catherine Carswell, who used Maurice Grieffenhagen, Professor at the School, as one of the central figures in a novel. The novel is based on real life, since she had a liaison with Grieffenhagen, and pursued him to London. But while it would be tempting to suggest that this was why Grieffenhagen left Glasgow, in fact the SED had reached the conclusion that Grieffenhagen had become too successful for the School of Art to afford - he wanted to reduce his attendance to three months in the year.

Mary Armour recalls that the Governors already allowed Grieffenhagen six weeks off to prepare his pictures for the Royal Academy, and during those weeks the Painting students taught each other, so that many of the pictures were the work of various hands. The students were highly amused when Grieffenhagen eventually descended and adjudicated on their work, awarding travelling scholarships to all the wrong people. Grieffenhagen never got to know the students or their work, and Mary Armour recalls once asking him, "Have you never thought of going up north and painting the Highland landscapes for a change?" Grieffenhagen pursed his lips, shook his head and said "Too amorphous". (Presumably that meant you couldn't put a big black line round everything).

The degree course in Architecture produced its first graduates during Revel's time as Director, and quite a few of these were women. The first woman to take a Diploma in Architecture in Scotland was Edith Burnet Hughes, who took the Aberdeen Diploma around 1910, while the first woman Architecture diplomate at Glasgow was Margaret J McEwan, in 1928. The first women BSc. graduates at Glasgow were Elizabeth S King and

*The Old Model Maker -
a wood engraving by
Lennox Paterson*

Margaret B Brodie, who later became a lecturer in the Glasgow School of Architecture. Elizabeth King went on to become the first woman Professor of Architecture in India, at Delhi.

The list of Governors during Revel's period as Director also shows former students in high office. George A Paterson, FRIBA, was a Governor of the School of Art and the School of Architecture 1930-32. He was the father of Lennox Paterson, a student at the School pre-war, and post-war Head of Design and Deputy Director and Registrar. George Paterson was a member of the Glasgow Architectural Association from 1895 - proposed for membership by his close friend Charles Rennie Mackintosh.

In 1927-28 two new members of staff were appointed in Architecture: Alexander Adam, future Head of Department, and Jack Coia. Adam had been a student under Bourdon, taking his Diploma in 1910. Jack Coia, later of Gillespie, Kidd & Coia, was Royal Gold Medallist in Architecture in 1969, and President of the Royal Incorporation of Architects in Scotland. The student President of the Glasgow School of Architecture Club, 1927-28, was

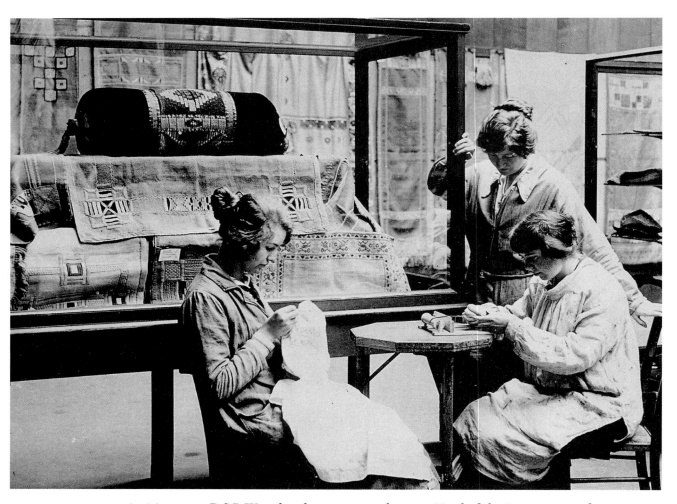

Mary Armour, on the right,
as a student in the Museum 1920s.

D S R Waugh, who went on to become Head of the Department of
Architecture after the war.

In December 1927 the student body was addressed by Sir David Murray
(1849-1933) who was then the School's oldest former student, having been a
student under Robert Greenlees. Mrs Mary Armour is now the School's oldest
former student resident in Scotland (there is someone in America aged 109),
and she began teaching in 1926-27, in a school in Rutherglen. Until then, elementary schools had no qualified Art teachers, so the role of the professional
teacher was as yet undeveloped.

W O Hutchison 1933-43

John D Revel was succeeded as Director in 1933 by William Oliphant
Hutchison, a portrait painter who had trained at Edinburgh College of Art,
and in Paris. Various sources, including The Glasgow Girls (1990), have stated
that Dorothy Carleton Smyth was appointed the first woman Director in 1933,
but died before she could take up her post. However, there is no documentary
evidence to show she was offered the post, and following the customary public
advertisement of the vacancy, W O Hutchison was appointed Director in 1933.

*Stained glass by
Dorothy Carleton Smyth.*

Dame Laura Knight ,
one time external assessor with
Glasgow School of Art.

Members of staff at table
left to right: A. Davidson, J. Barr,
I. Fleming, W. McLean (standing),
C. Baillie, H. A. Crawford.

The big event that year was the Mackintosh Memorial Exhibition in the MacLellan Galleries devoted to the work of the architect and his wife Margaret Macdonald Mackintosh, who had died in 1933. This major retrospective was mainly organised by William Davidson, owner of Windyhill at Kilmacolm, and the items then exhibited, all of which were for sale, are in many cases now in public collections.

During session 1936–37 Thomas Findlay Lyon, later Head of Town Planning, was engaged on research into Mackintosh, approved by Professor Hughes, and another student employed in Keppie Henderson's also wrote a thesis on

*Grosvenor Lunch, 1938
retiral of D. Forrester Wilson,
James Huck, Andrew Law and
J. A. Coia*

W O Hutchison and staff

Mackintosh around this time. Davidson eventually donated the unsold residue
of the Memorial Exhibition to Glasgow University, where Thomas Howarth
began his work on Mackintosh by cataloguing the collection, after joining the
Glasgow School of Architecture staff in 1939. Howarth's research over a decade
resulted in CHARLES RENNIE MACKINTOSH AND THE MODERN MOVEMENT,
published in 1952, and still the standard work.

Professor Hughes did not care for Mackintosh's work himself, being trained
in the classical style, but he was open to modern ideas, and acted as Howarth's
thesis supervisor for the University. In 1935, Hughes gave a paper to the RIBA
Conference entitled "The Modern Movement - A False Start?", in which he
argued that architectural development should be incremental and evolution-
ary, not a break with the past.

The Empire Tower designed by Thomas Tait co-ordinating architect of 1938 Empire Exhibition. Tait was student of Glasgow School of Art around 1903.
The inset cards are views of the Exhibition.

In 1938, the Empire Exhibition was held in Glasgow, at Bellahouston Park, and the firm of Sir John Burnet, Thomas Tait, and Francis Lorne, who had all been students at the School, were appointed architects. Tait is said to have started out in an office in Paisley run by a former draughtsman of Greek Thomson, and was a gifted designer. Tait prepared the master plan for the Empire Exhibition, and the design of individual buildings by other architects were sent down to him in London for his approval.

The "Women of Empire" building was designed by Miss M. B. Brodie, Jack Coia designed the Catholic Pavilion, and David Donaldson and Charles Baillie painted mural decorations for various buildings, as did William Crosbie. Tait was also responsible for the Tower of Empire (nicknamed "Tait's Tower" by the local papers), and this became the symbol of the Exhibition, much in the way the 'Skylon' mast symbolised modernity at the 1951 Festival of Britain. Compared with the Empire Exhibition, the 1951 Festival now seems rather puny. Scandinavian influence was especially strong in the buildings of the Empire Exhibition, and premonitions of postwar New Town architecture, and industrial estates, can be seen in the imagery of the Empire Exhibition site planning.

With the outbreak of war, the Exhibition was soon forgotten. In the early part of the war, air raid precautions were put in hand, and rotas of staff and students arranged for firewatching at night. Conrad McKenna has clear recollections of the diminutive figure of Henry Y Alison balancing on the eaves, overlooking the drop, saying, "Luk at that - nae fear at a'!" Two or three nights later Henry Y was on the roof during an air-raid, when out of the darkness came spinning a 'flying saucer', i.e., the base of a shell case from one of the anti-aircraft guns. It very nearly decapitated Henry Y, who jumped up and down yelling, "Did ye see that? Did ye see that? Could'a killt me! Could'a killt me!".

In 1940 the School Governors mistakenly celebrated the School's centenary. The date of 1840 seems to have been confirmed by the imperfect recollections of Sir James Fleming, Chairman of Governors, speaking around 1900 of his early days as a student in the School of Design, "which he entered in 1843, a few years after it opened." At any rate, a centenary lunch was given for the School by the Lord Provost in March 1940, when a short history of the School was read out by the Director, the notes for which had been compiled by John Groundwater, the then School Secretary.

Sir John Burnet, Thomas Tait and Francis Lorne who formed one of the leading architectural practices in the world at the time.

Robert Colquhoun and Robert MacBryde

Groundwater had started in the School as an office boy in 1875, and had completed 56 years' service when he retired. His daughter was the Deputy Director's Secretary in the early 1960's, so that between them they combined service with Greenlees, Simmonds, Newbery, Henderson, Revel, Hutchison, Walton, Bliss and Barnes. Indeed, it is not impossible that Mr Groundwater personally received Mackintosh's class fees at the office counter in Corporation Buildings, when the architect was a student there in the 1880s.

At the outbreak of war, W O Hutchison made contingency plans for announcing the closure of the School, but was advised by the SED that the Treasury would only continue to fund a School which was open. Keeping the School open thus became the first priority, although Hutchison himself was eager to get back into uniform, having been in the Royal Artillery in the first war, in command of a battery in France. In the event, he retired to Edinburgh to paint.

The year 1943 saw the destruction of Alexander 'Greek' Thomson's Queen's Park Church, caused by an incendiary bomb which produced a spectacular conflagration, lighting up the night sky for miles around. When the Church was built there had been a plasterers' strike, so that it was lined throughout with wood. As a result, it went up like a tinder box, and children were fetched out of their beds and held up to windows to see the sky lit up like daytime. Although this was a significant loss, it illustrates how lucky the School of Art was to get through the war unscathed.

Students at the School in the pre-war Hutchison period included David Donaldson, John Miller, Jack Fleming, John Laurie, Robert Colquhoun, Robert MacBryde, Ian Hamilton Finlay and Charles Baillie. After 1940, there were John Cunningham, Danny Ferguson, Bill Gallacher, Margot Sandeman, Joan Eardley, Sinclair Thomson and Cordelia Oliver. Due to the emergency conditions, under which students were conscripted into the forces at the age of 21, a three-year Diploma was permitted, and Joan Eardley was among those who took this, before going into war work.

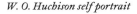

W. O. Hutchison self portrait

The late Danny Ferguson fondly recalled W O Hutchison inviting him into the Director's room for tea and a chat about his progress half way through first year. "W.O." had been alerted by Danny's old art teacher, a fellow-student at Edinburgh, that one of his "boys" was coming up to the Art School, and "W.O." kept a lookout for him - which made a lasting impression on the student.

Joan Eardley drawing

Farewell to Arms

ALLAN WALTON 1943-45

Allan Walton, wartime Director, GSA. Designed textiles, ship interiors, Maynard Keynes's Rooms, King's College Cambridge, and Founders Room LSE.

WHEN HUTCHISON was about to leave the School, he suggested Allan Walton, whom he knew from his time in Chelsea in the 1920s, as a suitable successor. Walton was already well-known at the School as the joint Assessor in Textile Design for the four Scottish Art Schools, and duly took over as Director in 1943.

Walton no doubt found the offer of the post timely, as his family textile business near Manchester had been bombed, and his own business, also in textiles, was at a low ebb due to wartime restrictions and quotas. Otherwise, it is unlikely he would have chosen to base himself in Scotland, being very much a metropolitan animal. During term time in Glasgow, he lodged in a Temperance Hotel, and recounted how he was forced to hide his whisky in his room, and smuggle out the empties - usually in a suitcase on the way to Central Station to catch the Euston train.

Walton had been educated at Harrow, but was not at all stuffy and entered into the spirit of student concerts where authority figures like himself were mocked. He regularly held tea-parties for students in the Director's room, and seems to have used the SRC President and the others as "prefects" to help run the School - not that there was much to run, given the depleted numbers.

In 1931 he had set up his own business, Allan Walton Textiles, with his brother, Roger. Their products featured designs by Duncan Grant, Vanessa Bell, Frank Dobson and Walton himself, and in the many books on the Bloomsbury group - Virginia Woolf, Vanessa Bell, Lytton Strachey, Duncan Grant, Maynard Keynes, etc., Walton usually merits a brief mention.

The decorative textile designs which Walton's firm produced are considered to be among the finest of their type, and Walton was elected one of the first Royal Designers for Industry. Earlier, he had trained as a painter, at the Slade, and in Paris, and kept active on that front. He had a country house by the sea, and seascapes with yachts figure prominently in his work. He also painted in the South of France where villas with overgrown gardens and terraces were frequent subjects.

Walton had a droll sense of humour, as shown in an interview he gave to the magazine DESIGN AND ART in 1928, on the theme of colour in interior decoration. Asked whether he had noticed particular colour preferences among people, Walton replied:

> *"Yes, I have. In fact, they can be classed in categories. I don't know why this should be so, but it is. Ladies always like green because it is so restful. Stockbrokers nearly always like brown and gold - it must be old, mellowed gold. Parsons like a sort of pale, washed-out Madonna blue. Architects do not like any colour at all - they adore masses of white plaster relieved at most with a little mahogany. They have no*

*colour sense... And actresses like mauve. Yes, especially the less intelli-
gent young actress adores mauve".*

About a year before he left Glasgow, Walton discussed a short-list of possible
candidates for the Directorship with the SED officers, suggesting among others H. Jefferson Barnes, although the SED thought he was too young at that
time. Walton himself left Glasgow School of Art in 1945 to resume his professional career in London, and in 1948 he was appointed Professor of Textile
Design at the Royal College of Art, but took ill and died before he could take
up the post.

The last project Walton was involved in before leaving Glasgow was the
refurbishment of No.11 Downing Street, and the design of curtain materials
was given to the Textile Section in the School of Art. One student who worked
on the project was Robert Stewart, later to become a member of the teaching
staff and Head of the Textile Design Section in the 1950s.

Although Allan Walton was at the School for less than three years, he is still
remembered as one of the more interesting Directors, not least because he kept
the spirits of staff and students buoyant during difficult times.

*Bob Stewart design for his
Retrospective Exhibition poster
1980.*

H Y ALISON 1945-46

When Walton quit in 1945, his deputy Henry Y. Alison was appointed Interim
Director until Douglas Percy Bliss took over the following year. Alison had
wide experience of the School since his own student days under Newbery, as
teacher, Evening School supervisor, and later Deputy Director. Alison had
probably known everyone connected with the School since Newbery's day, but

unfortunately recorded no reminiscences, and latterly became uncommunicative and rather intimidating. Former students who remember him in the 1940s refer to him as a "holy terror" or more bluntly as a "wee bastard".

Henry Y certainly took brusqueness to extremes, and it was said that his day was not complete until he had reduced at least one female student to tears. On the plus side, it could be said that, like Mr. Waugh in Architecture, he had no favourites - he disliked everyone with equal intensity.

In retirement, Henry Y affected twill riding breeches with woollen stockings, rather after the fashion of the Women's Land Army, which appears to have been fashionable wear among the artists in Chelsea in the early 1920's. While at the School he wore knickerbockers, and patrolled the corridors with his little Scottie dog Hamish. Originally he possessed two dogs, weaving in and out of his feet in figures of eight as he proceeded about the School. In brief, Henry Y was a "character".

Alison made an important contribution to the School in 1945-46, in heading off proposed alterations to the School Library by the architect, Graham Henderson. The Library balcony could be entered only from the an external half landing above, and to improve security and facilitate supervision, Henderson wanted to build a spiral staircase in the north-west window bay, for internal access. Alison thought this was an appaling idea, so he designed a little timber staircase (Alison's father was a master joiner), and with the help of a janitor built it over the Easter vacation in 1946. That is the origin of the existing library staircase, which was fitted with the removal of just one joist from the balcony floor to create the stair opening, and done so neatly and sympathetically that generations of students have gone through the School believing it to be part of Mackintosh's original design.

When Thomas Howarth was engaged on his research on Mackintosh he was given access to a collection of Mackintosh furniture, locked up in a basement room, and after the war, Howarth suggested there should be a display of the furniture. Alison raised the matter with the Governors, who gave permission for the original Board Room to be used for this purpose, and allocated some money. However, the creation of this exhibition was not completed until 1947, having been taken up by the new Director, D.P. Bliss, and his new Deputy, H. Jefferson Barnes. The exhibition in the Mackintosh Room, as it is now known, was opened by Miss Nancy Mackintosh, the architect's sister.

Henry Y. Alison resigned in 1946 once the new Director, Douglas P. Bliss, had been appointed. It appears that Alison was driven into resignation by the unrelenting attentions of one Elizabeth Brown, the former Acting Secretary, who had held the fort in the School office during the War, but who had become a major irritant through her habit of buttonholing people in corridors and subjecting them to endless conversations about trivia.

The Chairman of Governors alluded to there being a problem with Miss Brown in official correspondence, and moved her sideways to become Lady Warden - a sinecure with no specific duties except custody of the first-aid box and providing addresses of suitable student lodgings, though supervision of the Refectory was for a while also part of her remit. Miss Brown's garrulous tendencies increased with the years and she would not release her victims, even in extremis. "Do you know," raged D.P. Bliss on one occasion, "she even tried to follow me in there!" - pointing to the Director's private lavatory adjoining his office.

Change and Stability

DOUGLAS PERCY BLISS 1946-64

*Douglas Percy Bliss,
Director GSA 1946-64, painted by
Phyllis Dodd (Mrs Bliss) and
presented to the Governors of the School*

DOUGLAS PERCY BLISS WAS APPOINTED DIRECTOR of the School of Art in 1946, and served until his retirement in 1964, thus ranking with Robert Greenlees as the longest serving head of the School after Newbery. Bliss was unusual for an Art School principal in holding a University degree as well as the Associateship of the Royal College of Art, and it would be true to say that he was a cut above the average as regards intellect and scholarship. He was also a first-rate lecturer, in a style reminiscent of Sir Kenneth Clark, but more spontaneous, and indeed, teaching staff used to come specially to the Art School from the Technical College just to hear Bliss propose the vote of thanks at the annual Architecture prizegiving.

When Bliss took over as Director in 1946 he came to a School which was still organised very much along the lines of Newbery's scheme of Departments and Sections, devised at the turn of the century. And some fifty years later, the Bliss-period Prospectus shows a list of subject areas almost the same as Newbery's, except for the dropping of terms such as Decorative Art, and the substitution of Ceramics for Modelling. Thus, if Newbery had returned to the School in the 1950's he would have found almost all his Arts and Crafts subjects still taught somewhere in the School, but not necessarily in their original location or under the same title.

It was Bliss who put the Design School on a proper footing and created the three new or reconstituted departments of Interior, Textile, and Industrial Design, raising them to the status of Diploma subjects, and providing them with fully equipped workshops. By 1951, Bliss was able to write in the Prospectus that:

> *Provision is made in the Design Department for students specialising not only in the traditional Handicrafts, but in Industrial Design... The course in Industrial Design is now well established. Here students are encouraged to deal with problems of Design in the field of quantity-production. Contemporary materials and manufacturing methods are studied, with a view to familiarising the student with the problems met in machine production; at the same time, the visual qualities inherent in these processes and materials are analysed, and later used in suitable Design projects...*

*D P Bliss Book Plate
for T J Honeyman.
Bliss wa one of the best pre-war
wood engravers.
Dr Honeyman was Director of the
Glasgow Art Gallery and Museum and
originator of the term (Scottish)
"Colourist" now in general use.*

Douglas Percy Bliss was born in Karachi in 1900, in the last year of Victoria's reign, the same year the Science and Art Department disappeared and the Glasgow School of Art escaped from the South Kensington system. He went to George Watson's School in Edinburgh, and while his father was not keen that he should pursue a career in art, he agreed to support this ambition provided he first went to University and took a degree. Thus Bliss graduated M.A. with First Class Honours in History and English Literature at Edinburgh

Ted Odling's Class 1953.
Ted Odling –
the Art School's Magnus Pyke.
Had been an RAF instrument
maker during war –
and made anything.
BBC marvelled at his
early renderings of
Tam O' Shanter (TV 1953).
Expert on photography
and general gadgetry.

University, then proceeded to the Royal College of Art, and an Associateship.

Bliss senior had been a merchant in India, made his fortune before he was 35, and retired at 40. This was perhaps the one thing in Bliss's background that the Painting staff found truly admirable. Bliss himself felt that he was not fully appreciated in Glasgow and was quoted in SCOTTISH FIELD in 1952 as having said, "In Glasgow you are a nobody until you have been invited to a launch", i.e., at one of the Clyde shipyards. Evidently he was still waiting for an invitation. Bliss was a fairly regular contributor to the GLASGOW HERALD and SCOTTISH FIELD, and kept the School before the public eye.

Bliss used to spend a good deal of time in his studio above the Director's room, one of the most interesting features of which is a long trapdoor of floorboard width, which hinges up to allow large canvases to be hoisted up or lowered from the studio, to the waiting area outside the Director's office. Bliss once confided that he could squint through the trapdoor to see who was knocking at his office door below, and if he remained immobile for a minute or two, with luck they would go away. Bliss had no time for administration - between 1960 and 1964 he sent round one general circular to the staff, a one-page report on the ending of the National Diploma in Design and the introduction of the Diploma in Art and Design.in England.

Bliss was probably the last Director to be able to use his studio for painting - his timetable was very much of his own devising and he had little involvement with outside bodies. The educational quango had not yet been invented, and Bliss's attitude to outside busybodies would have been much along the lines of an advertisement for a seminary in Glasgow in the 1870's:

> *This School is maintained by private subscription and is not*
> *subject to interference by Government Inspectors or other*
> *ignorant persons...*

Bliss finished his service at the School of Art in the summer of 1964, just as the University of Glasgow severed its connection with the former Technical

*Glasgow School of Art Choir
in Central Station, Glasgow
Christmas 1954.*

*Willie Letham giving casts
a coat of paint.
A remarkable character usually
attired in full formal uniform
of the head janitor.*

William Drummond Bone and class 1958.
Drummond Bone was a nephew of Sir Muirhead Bone

Charities Day 1962

Glasgow School of Art and Garnethill
from the air c. 1960

*"Awfy clever wean, this.
Say 'Awa an bile yir heid'
that ye learnt aff the
budgie, hen....".
A cartoon by Bud Neill, in
the 1950's.
He had been a student at
Glasgow School of Art.*

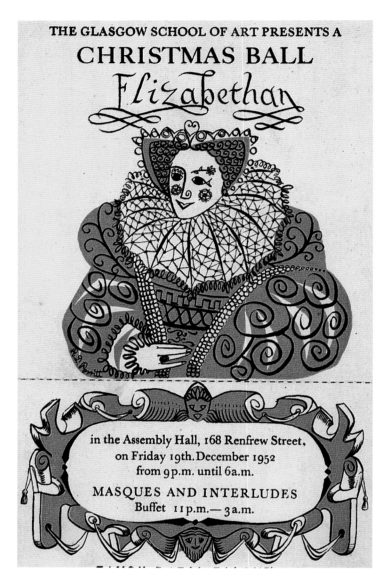

*Mr and Mrs Douglas Percy Bliss's
Christmas Ball Ticket 1950.*

College, which became the new University of Strathclyde. At this time, the
Glasgow School of Architecture also ceased to exist, and the future of the
Architecture Department in the School of Art became the most pressing ques-
tion for the new Director, H. Jefferson Barnes.

Bliss returned to the School in 1971 for a special luncheon with the
Governors before the opening of the Newbery Tower, and to give a lecture on

Douglas Percy Bliss and staff. Session 1961–62: Back row left to right—Bob Finney, Kit Grant, Jack Fleming, Conrad McKenna, Ernest Riley, R Sinclair Thomson, Bob Stewart, Jimmy Goodchild, Paul Zunterstein, Hugh Ferguson, J Cassidy, Leslie Auld, Jimmy Seel, John Miller, and Ted Odling. Middle row left to right—Willie Letham, Phil Reeves, Gordon Huntly, Geoff Squire, Cluny Rowell, W Drummond Bone, Lennox Paterson, Olivia Roberts, Johnny Crawford, Mary Armour, Margaret Grant, Elizabeth Hamilton, David Donaldson, Jimmy Barr, Trevor Mackinson and Henry Hillier. Front row left to right—D S R Waugh, Harriet Hansen, Wilson Steel, Elizabeth Brown, H Jefferson Barnes, Douglas Percy Bliss, Willie Armour, Kath Whyte, David C Black and Walter Pritchard.

Sir Walter Scott. While he was revisiting one of the Painting studios he bumped into a member of staff, and stopped to chat between the two sets of swing doors. "Mark my words," he said, "My time at the School was important in its way, but Barnes' period will be vital". When Bliss demitted office as Director, the standing of the Glasgow School of Art was high, and it was listed in WHITAKER'S ALMANAC as among the six highest-ranking Art Schools in Britain.

Bliss retired to his cottage at Windley, near Kedlestone, Derbyshire, and was soon invited to become a Governor of the local Derby College of Art, formerly Derby School of Art, where by coincidence Thomas Simmonds had been Headmaster after leaving the Glasgow School of Art in 1885.

H JEFFERSON BARNES 1964-80

H Jefferson Barnes joined the staff as a Drawing Master in session 1944-45, the year of the School's actual centenary, which had, as noted, been erroneously celebrated in 1940. However, even if the correct date had been known in 1945 it would have been ignored in the jubilation which marked the end of the war in Europe that year.

In 1946, after Bliss took over, Barnes was promoted to the new post of Deputy Director and Registrar, which suited his talents well, and he eventually succeeded Bliss in the summer of 1964. Barnes was thus one of four Directors who had intimate knowledge of the workings of the School, based on many years of experience. On his retirement, he was knighted and became Sir Harry Barnes, and Glasgow University conferred on him the honorary degree of Doctor of Letters. Sadly, he was unable to enjoy his retirement, through illness, and died in 1982.

H. Jefferson Barnes was the son of a medical man and was educated at Repton. He went on to study at the Slade, taking the Diploma in Fine Art, followed by a post-graduate course in stage design. He won a number of awards, including a Silver Medal for Life Drawing, and arrived at Glasgow School of Art on the recommendation of his former Professor at the Slade, Randolph Schwabe, whose daughter Alice, Barnes had married.

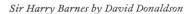

Sir Harry Barnes by David Donaldson

Textile Department 1960's

*Student in Product Design
workshop 1969*

*Margaret Grant and students.
A very gifted teacher for whom H J Barnes
had the highest regard.
John McNeece on the right*

Professor Schwabe had been a close friend of the Mackintoshes in their London days. Schwabe was executor for Margaret Macdonald's estate after she died in 1933, and Alice Barnes as a child was a great favourite of Mackintosh's. Barnes was thus steeped in Mackintosh lore through his family connections, and extremely well informed about the artist's work, which he also collected.

When he finished his pre-war studies at the Slade, Barnes was able to make a six-month tour of Europe, including Finland, then part of the Soviet Union, and the Baltic dependencies. He was thus one of the last independent travellers to see that part of the world before the frontiers were closed for the best part of forty years, and his travels in the Soviet Union must have provided him with interesting small-talk when he encountered Sir Anthony Blunt in 1947. Blunt had just been appointed to the Courtauld Institute and was one of the foremost authorities on the work of the 17th century French artist Nicolas Poussin.

Barnes came into contact with Blunt through Poussin and as a result of a

Painting of the Library Corridor by Tommy Burns
when a student. c.1970

most remarkable find. Barnes's home town was Sheffield, where his father was a Professor in the University, and at some point in 1946-47 he bought a painting in a Sheffield antique shop. Barnes thought it looked like a Poussin, and indeed a small plate fixed to the frame bore the artist's name, though that could not be relied on. Anthony Blunt was a Poussin expert, regularly consulted on points of authentication, and Barnes sent the Yorkshire painting to Blunt, who at that time had just been put on a retainer by the National Gallery of Canada in Toronto, to act as their agent in Britain. Blunt accordingly informed them of the Yorkshire Poussin and estimated that the vendor would be prepared to accept £6,000, a huge sum of money in 1947, and in due course the sale was concluded.

Blunt was also in touch with the Fitzwilliam Museum in Cambridge, which had expressed some interest, and he wrote to Toronto saying that if nothing came of the Fitzwilliam interest "both I and the vendor would prefer to see the painting go a gallery in the Empire..." This must be a rare recorded instance of Blunt trying to advance the interests of the British Empire - or as both he and Barnes would have said, "Empah".

Barnes' accent was of an upper crust variety now more or less extinct, and there is a sketch of him in Alasdair Gray's novel LANARK, in a scene where the hero goes to enrol as a student in the Evening School, then supervised by Barnes in his capacity as Registrar:

> *That evening he waited in a corridor of the Art School outside the Registrar's office in a queue of other applicants. When his turn came he entered a spacious room and started walking toward a desk at the far end, conscious of pictorial and statuesque objects on either side. The man at the desk looked up as he approached. He had a large, spectacled face and a wide mouth with amused corners. He spoke drawlingly, with an expensive English dialect. "Good evening. What can I do for you?"...*

The room described here is the former Board Room, now the Mackintosh Room, and on a workaday basis Barnes used it as his office, sitting surrounded by "pictorial and statuesque objects". Barnes was a tall, spare figure, and always wore the same old tweed jacket. One of his shoulders was higher than the other, and due to the weight of pocket contents on the other side, the hemline of the jacket assumed the same slope as the shoulders, presenting a curious optical effect as he receded down the corridor. The only thing lacking was an academic gown, given which he would have been everyone's idea of a typical Oxford don.

Barnes' position involved supervision of the General Course, as well as the Evening School, and thus he tended to be in the building from morning till night, administering an empire only rivalled in size by the Architecture Department, which had several hundred part-time and evening students and a small army of part-time teachers. The General Course was the common first two years of the Diploma Course, and involved Drawing, Painting, Sculpture, some Craft and Design work, and Architectural Drawing and Perspective. Lecture courses also included the History of Costume and the History of Ornament, and for a brief period after 1951, Artistic Anatomy, taught by Ted Odling.

Gordon Huntly, Lennox Paterson and John Tomlinson all of whom had been at one time chairmen of the Staff Association.
At the Foulis Press Exhibition of Private Press work 1973.

Danny Ferguson's drawing of the Staff Association party on the retiral of Robert Begg as Chairman of Governors May 7th 1976

These subjects – Ornament, Costume, Perspective, Anatomy – which survived until the beginning of the Barnes era, were staple elements in the art student's curriculum in Newbery's time, and even then they were traditional subjects, inherited from the 19th century. Perspective as taught to art students up to 1959 was a curious survival, as the method used was the "Measuring Point", or "Art Student's Method", which combined confusion with impracticality. Theoretically ingenious, it had been devised around 1855 for students with small drawing-boards who could not use plans, as in the "Architect's Method" of projection.

H Jefferson Barnes

Such subjects seem to have lasted in Scotland a decade or so longer than in England, and the two-year General Course continued until 1971, when it was reduced to a year, which also brought to an end the custom of talking about the "Upper School" and the "Lower School", terminology in use since Newbery's time. Indeed, the origins of the two-year "Lower School" can be traced to the Royal Academy Schools where two years in the "Plaster Academy", drawing antique casts, were a necessary prerequisite to admission into the Painting School. Thus in 1923, Winston Churchill writes to Lavery, saying he knows he is too old to learn to draw properly – "I can't afford to spend two years at the casts" – and so must do the best he can.

During Barnes' period as Director, the old Diploma courses were replaced by Degree courses, influenced largely by developments in England. This came about almost by accident, resulting from the resignation of the National Committee for Diplomas in Art and Design, and the transfer of responsibility for Art awards to the CNAA, which operated an external degree system in Polytechnics in a wide range of subjects. As a result of the creation of Polytechnics,, municipal Art Schools in England found themselves merged with technical and commercial colleges, and in some cases domestic science colleges, to make up the new institutions. Art students now graduated with Honours degrees and could proceed to doctorates and the like, "just like brain surgeons", as the critic Brian Sewell tartly observed.

In these circumstances, there was justified concern for the status of professional and technical Art and Design Diplomas, and holders of the unclassified Scottish Diploma in Art were likely to find themselves at a disadvantage in the market-place. In Glasgow, the decision was reluctantly taken to seek incorporation of the School of Art within the CNAA system, and the last Diplomas in Art were awarded in 1978, to be replaced by a CNAA degree.

The record of higher Art qualifications in England is not a good one. In the 1930's the Art Teacher's Diploma (ATD) was devised; then there was the post-war National Diploma in Design (NDD); this was replaced by the Diploma in Art and Design (Dip AD); this in turn gave way to CNAA external degrees, which, true to form, were in due course also abandoned. It takes many years for a new qualification to register on the public consciousness, and the net result of this turnover in diplomas and degrees was that none of them was recognised outside the closed world of the teaching profession and the Art Colleges.

However, the Barnes period was one of significant academic development, which although transitional, paved the way to the present workings of the School, and his retiral in 1980 is a milestone in the history of the School of Art for several reasons. In the broader picture, the era of expansion in

David Donaldson
by Danny Ferguson

Higher Education which began with the Robbins Committee Report) had come to an end by 1981, and a programme of cuts, rationalisations, and mergers characterised the next decade.

Eventually, from around 1990, another 'great leap forward' began, with wholesale expansion of student numbers and the promotion of some thirty-odd Polytechnics to University status, enabling the Government to announce that Britain now sends one third of its young people to University. Through a series of historical accidents, the former Regional Colleges of Art in England have ended up as divisions or Faculties of Art & Design in Universities, something unforeseen, never debated, and which has come to pass without a murmur. There are now scarcely more than a handful of free-standing Schools of Art left in the entire United Kingdom, and the Glasgow School of Art, thanks in no small measure to Sir Harry Barnes's efforts, remains one of them.

PROFESSOR ANTHONY JONES 1981-85

Sir Harry Barnes was succeeded in 1981 by Tony Jones, a former member of the School's teaching staff, and incidentally the first sculptor to become Director. Professor Jones was born and educated in Wales and gained his art training at Newport School of Art. In the course of his career he crossed the Atlantic several times, and first joined the School staff in 1968 as an Assistant in the Sculpture Department, after two years in similar posts in American Universities. He went back to the United States in 1972 as Professor and Chairman of the Faculty of Fine Art at the Christian University of Texas, Fort Worth, and it was from there that he returned to GSA as Director of the School. When he left in 1985, he was again bound for the United States, as the newly-appointed President of the School of Art of the Chicago Art Institute.

Danny's Drawing of Tony Jones

Towards the end of Barnes' period as Director, the Governors acquired the former premises of the Glasgow and West of Scotland Agricultural College in Blythswood Square. In passing, Barnes also used his connections with the National Trust for Scotland to acquire a long lease on a stable block at Culzean Castle in Ayrshire, which was fitted out as a students' hostel, and proved a valuable asset, while the School could afford to run it, enabling groups of students to pursue course work in a landscape setting.

After refurbishment, the Agricultural College building became the base for the Department of First Year Studies, which had been created when a new pattern of study replaced the old two-year General Course. Known as the Blythswood Building, this was later disposed of in the period of Tony Jones's Directorship, following a decision to centralise departments as far as possible in the vicinity of Renfrew Street.

The Blythswood Building is worth mentioning for its historical associations, since it had been in part the family home of Madeleine Smith, who stood trial for murder in 1857. The verdict of the court was 'not proven', and ever since there have been arguments about her guilt or innocence. Allegedly, she had poisoned her French lover, Emile L'Angelier, with arsenic in a cup of cocoa, handed out from one of the basement windows of the building later purchased by the Art School. This is interesting in itself, but Madeleine Hamilton Smith was also the niece of the distinguished architect David Hamilton, who had designed the Ingram Street building which housed the Government School of Design (later School of Art) in this period. Madeleine Smith's father, James Smith, was himself an architect and designed the Corporation Buildings in Sauchiehall Street, which housed the Glasgow School of Art and Haldane Academy from 1869. Thus, curiously, all three buildings occupied by the School had a connection with Madeleine Smith and her family. According to Somerset Maugham, she later admitted, to a mutual acquaintance, that she had indeed poisoned L'Angelier.

The period of Tony Jones' Directorship was distinguished by renewed energy and optimism, as the School became practised in the ways of CNAA, and 'TJ', as he was known, was a tireless publicist for both the Glasgow School of Art and its Mackintosh heritage, at home and abroad. His spell in the USA had been well used, and his particular talents were just right for the times and for Glasgow, then at the start of its civic resurgence. He mirrored the city's great promotional efforts, and both were well in tune with the spirit of Britain during the 1980s. In 1984, for example, the Design School mounted an exhibition

*Cassina Window during
Glasgow School of Art
Exhibition in Milan.*

*Opposite:
A poster for an
Exhibition of
Mackintosh Furniture
in Tokyo*

*Printing silkscreen in
Sauchiehall Street
during
Activities Week 1977*

*Printing on the
Arab Press in
Sauchiehall Street*

of student work in Milan, masterminded by the Head of Interior Design, Bill Macpherson, and Cassina, one of the first manufacturers of Mackintosh furniture, and long term supporters of GSA.

During his time as a Sculpture lecturer, Tony Jones with Bob Stewart had been instrumental in setting up an annual Activities Week, when the usual timetable was suspended in favour of a programme of special events and visiting lecturers. Among the notables persuaded to come to Glasgow to address the students were David Hockney, Eduardo Paolozzi, Ralph Steadman and George Melly, complete with his Dixieland jazz band. (Melly had written a very well-regarded book, REVOLT INTO STYLE, a history of 1960's Pop Art and music).

In his inimitable way, Tony Jones was something of a media personality himself, appearing frequently on television to promote the work of the School. He is a natural performer, never at a loss for a persuasive contribution or a well-honed soundbite, and was always immaculately turned out for his television appearances. This led the late Danny Ferguson to remark: "Aye, he's a very natty Welsh dresser". Professor Tony Jones enjoyed a highly successful spell at the Chicago Art Institute, and eventually returned to the UK in 1992 and to take up the post of Rector of the Royal College of Art, London, in succession to Jocelyn Stevens.

G S A : The Nineties

PROFESSOR DUGALD CAMERON

SIR HARRY BARNES'S TERM OF OFFICE was undoubtedly one of the most important in the School's history. In many ways, he became a father figure in Scottish art education, and his were the driving ideas. However, there seemed a lack of common purpose among the four Scottish art institutions, and although they might have reached a joint arrangement, which would have been responsive to their longstanding traditions, Glasgow eventually went its own way into CNAA. Barnes was truly concerned about art education, and after the School joined CNAA, he was in constant demand as a chairman or member of visiting parties. His knighthood recognised his services to art education in the UK as much as to his leadership of GSA.

The School's expansion during those years avoided the establishment of another school of art in the West of Scotland, or so it was said. It was certainly the case that the foundations for excellence were well laid then, and on balance, CNAA was a benign, if Anglifying influence. It did inaugurate the paper age, however, though its requirements were as nothing to the demands being made in the 1990s.

A less happy aspect of that period was the demolition of the old buildings on the north side of Renfrew Street and the erection, firstly, of the Foulis Building in 1964; next, the Newbery Tower in 1969; and lastly, athwart Renfrew Street, the Bourdon Building in the late 1970s. Thankfully, the old Assembly Hall was left intact and remains today as the Student Union and Vic Bar, the latter a marvellous re-creation of a Glasgow café rescued by students of the Mackintosh School of Architecture.

Sir Harry's brief retirement was cruelly marred by serious illness and he died in 1982. Drew Perry came to the School in March 1968 as his personal assistant, and in June of that year, Frank Kean arrived as Secretary and Treasurer; both became pillars of GSA's establishment and helped ensure the true purpose of our administration, which is to support the School's academic programmes.

One of the new administrative arrangements was the establishment of Schools within GSA. The Mackintosh School had already been created out of the erstwhile Glasgow School of Architecture Department, and along with the University of Glasgow, it formed what is now widely known and respected as the 'Mack'. Since 1973, under the remarkable leadership of Professor Andy MacMillan, the Mackintosh School has enjoyed consistent success in national competitions.

The Schools of Fine Art and Design were also created in this period, and Bill Buchanan, himself a GSA diplomate, and later an officer of the Scottish Arts Council, became the first Head of Fine Art in 1977. Notions of individual, as well as academic freedom run deep within artists, and the principle that one might agree in the morning and disagree in the afternoon has always seemed perfectly reasonable. Thus, it needed all of Bill's diplomacy to make the new

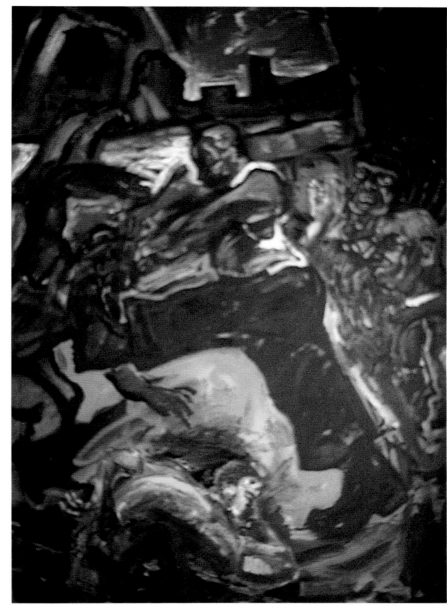

A painting by Peter Howson

School work, but during the '80s, there emerged from it an astonishing group of painters who won international renown as the 'new Glasgow Boys': Campbell, Wiszniewski, Howson, Currie, Conroy, later to be joined by the new Glasgow Girls – Beaton, Watt and Savile among them. Much of their inspiration came from Sandy Moffat, and Jack Knox, then Head of Painting. Bill Buchanan also introduced Photography as a Fine Art specialism, bringing the dynamic Thomas Joshua Cooper to run it in his inimitable way.

Again, during the late 1970's Bob Stewart, the Head of Printed Textiles, established a unique multi-disciplinary Masters' course in Design, became Head of Design under Sir Harry Barnes, and Deputy Director to Tony Jones, on the retiral of Lennox Paterson. Lennox, like others who had experienced fighting a war, took a civilised and relaxed view of life and was a valued confidant of both staff and students, as well as a hugely talented wood engraver.

Opposite:
Painting by Steven Campbell.

''Think Tank'
by Adrian Wiszniewski.

On following pages: left,–
'Crown of Thorns'.
Painting by Alison Watt.
and right,––
Jenny Saville's show
and one of her drawings.

Ken Currie's Degree Show.

124

*Thomas Joshua Cooper
Head of Fine Art Photography
with Frank Keen,
the School's 'pilot'
through many
a financial 'straight'
until retirement in 1993.*

After Bob Stewart's early retirement, along with that of Ted Odling, Jimmy Cosgrove was appointed Head of First Year and I became Head of Design. The MA Design course then came under Julian Gibb's leadership. Janice Kirkpatrick graduated from that course in 1984, and along with Ross Hunter from the Mackintosh School went on to found Graven Images, a determinedly Glasgow-based design consultancy which has won international recognition.

Design at GSA has traditionally encompassed a very wide range of activities, and the School of Design was formed as an intelligent response to the expectations of CNAA, and the difficulty its officers might have in accepting our relatively small specialisms. In England, an entry of 24 students was then a minimal requirement, and some GSA specialisms existed happily on a third of that. We were however determined to maintain the Scottish tradition, and the device of a School composed of several specialist Departments eventually satisfied both educationists and administrators, though it had to be explained all over again, each time we met them.

During my tenure as Head of Design we were able to introduce a development in engineering education which I had dreamt of for many years. In the words of Donald Firth: "Engineering education in universities had become an abstraction of the real world", and the real world of engineering is surely concerned with the creation of products for human use and delight. Design lies at the heart of manufacturing industry, and thence came the idea of extending our experience in teaching industrial design to that of educating engineers, with the product as its focus.

Norman McNally and his team have taken forward my initial concept, and in partnership with Professor Brian Scott and his colleagues at the University of Glasgow, have established a unique B.Eng. degree in Product Design Engineering. How right that this should happen in Glasgow, given its history and desperate need to rebuild its manufacturing base. How right also for

*Furniture used in residential homes.
Designed by a team led by
Norman McNally and manufactured
by Blindcraft, Glasgow.*

GSA, given the reasons for its founding, and for the University of Glasgow, where the world's first Chair of Engineering was created in 1840, just before the School itself.

The accreditation of the B.Eng. course by the Institute of Mechanical Engineers took place just after Tony Jones' departure for Chicago. Tony had been a great tonic for GSA and had given the School a new confidence. A few more years under his leadership might have been beneficial, but he was replaced by Tom Pannell, then Principal of the Central School of Art and Design. A true gentleman, Tom Pannell's short term of office ended when he refused to accept the new regime imposed by the Scottish Office in 1988, which reorganised the Governing Boards of the Central Institutions, removing many of their traditional members, and replacing them initially with appointees of the Secretary of State.

In addition, the Director became the School's Accounting Officer, with express personal responsibility for the financial and other aspects of the institution and the intriguing possibility of being arraigned before the Parliamentary Accounts Committee. The Director is also expected to clype on the Governing Board should they ever transgress the official diktat! This was the beginning of even greater centralisation of power in Edinburgh, though as with the much more far-reaching provisions of the Higher Education and Further Education Act of 1992, it was not presented as such.

At any rate, it perhaps marked a sea change in the way Scottish institutions were being viewed, by a Civil Service seemingly more politicised than ever before. "We are all Thatcherites now," said one. This is a great pity, since Scottish art education has long enjoyed the enlightened support of the Scottish Office and they have much to be proud of. Now, the Scottish Higher Education Funding Council, sponsored by SOED, as provided for in the 1992 Act, is authorised to fund all higher education, thus bringing together the Universities with the former Central Institutions, such as GSA, and the remaining Colleges of Education. Courts and Governing Bodies have had their authority reduced whilst their responsibilities have been emphasised.

Doubtless it is the unseen, clammy hand of the Treasury which really pulls the strings. Certainly, the useful buffer provided by the old Scottish Education Department has been removed, and SHEFC's role is that of a conduit for Government policy. No amount of consultation papers will alter that stark reality, and although the funding mechanism is in general satisfactory, the Scottish Office interpretation of the Treasury-driven Financial Memorandum appeared much more restrictive than its English and Welsh counterparts.

Teaching in art schools remains a mixture of the atelier system, and formal pedagogy, but the necessity for individual tutoring sits uncomfortably with current official thinking and constant reductions in funding. What is important is product, however, not process. That is not to say that process should be ignored, but it only exists to ensure that the product is right, and has no intrinsic merit otherwise. This is not a popular stance with administrators, and the complex machinery of accountability - Quality Assessment, Quality Audit, Quality Assurance - is yet another manifestation of decline in professional trust.

Such concerns are not objectionable in principle, but they have been translated into expensive and burdensome bureaucracies, diverting scarce resources from the production of quality, to the construction of process, in the fond belief that this will guarantee a quality product. Quality of this sort, however, is less about standards, than that which can be readily pursued by a bureaucracy. All art schools mount annual degree shows at which graduands offer their work up to scrutiny, as part of the assessment process - genuine public accountability, beyond the bean-counting stage. Five levels of official audit, on the other hand, is excessive and wasteful, and what may be necessary for a large university, with a £170 million turnover, isn't for GSA with £7 million.

At any rate, Tom Pannell's resignation was followed by a lengthy interregnum, during which Bill Buchanan held the fort, along with his most senior colleagues, while extensive advertising was undertaken to find a new Director. Head-hunters were eventually engaged and John Whiteman was appointed. Sadly, the appointment didn't work out and he unexpectedly resigned, in August 1991. I was then invited by the Governing Board to become Director, and formally appointed on September 6th, 1991.

At this point it must be said that the voluntary, unpaid service rendered to the School by its Governing Board over the years has rarely been fully recognised. Robert Begg, Bill Leggat-Smith, and Harry Abram all gave freely of their time and energy to chair the Board, and David Leslie now continues that tradition in even more trying circumstances!

On taking up the post of Director, I determined that my first priority was to ensure the academic and financial health of the School. "Tell us what's wrong and we'll fix it," said one of my colleagues, and this statement characterised the attitude of staff generally, whose support was, I now know, considerable and widespread. Internally, it was clear that an overhaul of our academic administration was required, and this was accepted, and even welcomed, by the staff, through a process which now provides the basis for the School's quality assurance systems.

The 'Directorate' was also established, and a relatively simple management structure for the School, with the redefinition of the Secretary/Treasurer's role postponed until the retiral of the incumbent, Frank Kean, in December 1993. While the School was thus absorbing widespread internal change, however, the

Bill Buchanan and his senior staff 1989. Back row left to right–Drew Perry, Chrissie White, Penny Hudd, Phil Reeves, Iain Money, Paul Reeves, David Harding, Mike Healey, Thomas Joshua Cooper, Jackie Main, Steve Mulrine, Dan Smith, Neil Morrison, Drew Plunkett and Stan Bell. Middle row left to right– Dugald Cameron, Jimmy Cosgrove, Andy MacMillan, Bob Shaw and Sam Ainslie. Front row left to right– Bill Buchanan, Cliff Bowen, Kenny Mitchell, Roger Millar and Barbara Santos-Shaw.

entire spectrum of tertiary education in the UK became the subject of some upheaval, when the provisions of the Further and Higher Education Bill became the Act of 1992.

A major aspect of this legislation was the removal of the binary line hitherto separating the Scottish Central Institutions from the Universities, together with the closure of CNAA and the extension of degree-awarding powers, and university title, to institutions meeting size and other requirements. GSA is unlikely to want or ever contain the range of disciplines and student numbers required for university status, and did not have accredited status with CNAA, the prerequisite for degree-awarding powers. Hence, the School faced the immediate need to secure the future validation of its degree programmes in Fine Art and Design. Architecture had of course been associated with the University of Glasgow since the late 1960s, and eventually a very satisfactory new association was concluded with the University, which respects the autonomy of the School, and also recognises its policy to seek degree-awarding powers, whilst ensuring the continuation of its present and future degree programmes.

The School also concluded its protracted Institutional Review, begun under CNAA in May 1992, and completed successfully in March 1994. This is the first step towards gaining degree-awarding powers, the achievement of which will keep the School's keep its functional independence in good working order. The creation of SHEFC, replacing the SOED directly as our funding body, has also brought in its train far greater changes than were anticipated, in particular a marked emphasis on financial control mechanisms.

Accommodation difficulties, and the many serious concerns over the School's estate, which the new administration inherited, have inhibited almost all of its operations, even threatening some of the School's core activities. The long saga of the School's problems in this area reaches back to the selling of the Blythswood Square building in 1982 and a catalogue of error and misfortune seen against official procrastination, and perhaps even indifference. This remains the major operational challenge for the Directorate, although significant headway has been made during 1994 with the acquisition of No.11 West Graham Street, named the 'Sir Harry Barnes Building', unfortunately to be set against the loss of the former Girls' High School, a much valued facility.

While the establishment of SHEFC appeared to promise a more 'hands off' relationship with the funding body, the experience of the School in the purchase of the former Health Board building did not show this to be so. Frankly, it should be cause for concern that one public body (GSA) has to take out a commercial loan to buy a property originally funded by the Health Board, another public body. This was a 'first' for GSA, and no doubt, a sign of the future.

There is a nice irony in that while resources are being squeezed and 'efficiency gains' imposed, institutions are undergoing quality audits and assessments in which they would naturally wish to demonstrate their continued excellence, rather than admit the consequences of reduced circumstances. However, the current climate actively discourages candour in this process, and the rewards are small in comparison to the penalties.

On a happier note, I have been at pains to extend productive relationships between the School and the business and commercial world, and between the School and its local community and the City of Glasgow. The latter has included establishing links with Garnethill Community Council, and neighbouring establishments such as St Aloysius, the Dental School and RSAMD. The School enjoyed its first civic lunch in February 1994, preceded by a visit from the late Lord Provost. It is essential for the School to keep its many friendships in good repair and to extend them locally, nationally and internationally. GSA has also a longstanding relationship with the Trades House of Glasgow and with individual Incorporations, which we seek to maintain and develop.

GSA Enterprises Ltd was established in 1985 to provide a means of generating income for the School, and FOLIO records our activities in newsletter form for both internal and external readers. 'Friends of GSA' is a further witness to the School's desire to encourage wider involvement in its affairs, and the establishment of a United States 'Friends of GSA', by Eleanor Taffner in 1994, is an important contribution to the School's fundraising effort, and we are grateful to the Taffners for their sustained support.

Soon after my appointment, I was invited by Graham Roxburgh to view the nearly completed Art Lover's House in Bellahouston Park, which struck me as having considerable academic potential, notably in the area of postgraduate

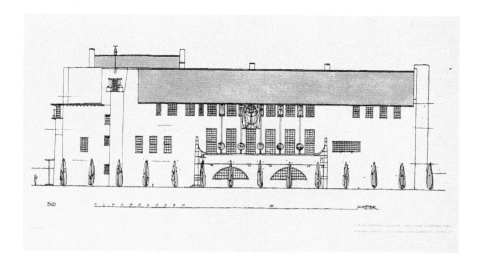

Art Lover's House.
Drawing by C R Mackintosh

Interior of Art Lover's House. C R Mackintosh's drawing of Music Room

and research activity, which might be developed there, complementary to our main campus on Renfrew Street. After much discussion with the City Council, this is now on the way to achievement, and how appropriate this will be, should it be ready in time for the various centenaries of Mackintosh's masterwork, between 1996 and 1999. The School also played an important role in Glasgow's successful bid for the nomination of City of Architecture and Design in 1999, and our new Centenary Building, looking to the 21st century, as did Mackintosh's to the 20th, erected on a Garnethill site, would be a fitting centrepiece to this enterprise, if funding can be found.

Perhaps not surprisingly, the theme of recent years has been consolidation, in both academic and resource terms. The quality of our academic programmes, supervised by the Deputy Director, Jimmy Cosgrove, and Heads of Schools, remains high, and significant new developments in postgraduate and

*Untitled painting by
Jimmy Cosgrove,
Deputy Director, 1992*

research work have been established. Frank Kean, whose long and distinguished service to the School ended in December 1993, was replaced by Mike
Foley, and the post of Secretary and Treasurer was re-defined as Assistant
Director (Resources) in recognition of the extended role now required of the
School's administration. Ewan Hainey, as Academic Registrar during this
period, played a key part in steering the School through the bureaucratic
minefield.

Running a good art school, and by any reasonable test GSA is one of the
best, cannot ever be easy. Mediocrity, perhaps, is easily managed – GSA isn't!
Almost every week, the achievements of our students, graduates and staff are
recorded in the media, and such successes, often gained in national competitions, are both a measure of, and witness to, the commitment of everyone
involved in our creative enterprise.

The School community comprises three estates: the Governing Board; the
academic, technical, administrative and support staff; and the student body.
The lifeblood of the School is its students, however trite that may seem, and
Glasgow School of Art attracts some very remarkable people, with increasing
numbers from abroad. As a body, students have a voice in all of the constituted
committees, other than the Chairman's, and those concerned with academic
progress and examinations. The Students' Representative Council has traditionally been responsible for the annual Fashion Show, and used to organise
the Christmas Ball, once the highlight of the social calendar. These days,
however, students' social life is far more intense with discos every weekend,

and even an occasional radio station – 'Ton and a Half' – for the 150th Anniversary!

In recent times, John Quinn, SRC President 1992-94, assisted by his Social Convener, Mia Messinger, has made these events a mighty work. Bob Grieve, his successor in 1994, has an unenviable task as financial support for students is cynically reduced by central government, in parallel with funding to the institution itself.

Directors of GSA enjoy a rare privilege and a heavy responsibility in their custodianship of the Mackintosh heritage. Mackintosh's masterwork, at the focus of our campus, has become a place of pilgrimage, yet remains proudly in use for its original purpose, from the great Painting studios, to the table and chairs I use in the Headmaster's room, and the studio above, in which I draw.

One might question whether art schools really are special, or perhaps the beneficiaries of special pleading. Experience and reflection, however, suggest that institutions like ours are indeed special places and their value to the communities which support them is that they offer an alternative education, based on the acquisition of a blend of intellectual and practical skills – an education by 'hand, eye, and brain'.

Only in Schools of Art, for example, are undergraduates expected to display the fruits of their creative strivings to the public at large, in their annual degree exhibitions. And only in Schools of Art do the oldest making activities of mankind, the crafts, remain entirely relevant alongside the newest – the electronic image. They provide society with an alternative view of itself, and how its future might be, and why it might be so. This may not always be easily comprehensible or comforting, but it fulfils a need acknowledged by any civilised society.

Glasgow School of Art was founded as a Government School of Design almost 150 years ago. It is still faithfully fulfilling that task and concerning itself with making things. The School's business is teaching, scholarship, and research, across a coherent range of related disciplines from the fine arts, and architecture, through the applied arts, to industrial and commercial design. Never has the business of making been more vital to our future as a nation, and the School has a leading role to play in that, as its potential is realised.

Welding in Sculpture Workshop

Architecture

ARCHITECTURAL EDUCATION IN GLASGOW

THE BEGINNINGS of architectural education in the city can be seen as early as 1871, when the Glasgow Institute of Architects, an employers' organisation, first approached the Trustees of Haldane's Academy, for financial help to set up evening classes for apprentices. What became of this initiative is not known, but it was soon overtaken by the activities of the Glasgow Architectural Association, founded c 1877 for the benefit of apprentices, assistants, etc., with a programme of visits to works in progress, sketching parties in summer, and lectures in winter. They also produced an annual publication, The GAA Sketchbook, featuring a selection of the best sketches from summer visits, and the names of the young artists include the first two Professors of Architecture in Glasgow.

The Glasgow Architectural Association also provided instruction in hitherto neglected areas, such as architectural history, and members would be asked to contribute a paper, followed by a debate. C R Mackintosh, e.g., gave a lecture on "Scotch Baronial Architecture" in 1891. Generally, a member appointed as 'critic' for the evening would begin the debate with some technical criticism of the paper, then the others would join in. The lecturer was required to furnish the critic with a copy of his paper in advance, so that he could do his homework, and the surviving manuscripts of Mackintosh's lectures were probably for this purpose.

Francis Newbery took up his post at the Glasgow School of Art in 1885, and seems to have recognised an embryonic School of Architecture in the work of the Association. At that time the School of Art taught subjects called Architecture and Building Construction, conforming to the South Kensington syllabuses, in which the notion of 'Advanced Architecture', according to old exam papers, was typically the detailed design of a village schoolhouse, including drainage. Building Construction, moreover, was less concerned with technology, than with teaching builders and tradesmen to do architectural drawings, and this no doubt explains why the Association members ran their own Construction class. Newbery accordingly invited this class to transfer to the School of Art en bloc, and among the students at that time were John Keppie, Charles Gourlay, and Alexander McGibbon.

Keppie became a partner in the firm of Honeyman, Keppie and later with Mackintosh, President of the Glasgow Institute of Architects, Chairman of Governors of the Glasgow School of Art, and a member of the Royal Scottish Academy. McGibbon became the first Professor of Architecture in the School of Art, and Professor in the Glasgow School of Architecture. Gourlay became Professor of Architecture and Building Construction in the Technical College, and later Professor in the Glasgow School of Architecture.

The Architecture curriculum in the School of Art was developed by William J Anderson, who became Director of Architecture in 1894, and set up

John Keppie, FRIBA,
Chairman of Governors.
By Maurice Grieffenhagen, RA.
Picture presented to the School
Governors by Jessie, his sister.

Charles Gourlay FRIBA
Professor of Architecture and
Building Construction
in the Royal Technical College.
Teacher GSA and
Glasgow School of Architecture.

a programme of evening classes with distinguished local architects as visitors, including J J Burnet and John Keppie. Anderson is best remembered for his book ARCHITECTURE OF THE RENAISSANCE IN ITALY, which is still a useful guide. Following his death in 1899, his unpublished lectures on Greek Architecture were assembled by other hands to form the basis eventually of W B Dinsmoor's encyclopaedic ARCHITECTURE OF ANCIENT GREECE, the reference work of first resort.

Glasgow's Technical College had offered an evening-class Diploma in Architecture since 1888, and passes gained at the School of Art theoretically counted towards the Technical College Diploma. Since no-one ever took it, it was a dead letter. However, the system whereby passes gained at one examination centre could be credited at another, had all the ingredients of credit accumulation transfer, now promoted as the way forward in further education. In 1892, the Technical College introduced a day-class Diploma in Architecture organised in two main divisions, Design and Construction, the latter taught by Charles Gourlay, whose mathematics were good enough to gain him a BSc in Civil Engineering. Gourlay clearly had ample time to study, since no-one took the new three-year Diploma either.

Design classes could be taken at the School of Art, and there was, in fact, considerable traffic between the two institutions. This was probably because the School of Art had phased out its science subjects, including Building Construction, which was pursued to a much higher standard at the Technical College. Among the College students, worthy of note are: J B Fulton, who became Professor of Architectural Design at Glasgow School of Art and Head of

Alexander McGibbon,
Professor, Glasgow School of Art,
by Maurice Grieffenhagen.
Portrait exhibited RA

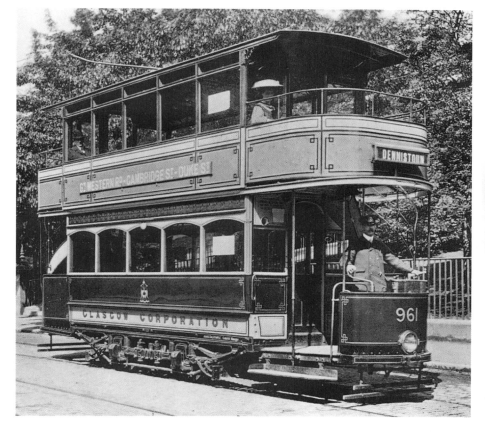

Sir John Burnet. Bronze bust.

Standard Glasgow Corporation
Tramcar with enclosed top deck
designed by J J Burnet
(conversion of open top deck type 1904).
Burnet was a close friend of the
Tramways manager.

Glasgow University Chapel designed by J J Burnet

the Glasgow School of Architecture; A Graham Henderson, partner in Keppie Henderson, successor to Keppie as Chairman of Governors of Glasgow School of Art, and first Scottish President of the RIBA.

In 1901, the designation of the School of Art as a Central Institution, empowered to grant its own diplomas, with the expressed intention of award-ing diplomas in Architecture, led to a major re-appraisal, and a working party of architect Governors from the School of Art and the Technical College worked out a draft curriculum for a new course, leading to a joint diploma.

The question of who would direct a new School was a tricky one, but as both Keppie and J J Burnet had been trained at the Paris Ecole des Beaux Arts in the atelier of Professor J L Pascal, the latter was duly invited to Glasgow by the Governors of the School of Art and asked to report on architectural educa-tion in the city. Professor Pascal was unable to travel but sent in his place his assistant Eugène Bourdon. Bourdon made his report, suggested minor modifi-cations of the curriculum, and also recommended the appointment of a French-trained professor to head the new School. Asked if he himself was available, he agreed to accept the post of Professor of Architectural Design in the School of Art, and the Governors then presented him to their opposite numbers at the Technical College, who agreed to appoint Bourdon indepen-dently. The Glasgow School of Architecture thus came into existence in 1903, and enrolled its first students, mostly to the Certificate Course, in which Bourdon taught Design. The first intake was in 1904-05.

Broadly, the arrangement was that Design was taught at the School of Art and Construction at the Technical College, and students on the Diploma Course were regarded as full-time students of both institutions. The first Diplomas in Architecture were awarded to three candidates in 1910, one of them Alexander Adam, who became Head of the Department of Architecture in the School of Art, and lectured in Architectural History until his retire-ment in 1960. One of the Certificate students just before the First World War was William J Smith, later Professor of Architecture in the Technical College. Smith entered the School as a student in 1909, the year the Library wing was

*Eugene Bourdon ,
Professor of Architectural Design
in G S A and first Head of the
Glasgow School of Architecture.*

*Stained glass window designed
by Robert Anning Bell, RA,
Professor of Design
as a memorial
to Eugene Bourdon.*

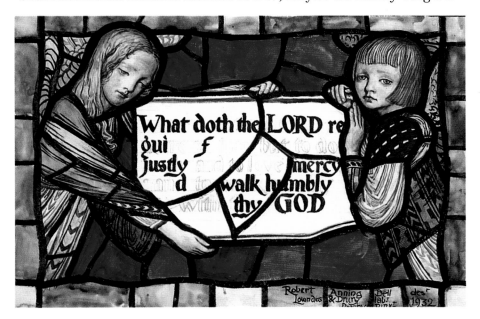

completed, and retired as Professor and Head of the Glasgow School of Architecture in 1959. Thus, two of Bourdon's former students were still in post as teachers in 1959.

Bourdon's new School of Architecture was very modest in scale and had hardly got properly under way before the War arrived. At the outbreak of hostilities, Bourdon returned to France to enlist, and was killed on the Somme in 1916. After the War, Bourdon's mother contributed towards his memorial, which took the form of a bronze head on a plaque erected in the Technical College. At the School of Art, a stained glass window in memory of Bourdon was designed by Professor Robert Anning Bell, and the bronze memorial was transferred to the School of Art at the opening of the Bourdon Building. It should be noted that the inscription on it refers to Bourdon as a Professor in the Technical College, and not the School of Art.

During the First World War there were very few day students and the Headship of the School remained vacant until the appointment of Edward G. Wylie, formerly Assistant Professor under Bourdon. Wylie resigned after only a year and in 1921, James B Fulton was appointed Professor in the School of Art and Director of Architectural Studies in the Glasgow School of Architecture.

THE GLASGOW SCHOOL OF ARCHITECTURE

Fulton had been an outstanding student in the 1890s, winning almost all the RIBA competitions in his day. He was a brilliant draughtsman, better than Mackintosh, according to Professor Smith, at least in the restricted architectural sense, a master of the linear style, and there are echoes of D Y Cameron here and there in his free-hand drawing. In the years after 1900, Fulton travelled extensively in Greece and the Eastern Mediterranean, and the sketches he made at this time are among his best, notably one of the townscape and roofscape of Constantinople, in which fading light, possibly, forced him to work quickly to a conclusion. Some of his studio drawings were perhaps a little overworked, and lack vitality as a consequence.

Fulton's death in 1922 meant the loss of a rare talent. At the outbreak of war, he had enlisted as a private soldier, declining the offer of a commission. Rigorous basic training, followed by service in harsh conditions, damaged his health and he was discharged with a small disability pension. Following a routine medical board, he collapsed in the street outside the Technical College, and died after a brief period of illness. It will be observed that the survival rate of Architecture professors was not encouraging: thus, Anderson, died 1899, by his own hand; Bourdon, died 1916 in action; Wylie, resigned after one year; Fulton, died after one year in post.

Speaking long after these events, however, Professor Smith described Fulton as a "hopeless administrator". Before the First World War, professors simply professed (i.e., taught their subjects), and designed or drew. The Head of the Glasgow School of Architecture was also the Professor of Architectural Design, and since Gourlay at the Technical College was not a designer, he was simply never considered for the Headship, much to his annoyance. The possession of a BSc in Civil Engineering merely helped reinforce his 'nuts and bolts' image as superintendent of a vast night-school operation for building students which had nothing to do with the School of Architecture.

At any rate, the vacant post was filled by T Harold Hughes, who almost immediately had difficulties with Gourlay which the Governors resolved by giving the latter a written 'job description', making clear the extent of Hughes' jurisdiction over him. These arrangements were overtaken by Gourlay's death in 1926. He was only sixty when he died, yet he looks quite elderly in the photographs. Forty-odd years of teaching four nights a week had taken its toll.

Professor Gourlay was revered in the building industry in the West of Scotland, and many of his students went on to become foremen and eventually run their own businesses. Gourlay also published a number of books on building construction, mostly drawings however, with only a few pages of text, and it is clear from surviving class material that Gourlay framed his publications around his teaching. As was customary, he received fifty off-prints free from the publishers, and extra prints could be obtained from the blocks at little or no cost. The drawings and texts were then numbered and loaned out to students to take home. In the days before Xerox, Gourlay had devised his own method for multiple copying.

T Harold Hughes.
Portrait by W O Hutchison.

Buchanan Street and Gordon Street by Muirhead Bone.
Bone was a student at GSA in the 1890's
and is recognised as the modern master of architectural subjects.
He had a perfect eye for perspective and worked at great speed.

Historical Studies:
Roman composition by
Marion Shaw first year
1927–28.
Miss Shaw was one of
the first students to graduate as
BSc (Arch) (Glas).

Following Professor Gourlay's death, Hughes offered to take on Gourlay's Technical College responsibilities, in addition to his own as Head of the Glasgow School of Architecture; this was agreed, and the title of the College Chair was changed from Architecture and Building Construction to simply Architecture.

At the time, no particular notice was taken of this move, since as long as Hughes was Head of School, no real change was evident. However, there was trouble in store, and in 1959, the Technical College was to claim that the Professor of Architecture in the Royal College of Science and Technology was ex officio Head of the Glasgow School of Architecture. This was simply not the case.

Hughes had his reasons for wishing to escape from the embrace of the School of Art and its Governors, particularly John Keppie, and his own flourishing

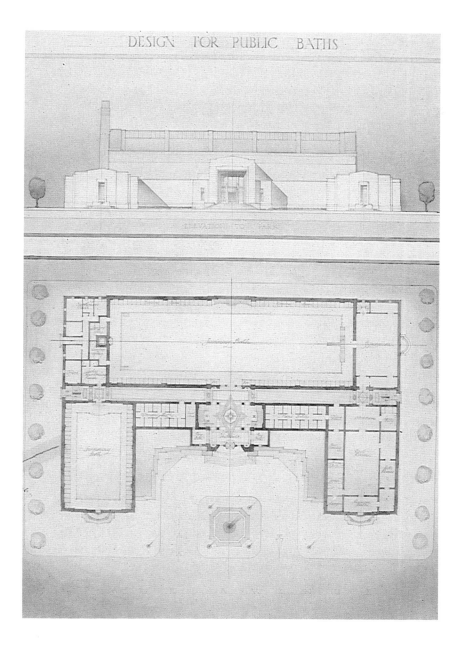

DESIGN FOR PUBLIC BATHS

private practice did not endear him to the local architects. Negotiations with the University of Glasgow, concerning the setting up of a degree course in Architecture, brought Hughes into contact with its senior academic officers, and when the BSc in Architecture was set up in 1924, it was under the control of neither the Governors of the School of Art nor the College, but a joint Board of Studies, including Hughes, who thus acquired another hat for himself, which effectively rendered him fireproof against the machinations of the Governors seeking to dislodge him. Further aggravation was caused by the RIBA Board of Inspection, which visited Glasgow in 1927, and created problems which were to rumble on for decades.

The RIBA Visiting Board claimed to have identified a weakness in teaching, in that Construction was taught in the Technical College, and Design mainly in the School of Art. The Board felt that this separation might engender a similar split in the students' minds between Design and Construction, and that it would be best if all Architectural teaching took place in one building. The RIBA also made some less than enthusiastic remarks about the Architecture Section at the School of Art. Many years later, Professor Smith divulged that Hughes had not told the Art School of the RIBA Board visit until until the day before, so that there was no exhibition of students' work for the London inspectors. Certainly, Hughes never really took him into his confidence, and when Smith came to write Hughes' obituary, the word he used of him was "elusive" - he was always giving 'Smithy' the slip.

Debate then ensued as to where a reorganised day school might be housed, with the School of Art and the Technical College each staking their claims. As part of the Technical College case, it was argued that Architecture should be housed alongside departments such as Civil Engineering, reflecting modern trends in which structural considerations, the increasing use of ferro-concrete, for example, would bring architecture closer to engineering. Ironically, an earlier group of College Governors had agreed to Architectural Design becoming the responsibility of the School of Art, precisely so that those students might have the benefit of being trained alongside painters, sculptors, and designers.

Changed times require changed approaches and some found the technological argument persuasive, including, strangely enough, the Director of the School of Art, J D Revel, as already noted. The Scottish Education Department was also drawn into the debate, but were not convinced by the Technical College case. As one officer put it:

> *Architecture is not the same as Engineering; if it were we would not have a different word for it. Architecture is both an art and a science...*

The School of Art Governors made the same point : "Architecture is not Technology, it is about technology in the service of Art."

At any rate, the formula eventually arrived at was that within the joint Glasgow School of Architecture, the Technical College would assume responsibility for housing the day classes, and full-time Diploma and Degree students would study Design and Construction at the College. Teaching of art subjects on the full-time courses would be increased, and History of Architecture would become a School of Art responsibility, along with the conduct of the part-time certificate course. Diploma and Degree students, who henceforth spent most of their time at the Technical College, were nonetheless regarded by the SED as full-time students of both the School of Art and of the Technical College.

Not surprisingly, by the end of the 1950s, only two or three people really understood the constitutional intricacies of the Glasgow School of Architecture, and they were not in a position to affect the course of events. After one meeting, where its history from Bourdon onwards was gone over, even the Director of the School of Art, D P Bliss, exclaimed to the Head of Architecture: "But my dear chap, this is archaeology!"

Bliss had his problems with the Technical College from around 1954, when its Director, Sir David Anderson, began agitating about Assessors in Architecture. As early as 1912, Francis Newbery had argued that the same Assessors should adjudicate in all the Scottish Art Schools, thus preventing any suggestion that one Diploma was better than another, and this arrangement became standard practice. And since the Architecture Department in the Technical College was considered a branch of a Central Art Institution, its authorities had no say in the appointment of Architecture Diploma Assessors. Sir David Anderson wanted External Examiners to be appointed by individual colleges. This the Art Principals opposed, and the SED supported their view. However, Anderson kept worrying away on this point, and finally got his way. Bliss wrote him a sarcastic letter, "Now you have your heart's desire." Anderson retired in 1959, and at their last meeting he said to Bliss, "I've always meant to find out about art - can you recommend a good book?"

During the career of Anderson's predecessor at the Technical College, Sir Arthur Huddlestone, the question of the best location for the School of Architecture had also arisen. In 1937, the School of Art Governors asked Sir Hector Hetherington, the University Principal, to chair a committee of enquiry, and in due course, this committee recommended that the School of Architecture should be provided with its own accommodation, preferably at the School of Art and that links should be developed with the University - more or less what Burnet had recommended in 1931. World War II, however, intervened and nothing was done. Student numbers fell away and by 1943 there were only 23 students in all the full-time years put together. Far from needing a new building, the entire School was accommodated in one room at the College.

In 1941, Professor Hughes intimated his intention to retire and finally left when William J Smith was released specially from the army to replace him. Professor Smith took over as Head of the School of Architecture in 1942, and continued until his retirement in 1959. He had entered the School of Art as a student in 1909, and had thus been connected with the School more or less continuously for fifty years, apart from military service. Smith loved the School of Art, and it was largely due to his presence that the post-war years were a period of good relations between the two institutions at the operative teaching level.

Smith was succeeded by Professor Frank Fielden, previously Senior Lecturer in Architectural History in the University of Durham, and whereas Smith held the Military Cross from the First War, Fielden held the Croix de Guerre from the Second War, something which obviously commended him to the Appointments Committee. What used to be called the 'officer class' were still noticeably represented on public bodies at that time, and the military virtues were esteemed. Following his arrival in Glasgow, Fielden very quickly found himself on the Military Education Committee, which oversaw the University Officers' Training Corps. The School of Art was never involved in this, presumably not considered worthy of inclusion, since around half the students were women and the men students in the main did not look like a recruiting sergeant's dream.

Through the Military Education Committee, Fielden got to know the Principal and the senior professors, and also renewed acquaintance with J L Gleave, RSA, planning consultant to the University, who was then drawing up a quinquennial development plan. This eventually gave rise to the new University Library and Hunterian Art Gallery, including the reconstructed Mackintosh House. Another proposed building was the new students' Refectory, for which Gleave recommended Fielden as architect. In terms of the history of the School of Art and School of Architecture, Fielden can be seen to be following in the footsteps of Professor Hughes, who had taken an identical path thirty-odd years before, negotiating the degree course, obtaining building commissions, and fraternising with the decision-makers. This did not go unnoticed, and relations within the Joint Committee of the School of Architecture became difficult.

Professor Fielden had inherited the Glasgow School of Architecture degree and diploma course set-up, where the degree students, in common with all other BSc students, had to take first year Mathematics, Chemistry, and Physics. Fielden very quickly managed to negotiate the removal of Physics and Chemistry and to have them replaced by Building Science. The result was that the content of the degree course was now virtually identical to that of the diploma course. To the potential student, the prospect of an Honours degree from an ancient University was much more attractive, and from 1962 on, enrolments for the BSc increased substantially.

At the same time, the RIBA, resolved to phase out part-time and evening school training, began to tighten the screws on the School of Art, although the Institute made little headway, thanks to the tactics of the then Head of Architecture, D S R Waugh. The Principal of the Royal College of Science and Technology, Dr Samuel Curran, had by this time conceived his plan to make the College into Britain's first technological university, which he achieved in 1964. With the creation of a University Court and Senate, the old Governors would have to go, and as an incidental consequence, the Joint Committee of the Glasgow School of Architecture. To a man who had worked on the Manhattan Project, helping to create the first atomic bomb at Los Alamos, this would not seem significant. However, everything was significant to the Governors of the School of Art, and the Joint Committee, and although the transfer of students to degree courses was RIBA policy, they interpreted Professor Fielden's expansion of degree course enrolments as an attempt to escape their authority.

At any rate, Dr Curran achieved his ambitions with the conferring of university status on the Royal College of Science and Technology, which became the University of Strathclyde. The Architecture staff then in post were not entirely happy with developments, for they were already recognised teachers of the University of Glasgow. Nevertheless, this put paid to clandestine plans to move the entire School of Architecture from the College to Glasgow University. Indeed, Professor Fielden was on the brink of achieving this when the granting of university status was announced, which scuppered his plans.

The new University of Strathclyde admitted its first students in session 1964-65 and by the end of that year practically all Architecture full-time students had transferred to Strathclyde degrees, except for a few who chose to complete their Glasgow BSc degrees, as was their right. Professor Fielden became the first Professor of Architecture in the University of Strathclyde, and designed a new building for his department. This was opened in 1966, and academic dress was order of the day. One of the invited guests was Stanley Unwin, a noted comic "Professor" who specialised in near-credible gobbledygook. Unwin was fitted with a gown and invited to explain the use of laboratory apparatus. One Engineering Professor passed through the labs, listened and moved on, puzzled. Only later was he told it was a spoof, and was most upset, declaring that such things shouldn't be allowed in a serious academic institution.

Curiously, in his quest for university status, Dr Curran had been informed by the Privy Council that the College was too monotechnic and must have a substantial arts component to leaven the mix. For this reason, the Commercial College Departments of Language and History were necessary admixtures, and likewise Architecture as an arts subject. The irony of this turnaround was not lost on observers, and indeed the Arts Faculty status of Architecture was eventually eroded by its reclassification when a BSc degree was reintroduced, and Architecture was finally relocated in the Faculty of Engineering.

The last students of the Glasgow School of Architecture transferred to the new Strathclyde degree and graduated in 1968. At the end of the same year, Professor Fielden accepted an appointment as Secretary of the Royal Fine Art Commission and left after ten years in Glasgow. At Strathclyde, Fielden was succeeded by Professor Morcos Asaad, from Liverpool University. On hearing the name of the new Professor, the architect J B Wingate said, "Good God! Not the Marquis de Sade?!", and this brings the story of the Glasgow School of Architecture to a fitting conclusion.

THE MACKINTOSH SCHOOL OF ARCHITECTURE

Professor Fielden's aborted negotiations for a new School of Architecture at Glasgow University, however, served to pave the way for an analogous arrangement connecting the School of Art and the University. Harking back to the earlier history, this was the formula Sir John Burnet had suggested in 1931, and the new Director of the School of Art, H Jefferson Barnes, was surprised how quickly it proved possible to reach agreement. This new School, maintained by the University and the School of Art, was to be called the Mackintosh School of Architecture, and a Chair of Architecture was to be created.

The most pressing problem when Barnes took over as Director was securing the future of the School of Art's Department of Architecture, and the safeguarding of the status of the part-time students of the dissolved Glasgow School of Architecture. The constitutional position of the School of Art was raked over many times but its weakness was that there was no enforceable agreement, merely a historic position from which one side had resiled.

When the University of Strathclyde replaced the Royal College of Science and Technology, the Glasgow School of Architecture ceased to exist, since no provision for its continuance had been made in the Royal Charter (no doubt deliberately). The Strathclyde authorities were taking their lead from the RIBA policy which was pro-University and anti-Art College, the latter being deemed to lack "intellectual rigour". Thus, with the demise of the Glasgow School of Architecture, for the first time since 1904 the School of Art had no involvement with full-time architectural training.

Once Barnes was appointed Director, he entered into negotiations with the University of Glasgow, and eventually enjoyed complete success. Among the most important external factors in Barnes' favour, which ultimately helped to secure official approval for the new Mackintosh School, was a meeting held in London in March 1965, between officers of the University Grants Committee and the RIBA, along with representatives of both the SED and the English DES.

Jack Coia, RSA PPRIAS.
Royal Gold Medallist (1969).
Portrait by Alexander Goudie
for RIAS, Edinburgh

According to the UGC Report of 1968, the RIBA's view was that architectural education should be provided in Universities, but the Committee endorsed the principle that:

> *Under the national policies being evolved in higher education, it should be possible for Universities... to develop forms of academic association, including provision in suitable cases for the award of degrees to students in other institutions, without the need for formal transfer...*

Thus, the UGC suggested precisely the arrangement Barnes had in mind - a teaching department at the School of Art, recognised by Glasgow University for the award of a degree.

Arising from this background, Barnes was able to reach agreement with remarkable speed, though at the time not all the factors working in his favour were known. He was assisted in his representations by two architect governors of the School, Jack Coia, RSA, and Ninian Johnston, RSA, and the triumvirate congratulated themselves on their diplomatic skills, though in fact timing and luck probably had most to do with their success. Jack Coia was exhilarated at the idea of a new School of Architecture and talked excitedly of a "Bauhaus of our own" to the point of tedium. Actually, he pronounced it "Bawhaus", which prompted one wag to ask if the head of the new School would be called the Bawheid?

There were other comical aspects to the creation of the new Chair of Architecture at Glasgow University. On the day the advertisement inviting applications appeared in THE TIMES, the University received a phone call from the RIBA asking why they had not been consulted. The RIBA then sent a letter to the Principal, Sir Charles Wilson, enclosing a list of individuals whom they considered "suitable". Sir Charles did not take kindly to this impertinence and told Barnes at a meeting, "Whatever else happens, one thing is certain, no-one on this list is to be considered for the post".

When the applications were all received, Sir Charles was amazed to find one applicant with no professional qualifications whatsoever, and one application from a student. Barnes later said he got the feeling that Sir Charles Wilson might be having second thoughts about closer involvement with the strange world of architectural education.

The eventual appointee was Professor John Voelcker, who became the first Head of the Mackintosh School of Architecture, which admitted its first intake of degree students in 1970-71, and is thus a continuation of the original Department of Architecture in the School of Art, dating back to 1891.

Once the future of Architecture was secured on the academic front, the next step was to secure appropriate teaching accommodation. Part of the original agreement to mount the Mackintosh School of Architecture was that the School of Art would provide a new building, and the SED were party to this. There were the usual planning and building permissions to be obtained, and the Royal Fine Art Commission also had to pass judgement on the designs, since the new building was to sit opposite the Library wing of Mackintosh's masterwork, on the west side of Scott Street. At any rate, the new Architecture building was finally opened in 1979 - almost ten years after the concordat with the University - and was named the Bourdon Building, in honour of the first Professor of Architectural Design in the School of Art.

It was a tremendous relief to Barnes to see the Bourdon Building finished, as the economic and financial climate had changed by the mid 1970's. The extent of Government borrowing had reached a level which caused the intervention of the International Monetary Fund, and right up to the last Barnes felt it was touch and go whether the Architecture building would get the go-ahead, or be deferred indefinitely. However, the SED were as good as their word, and saw the contract completed. Having pulled off this minor coup, Barnes was somewhat miffed by the ungrateful response of the architects in the School, who looked their gift horse in the mouth, and found it wanting. They did not like it, though Barnes thought it a "fine building".

In fact, the Bourdon is a tremendous lump of a building whose hulking mass seems to have reduced the monumental effect of the Library wing of the Mackintosh Building. Remarkably, the original design for the Bourdon Building was one floor higher than built - so the first proposals must have been 'talked down' by the City Planning Department or the Royal Fine Art Commisssion.

The city's architectural history has now become something of a growth industry, and a milestone in that process was the 1964 RIBA Annual Conference, which was held in Glasgow for the first time since 1935. Just as in 1935, when Thomson and Mackintosh were 'discovered' by the London visitors, so in 1964 the metropolitan literati discovered Victorian Glasgow. At this time, the successful little book GLASGOW AT A GLANCE appeared, edited by Archibald Doak and A MacLaren Young, and Gomme and Walker's major work THE ARCHITECTURE OF GLASGOW appeared in 1968, the year of the Mackintosh Centenary Exhibition, in the Royal Scottish Museum. A decade

St James's Street, London, SW1. H C S Ferguson, 1971.
Traditional Architects style of pencil drawing.

later the label 'Merchant City' was invented, a term not used before 1977, but which has stuck, quite literally, with name-plates carrying this legend now fixed to every street in the area.

Research of any kind, other than occasional articles, or the odd book review, was unknown in the Glasgow School of Architecture until after 1960, when Professor Fielden persuaded two of the staff to register for higher degrees with the University, and conditions of appointment never mentioned research, since the RIBA required all Design teachers to be practising architects - that is, practice was essential while research was optional, something one did in the vacations.

As regards postgraduate research, there was none in the Glasgow School of Architecture, and the only postgraduate course was an instructional Diploma in Town Planning instituted in 1949. With the ending of National Service in the early 1960's, postgraduate numbers mushroomed nationally, till by 1970, they exceeded the Robbins Committee targets, while undergraduate targets had not been met. For the first time, expenditure on education exceeded that on defence.

PROFESSOR ANDY MACMILLAN:
A REMINISCENCE

When I arrived at the School of Art in 1973, it was as a new Professor of Architecture, appointed straight from practice to head up an almost equally new Mackintosh School, and manage an older Department of Architecture of the Glasgow School of Art where, twenty-nine years earlier, I had embarked on the Certificate course, and my apprenticeship, at one and the same time.

Now, as a partner in the practice of Gillespie, Kidd & Coia, I held strong views on architectural education and was fresh from the 'Flying Circus' - that small invited body of UK architects and teachers who had just set up a new School of Architecture in the University College of Dublin, in the wake of the student revolts of 1968. That experience had shaped my views on teaching, which had also been informed by my wife's concurrent undertaking of a teacher training programme at Jordanhill. Nightly discussion had given me some understanding of educational theory and enlightened me particularly to the primacy of learning over teaching as an energising force.

Coming back to the School of Art, I found friendship, talent and faith among the staff which included some of my former tutors, like Clunie Rowell and Bill Paterson. Jack Anderson, the first Director of Studies of the Mackintosh, went off to head the Manitoba School after offers he eventually could not refuse and was replaced by Ray Harrington, teaching guru, saxophonist, and bon viveur, whose fine nose for the rare student brought a generation of young people to the School who are now teaching round the country or starring in the profession. Later, when Ray returned to Kent, Ian Ballantyne took over the role.

Tony Vogt, who was running the new Diploma course, was another tutor with a style of his own and an eye for the unusual talent. Bill Lever, Bill Murdoch, Paul Simpson, Dougie Niven and Isi Metzstein are still with us, and many of the visiting lecturers from those early days have assumed the status of gurus: Mario Botta, Herman Herzberger and Alvaro Siza, for example, and nearer home, John Richards became Chairman of RMJM, one of Britain's best known firms; Robin Webster is now Professor in Aberdeen, Isi Metzstein Professor in Edinburgh - clearly the School was a lively place from the outset.

The joint concern of the University and the School of Art for the Mackintosh venture was supportive and important in the beginning and RIBA recognition for all the course was a priority. This was achieved in a series of visits and by 1981 the entire School was not only recognised, but Senate, Academic Council and the RIBA had all agreed that the Certificate Courses could now become a part-time mode of study for the Degree and Diploma, thus the entire School was unified, and the following year saw the introduction of post- graduate study.

The local student was and still is an unsurpassable asset to the School, and the mixture of native and immigrant talent developed over the years is a tribute to both them and us - e.g., Laurence Bain of Wilford's, Andy Bow of Farrell's (the only architect to win the Newbery Medal), David Harper of Harper and McKay, Ulrike Wilke, who was second in the Museum of Scotland Competition, and Kenny Fraser of Piano's, along with Stephen Clow of Hampshire, and John Stewart in Buckinghamshire; these are only a few of the more talented students that come to mind.

Many of them are a product of a particular strength of the School, its ability to offer both part-time and full-time study, which also helps to maintain a fair balance between the needs of architectural practice and the academic ambitions of the School. Sandy Page, Mark Baines, Sandy Wright and Alison Blamire are some of those students who have returned to the School to teach (and continue to practice). Over the years, the staff have engendered the perception of the School as a place where expectations of students are high and rigor is sought, and above all, the possibility of self-fulfilment, and off-beat personal goals are encouraged and supported.

Over the years too, the technical, administrative and secretarial support has been also built up, and provides another aspect of the ethos of a caring School, one that cares for its students, fellowship of a committed staff, and for the the discipline of Architecture, the mother of the arts.

Perhaps the best insight into the School, and certainly the most flattering tribute, to end this brief account of the last twenty years, is an extract from a letter received a little time ago from the Dean of the Turin School, concerning an exhibition of student work we had sent to our twin town:

> *This is to thank you and the Mackintosh School of Architecture for the exhibition of works made available to the Turin School of Architecture. Looking at those works the main feeling is that one is confronted with a 'School' in the relevant meaning that this term has in our 'trade'.*
>
> *A 'School' of Architecture is knowing what to teach and how to teach it in the given historical contingencies, is the wise management of freedom within the responsibilities deriving from the task of transferring competence and skill through the generations; a 'School' is continuity, reference values and guidelines for creativity...*

C H A XVIII P T E R

Town Planning

THE DIPLOMA IN TOWN PLANNING

FROM 1962, the School of Art, quite independently of the Glasgow School of Architecture, acquired a part-time course in Planning, which developed into a full-time undergraduate course in Town Planning, eventually transferred to the University of Strathclyde. The principal developments fell during the Directorships of H Jefferson Barnes and Tony Jones, and the full story is perhaps even more tortuous than that of the Glasgow School of Architecture.

The postgraduate Diploma in Town Planning was set up in 1949, to meet the manpower requirements arising from the Town and Country Planning Act, which created the modern system of authorities responsible for development plans, in the period of post-war reconstruction, slum clearance, and the New Towns programme.in the era of post-war reconstruction.

A School of Town Planning had been in existence at Edinburgh College of Art since 1935, but there was no provision in the West of Scotland, and the Department of Health for Scotland requested that a course be set up. Accordingly, a small committee of Technical College representatives drafted the curriculum, and Thomas Findlay Lyon was appointed Head of the new Department of Town and Country Planning.

Lyon was an acknowledged authority on Patrick Geddes, the town planning pioneer, and was indeed invited to give the public lecture at the centenary celebrations in Edinburgh in 1954. As a consequence, the valuable Geddes collection of books and papers relating to the Outlook Tower was gifted by Lady Whitson to the Technical College in Glasgow. It was in fact unusual for someone from Glasgow to be invited to lecture on an Edinburgh figure, and the gift suggests that there was no-one in the capital at that time with a serious academic title to the material. Indeed, Lyon was one of the few people who could claim to understand Geddes's diagrams, or "thinking machines", for the mapping of complex inter-relationships and ordering of subject matter.

Lyon had taken the Diploma in Architecture in 1937, and records show that he wrote his final year dissertation on Mackintosh, two years before Howarth arrived in Glasgow. Lyon was particularly interested in the history of Town Planning, and lectured in that subject throughout his service. His Professor before the war had been Harold Hughes, co-author of TOWNS AND TOWN PLANNING: Ancient and Modern (1923), and it was he who first sparked off Lyon's interest in the subject.

Following War service, in the Royal Engineers, Lyon was appointed Senior Lecturer in the University of Durham in 1947. Later, when a Town Planning course was being suggested for Glasgow, Sir David Anderson of the Royal Technical College presumed on an acquaintance with the Vice-Chancellor at Durham, Lord Eustace Percy, to send him a copy of their Town Planning course regulations. A Glasgow course was duly formulated, and the Technical College then poached the Durham Senior Lecturer!

151

Thus, the Glasgow School of Architecture established its Diploma in Town Planning, which was a joint award of the Glasgow School of Art and the Royal College of Science and Technology. At the beginning of his appointment, Lyon was accommodated in the School of Art, and had in effect a sabbatical year to prepare his material. During that first year, visiting lecturers also had to be recruited, and from Glasgow University, the School obtained the young Geology lecturer Dr Alwyn Williams, who later became Principal and Vice-Chancellor of the University., retiring as Sir Alwyn.

Lyon had an interesting circle of acquaintances, and corresponded with some important people, including Lewis Mumford, who had been present at his Geddes Memorial lecture in Edinburgh in 1954. Mumford was of course a name to be reckoned with, and his book The Culture of Cities was regarded as a standard work. When Professor Smith retired in 1959, Lyon applied for the vacant Chair, and gave the names of three referees, as requested. After due process, however, Frank Fielden was appointed to the post. Lyon eventually received an account of the search committee's deliberations, and learned that his application had been well received, with the incidental titbit that several of the Technical College Governors had never heard of Lewis Mumford, and the weight attaching to his name had been somewhat reduced as a result.

The Diploma course in Planning was of four terms full-time study, or two years part-time, and there were never more than five or six students in either mode. Teaching was thus one-to-one, or in small seminar groups, a type of teaching which now only exists in some ancient universities, and Lyon's little academic backwater was swept away in 1964, with the end of the Glasgow School of Architecture, and the creation of the University of Strathclyde. Along with the University Diploma in Town Planning, a new degree of MSc in Urban Planning was introduced, and a new Department of Urban and Regional Planning established, physically separate from Architecture.

A new Chair of Urban Planning was also created, and it was clear that the University needed an energetic empire-builder to put the new department on the map. According to gossip, after a fruitless search, the Principal's patience finally snapped at a committee meeting and he demanded: "Where did Glasgow get their Professor of Planning?" Dr Curran was informed that Professor Grieve had been Chief Technical Planner at the Scottish Office. "Who has that job now?" he asked. "Ronald Nicoll," came the answer. Whereupon, Dr Curran made a telephone call, hired Professor Nicoll, and proceeded to the next item on the agenda.

Nicoll proved to be an excellent Professor, a good performer on television, and a decisive administrator. As Director of Planning for Glasgow Corporation he had negotiated all the city's overspill agreements, and he had indeed been one of Lyon's first students, with continued involvement in the School as a visiting lecturer for many years, prior to moving to the Scottish Office.

This marks the end of the story of the Department of Town Planning in the Glasgow School of Architecture, and the last joint Diploma, issued in the name of the College and Glasgow School of Art, was awarded in 1964.

TOWN PLANNING
AT THE GLASGOW SCHOOL OF ART

Prior to 1960, most Town Planning courses were at postgraduate level, but there was increasing talk of undergraduate courses, for both school-leavers, and planning assistants or technicians, and in 1961, the Planning Officer for Hamilton called on T F Lyon at the Technical College to discuss the possibility of his running a part-time course at that level. The visit left Lyon in a state of alarm, with visions of a horde of junior employees fresh from school, demanding instruction in isometric projection. etc. However, quite by chance, a colleague from the School of Art happened to mention that the attendance of day-class College students at the School of Art each week had been reduced, and it was thought that Mr Waugh, the Head of Architecture, might be interested in providing a course for Planning Assistants to keep up student numbers. A meeting was duly held at the School of Art, and a part-time Planning course was approved to commence in October 1962. Approval was pending for a full-time course in 1964, when H Jefferson Barnes took over as Director of the School of Art.

The School of Art's Planning Department began as a section within the Architecture Department, headed by D S R Waugh, and the Lecturer-in-charge was Geoffrey Bargh, who did much of the teaching until a part-time staff was built up. Bargh had taken his postgraduate Town Planning qualification in the Glasgow School of Architecture as a student under Lyon, and was one of the very few students to gain the Diploma in Town Planning with Distinction. Once the Planning Course received full exemption from the examinations of the Town Planning Institute, Bargh was made Head of the Planning Department, separated from Architecture and housed in its own premises.

As a product of the Robbins Committee Report, the Council for National Academic Awards was set up, and although not an examining body, the Council was empowered to award degrees to candidates in accredited institutions, provided they were able to meet very stringent requirements as to buildings, library facilities, course structure and content, staff qualifications, and so forth. The Planning Department, following negotiations with the CNAA, was able to have the School accepted as an eligible institution and it was indeed this initiative that opened the door to the devising of CNAA degree courses in Fine Art and Design, and eventually led to the demise of the SED-approved Diploma.in Art..

However, not entirely satisfied with CNAA validation, the Town Planning Department at the School, now headed by Brian K Parnell, also investigated the possibility of an arrangement with the University of Glasgow along the same lines as the Mackintosh School of Architecture, and progress was made towards a form of integration. Complications then arose when a circular letter was sent to University Vice-Chancellors in July 1981, intimating a standstill on expenditure, and a subsequent letter 'advised' a merger of the Town Planning departments in the Universities of Glasgow and Strathclyde, which meant, in effect, closure of one and transfer of staff and students to the other.

The situation in Glasgow became the subject of a special enquiry involving several quangos, the SED, DES, Glasgow and Strathclyde Universities, and the School of Art. The eventual decision of the funding bodies was that all three

Departments be combined at the University of Strathclyde under the title "Centre for Planning". As a result, the entire strength of the School of Art Planning Department, students and staff, was transferred to the University of Strathclyde.

The new 'Centre' is said to be the largest planning school in Britain, a long way from the tiny sub-department in the Glasgow School of Architecture where the story of Planning education in the West of Scotland began. Thus, the School of Art gained and lost a Department of Town Planning, the second to be emptied in this way, since the full-time students of the Glasgow School of Architecture had been similarly removed in 1964. This could be regarded as a form of 'asset stripping', in so far as the exporting School has borne all the development costs - resources which could have been better expended on subjects of lasting concern.

Similar rationalisations were of course carried out elsewhere in the country, with the aim of reducing public expenditure. Ten years later, however, there was much less concern about over-production of town planners, architects or artists, and universities and colleges were broadly to be allowed to teach as many students as possible, as cheaply as possible.

A progressive policy shift can accordingly be observed, from overt manpower planning to wholesale expansion of student numbers with little regard to graduate employment prospects. Almost certainly, this is due to the realisation, from Government statistics, that many graduates now end up in jobs unrelated to their degree subjects. With the admixture of student loans, leading to self-financing students, all the ingredients of a market are present, in which customer choice rules. The good universities and colleges will attract customers/students, while the poor ones will have dwindling numbers and reduced central funding as a consequence.

This would have mightily pleased Sir Henry Cole, since it meets his criterion that the survival of a School should be dependent on its own efforts. Likewise, the performance-related pay schemes currently being promoted in the public sector employment and in higher education would have met with Cole's approval. Nevertheless, according to an inquiry witness in 1910, the effect of the payment by results scheme was baleful, for the entire education system had become "an engine driven by money". Can we perhaps detect in our present-day system another engine driven on the same principle?

Personal
Reflections

DAVID J LESLIE,
CHAIRMAN OF THE BOARD OF GOVERNORS

MY ASSOCIATION WITH THE SCHOOL has been long, although the famous who have made its reputation would no doubt say it has been peripheral. In a sense, I am its product turned keeper, having begun my architectural education here in the large ground-floor studio which Mackintosh himself intended for Architecture students. I well remember the sheer grind of the part-time Architecture course, working into the small hours to meet deadlines, but I also have fond memories of sketching Mackintosh detail around the building, of life drawing, and colour application, and best of all, personal tuition in modelling from the legendary Benno Schotz himself.

As an Architecture student I rubbed shoulders with artists and designers, and almost without appreciating it, absorbed the influence of these many disciplines on my architectural understanding. And we need only look back to the halcyon days of the late Victorian period, to see how important that is, to have architects working with artists and craftsmen to adorn their buildings and create a quality experience for all.

Since then, my particular enthusiasm has been the relationships between architects, and the sculptors who helped to adorn their buildings, and I remember once walking back to my office through the city centre with Walter Underwood, a former Governor of the School. As we passed one building he drew my attention to some ornament on a façade, which bore the letters 'IOU'. This, he told me, was the work of Archie Dawson, carved in a fit of pique at the non-payment of his fee. However, although I saw these letters for myself, when I later began photographing architectural sculpture I was never again able to find them, and now wonder if they ever existed!

In fact, my lifelong interest may have been first awakened when I opted for sculpture as my craft study. I should have been under the scrutiny of Paul Zunterstein, but he presumably found Architecture students a bore, and was seldom in the studio. However, an elderly gentleman in a little room behind a glazed screen noticed my efforts at modelling a nose. "Naw, naw, lad - see here... " He took the clay from my hands, and I marvelled as the nose sprang from the board with a strength which all fine noses should possess. This was the start of a session which proved to be an experience of my lifetime, when Benno Schotz gave me his personal attention, and I soon became proficient with clay.

Benno Schotz studied at Glasgow after training as an engineer, and eventually became Head of Sculpture and Ceramics. His architectural sculpture can be seen on the Mercat Building at Glasgow Cross, where he created the figures of 'Painting' and 'Sculpture' in 1922, and at the Bank of Scotland in Sauchiehall Street, figures and an armorial panel in 1931. This continued a fine School tradition, and many members of the Sculpture Department have lent their talents to the adornment of the city, including Alex Proudfoot, Archie Dawson and Kellock Brown, who carved the figures on the People's Palace 1898, and the Personification of Glasgow at Parkhead Library.

*Benno Schotz in Studio c 1960.
Benno had a BSc in
Mechanical Engineering
gained at the
Royal Technical College.
Had very sharp brain and great
vitality into old age.*

Before them, the Dutch sculptor Johann Keller, Head of the Sculpture department from 1901, did some fine work in the city, including the figure of 'Religion' on the south-west corner of Kelvingrove Art Gallery. And Francis Derwent Wood, who taught modelling at the School in the late 1890's, left us some of the finest examples of architectural sculpture to be found in Glasgow, at the Savings Bank in Glassford Street, and the British Linen Bank in Govan Road, as well as the figures of 'Music', 'Architecture', 'Sculpture' and 'Painting' on the north portico at Kelvingrove.

For me the most interesting demonstration of the relationship between architect and sculptor is the work of Francis Derwent Wood, who collaborated with the architects James Salmon Jr and James Gaff Gillespie on a number of buildings, beginning with the Mercantile Chambers in Bothwell Street, where Derwent Wood applied sculpture in the Beaux Arts style to the office block At the British Linen Bank on Govan Road, where he sculpted the figures of the Trade Winds under Salmon's corner oriel window, he must have been even more closely involved in the design process, since the figures are carved into the structural corbel. Later, with the Hatrack in St Vincent Street, the architectural design itself became the sculpture. Could a clearer example of the sculptor's influence over the architect be found?

During the last decades of the 19th century, when the Glasgow Boys were at their zenith, Keller and Derwent Wood were working with James Salmon and James Gaff Gillespie, and along with the Mackintosh group, they have given us not only the city we know, but a worldwide reputation for architecture, art and design. Those of us who have been educated at the hub of that influence, the Glasgow School of Art, are fortunate indeed.

Design by Jack Fleming

Designs by Gordon Huntly

*Designs by David Gentleman
whoes father had been at GSA*

KENNETH GRAHAM,
CHAIRMAN OF THE SCOTTISH POST OFFICE BOARD

DURING GLASGOW'S YEAR as European City of Culture in 1990, the Glasgow School of Art was honoured by a postage stamp tribute, and this link between the Post Office and the School, which has contributed so significantly to visual education in Scotland, seemed a good basis for a further philatelic celebration to mark its 150th anniversary year. We were thus delighted to issue a Scottish Pictorial Aerogramme, designed by the School's own Mike Healey, in April 1995, and an illustration appears in this book.

Since becoming Chairman of the Scottish Post Office Board in 1988, I have never ceased to be amazed at how the Post Office seems to touch every aspect of social and business life in Scotland, and there are other fascinating links. Gordon Huntly and Jack Fleming, for example, both designers at the School, had designs accepted for the first issue of Scottish definitive stamps in 1958, and Gordon Huntly also designed the Burns stamp in 1966. Dugald Cameron, the School's current Director, provided the illustrations to the 1984 Scottish Pictorial Aerogramme celebrating aviation in Scotland; and Stephen Conroy painted splendid portraits of six famous Scottish Communicators - including John Logie Baird - for a set of postcards issued in 1989.

There is an even more direct link, however, in the career of one of the School's great alumni, who worked for the GPO before achieving international fame in his chosen specialism. I refer of course to Norman McLaren, by common consent one of the greatest film animators this country has produced.

McLaren enrolled in the Diploma course in 1933, and although he remained at Glasgow School of Art for four years, he did not actually receive his Diploma, and indeed failed his examinations in second year. An enthusiastic member of the School's Film Society, however, McLaren believed that film was "more interesting than drawing or painting", and his first film, a documentary record of a day in the life of the School, "Seven Till Five", already showed the irony and technical innovation which were to become his hallmarks.

It was with animation that McLaren made his first real impact, and a short abstract film called "Colour Cocktail", in which he painted directly onto the celluloid, caught John Grierson's attention at the Scottish Amateur Film Festival in 1936. It also led to the offer to join Grierson at the GPO Film Unit.

The Grierson unit was an extraordinary organisation, not only using the talents of people like W H Auden and Benjamin Britten, but also affording a unique film-making opportunity to a host of stars, from William Coldstream to Humphrey Jennings; from Norman McLaren to the great New Zealand animator Len Lye, to whom McLaren always expressed his indebtedness. It also produced "Night Mail", arguably Britain's greatest film documentary.

At the Post Office Grierson was keen for McLaren to "get disciplined", but it was in a surrealist film of delightful whimsy called "Love on the Wing" that McLaren made an indelible mark on the Post Office. The film was commissioned to promote air mail and involved him painting directly onto the film stock and synchronising the images to the music of Jacques Ibert. McLaren had indeed learned discipline at the Post Office, but alas, the five minutes–plus of fun were thought too risqué in an age in which almost any object could have dangerous Freudian undertones, so the film was shelved until after the War.

Stephen Conroy's painting of John Logie Baird.

McLaren filming for the Glasgow School of Art Kine Craft Society in 1933.

By 1938, war was looming. Grierson had already left for Canada, and he invited McLaren to join him at the National Film Board. As Director of Animation there he went on to achieve worldwide fame – but never forgot his days at the Glasgow School of Art... or the Post Office.

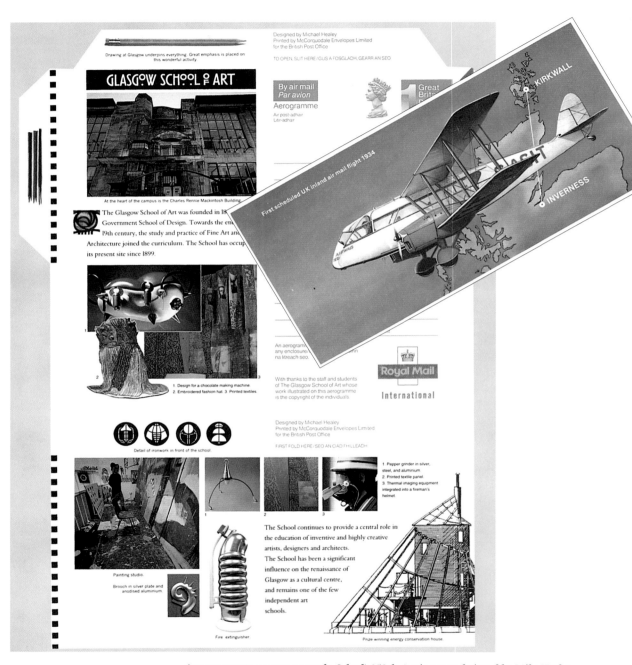

Designed by Michael Healey
Printed by McCorquodale Envelopes Limited
for the British Post Office

TO OPEN, SLIT HERE / GUS A FOSGLADH, GEARR AN SEO

By air mail
Par avion
Aerogramme

Air post-adhar
Litir-adhair

1 Great Britain

First scheduled UK inland air mail flight 1934

Drawing at Glasgow underpins everything. Great emphasis is placed on this wonderful activity.

GLASGOW SCHOOL ⚬ ART

At the heart of the campus is the Charles Rennie Mackintosh Building.

The Glasgow School of Art was founded in 18[...] Government School of Design. Towards the en[...] 19th century, the study and practice of Fine Art an[...] Architecture joined the curriculum. The School has occup[...] its present site since 1899.

1. Design for a chocolate making machine. 2. Embroidered fashion hat. 3. Printed textiles.

An aerogram[...] any enclosure[...] na litreach seo.

With thanks to the staff and students of The Glasgow School of Art whose work illustrated on this aerogramme is the copyright of the individuals.

Royal Mail
International

Designed by Michael Healey
Printed by McCorquodale Envelopes Limited
for the British Post Office

FIRST FOLD HERE / SEO AN CIAD FHILLEADH

Detail of ironwork in front of the school.

1. Pepper grinder in silver, steel, and aluminium.
2. Printed textile panel.
3. Thermal imaging equipment integrated into a fireman's helmet.

The School continues to provide a central role in the education of inventive and highly creative artists, designers and architects. The School has been a significant influence on the renaissance of Glasgow as a cultural centre, and remains one of the few independent art schools.

Painting studio.

Brooch in silver plate and anodised aluminium.

Fire extinguisher.

Prize winning energy conservation house.

Aerogramme to commemorate the School's 150th Anniversary designed by Mike Healey
and Dugald Cameron's painting of a De Havilland Dragon of Highland Airways
for an aerogramme celebrating the first UK inland air mail flight 1934

DR MARY ARMOUR:

RECOLLECTIONS OF A "GLASGOW GIRL"

AT ONE TIME THERE was so much water running down Garnethill, that Sauchiehall Street was virtually a swamp, covered with willow trees. The willow is known in Scots as the 'sauchie tree', of course, hence the name of the street, and the Willow Tearoom, designed by Mackintosh, and still in use.

The task of building the new School was very difficult, and a great many piles had to be sunk to form the foundations, since the building was so high. If you look up from Tréron's corner, you see a huge blank wall and I can remember that the harling had to be redone several times due to the weather. The only time it ever looked good was in 1937 at the Coronation of the late George VI and the Queen Mother, when it sported a decoration from top to bottom, a beautiful painting which remained somehow undamaged by the wind, and of course, we all had decorations on our window-sills, as well as all the shops.

When I first came to the School as a student, Glasgow was an industrial city and the air was thick with soot, and the soap-makers were making a fortune out of women trying to get the black soot out of their underwear, so everyone went into trousers. I can also remember going to the Cosmo cinema with my husband and brother and when we came out, the fog was so thick it was like a dirty old carpet hanging in front of you, and you had to keep a hand on the wall, otherwise you got lost. We hadn't done this, so we ended up in the close next to the picture house, lost, and my brother thought he was never going to find his way home.

Glasgow's dirty air was cleaned up eventually, not because it was killing people, but because the Royal Smithfield Show happened to take place during a dense fog in 1953, and some of the cattle at the show collapsed and died, so they came to the conclusion that something needed to be done. Now, when you look at Glasgow, it's a lovely city, but by Jove, when I was young it was as black as coal. After the Second World War, the new Mackintosh School was then about fifty years old, and its amenities were in much need of renovation. The job was given to an eminent Glasgow gentleman, Major-General Jock MacFie of the Royal Army Medical Corps. He had served in Belgium and after the war was given the task of rebuilding the hospitals that had been knocked down by the retreating Germans, and one of his peace-time jobs was to sort out the dirty School of Art.

He started with the lavatories. If you went into the lift shaft just next to the boys' lavatory at the front door, you were nearly asphyxiated, and Jock told me that if we hadn't done something soon, there would have been a major outbreak of typhoid fever. All the girls got new washhand basins and lavatories, as did the boys, and the next thing he tackled was the heating system. We had a balcony up in our studio, a great place to have impromptu concerts and store pictures, but when we climbed up the ladder, there were all these wee black balls running all over the place like mice. They were balls of soot, which we were breathing in, so Jock renewed the whole system.

We could also cook, or at least boil an egg in the studio, and at the end of the session we always had a party, with people playing instruments, Sandy Goudie dancing with the Beauty Queen and plenty of food, and it was just lovely.

The four Colourists, Peploe, Hunter, Cadell and J D Fergusson were recognised by this time. Fergusson had been working in France, and had to get out quickly because of the war, so came to live in Glasgow in a tenement in Clouston Street.

My brother lived on the bottom storey, and his daughter used to bring Fergusson's fruit order as her mother had a fruit shop in Queen Margaret Drive and she said there was nothing in his house but some deck-chairs and some canvases. Fergusson had nothing. He had had to rise and run from France, so we were sorry for him and invited him to our studio party, where all the young folk were thrilled that anyone so eminent should be among them. When it was all over, he came over to me and had his hands in mine and said, "God bless you", and he was weeping. He was so happy to be back among real friends.

So, now the School has reached its 150th anniversary and a new round of improvements is in hand. I am excited that the School is thriving and goes on happily getting happy people, interested people, good students and good teachers, and I hope the next 150 years will be as good as the last.

Dr J Mackintosh Patrick

I BECAME A STUDENT at Glasgow School of Art in 1924 and took my diploma in 1927 followed by a post-dip year. In general, the staff were helpful and constructive, and Haswell Millar, whose work I admired, influenced me considerably. Etching was at least as important as painting for me, and Millar's wife Josephine taught the etching class, which had excellent facilities. This was a boom period for etching and I later received a contract with a noted London publisher.

In the students' view, Maurice Grieffenhagen was a great artist and his dandified mode of dress and manner all contributed to his mystique, though he was often absent from the School. I spent the summer vacation of 1926 in Provence, where Grieffenhagen also happened to be, and I remember him showing much interest in the paintings I brought back.

For the social life of the School, the Dramatic Society was very important, and Dorothy Carleton Smyth of the Illustration course, who had stage experience, produced a number of plays and revues, including "Macbeth" and Shaw's "Arms and the Man", as well as a cabaret show in the McLellan Galleries for Glasgow Art Club. All the costumes and scenery were created in the School, involving every department, and these shows were very popular. This was also the boom period of the ukulele, and at break-times students played and sang in the corridors.

So far as studio work was concerned, a life-painting class from 9 am to 12.30, and a drawing class, also with a model, from 4 pm to 6 pm, left afternoons free for our own work, when we could use the etching room and other facilities. Altogether, I found my time at Glasgow School of Art an excellent training for my future career as a professional artist.

'Tay Bridge from my Studio Window'. Painting by James McIntosh Patrick 1948.

DR EMILIO COIA

*Drawing of Dr. Emilio Coia
by Hugh Adam Crawford.*

THE HAND that held mine in a vice-like grip all the way up Dalhousie Street and into the School of Art belonged to my sister Minnie, the first-born of nine Coia children, of whom I was the youngest. I was trembling with shyness when Minnie demanded to see the Director, and was assured that no-one of my age could possibly be admitted as a student. Minnie stood her ground, however, convinced her brother was the reincarnation of Michelangelo, and eventually the Director himself, John D. Revel, wearing a clean white painting smock and smoking a cigarette in a holder, made his appearance and patted my head. Minnie insisted that lack of years had nothing to do with genius, and Revel, patiently smiling, looked at my caricatures of film stars, including my hero Rudolph Valentino, landscapes and still-life sketches, and agreed I possessed some talent. "Bring the boy back in a couple of years and I'll have a word with the Governors meantime, Miss Coia," said John D., patting my head again. With that he departed upstairs, and I was admitted two years later.

James Huck was one of our first teachers, a big round man with a pointed beard and bald head. Affable to a degree, he never once lost his temper or uttered an expletive even when he discovered us - during the model's break - playing a kind of ping-pong over the draught screens. Jimmy was a devout spiritualist, on familiar terms not only with the Supreme Being, but also, he declared, with Tintoretto, whose name he always pronounced without the last three 't's. Asked to name the greatest Italian Renaissance painter, we students answered with one voice, and our reward was a truly beatific smile.

An influential and much-liked teacher was Charles Murray, who eschewed sobriety, day and night, to the despair of all, but was widely respected as a very fine etcher. Often absent from duty, Charlie only avoided dismissal thanks to the exertions of Hugh Adam Crawford, who enlisted Grieffenhagen's help in persuading the Governors to withhold action. An appealing, waif-like character, dear to everyone despite his unquenchable thirst, Charles Murray remains a much underestimated artist.

Hugh Adam Crawford was the most inspirational and generous personality I have known in the art world. In those distant bohemian times, Crawford went to considerable trouble to bail out artist-friends who found themselves behind bars, in both senses of the word, and who took it for granted he would come to their rescue. I count myself privileged to have been his unofficial protegé and friend, and regard Hugh Crawford as my mentor.

Another much-admired artist was Professor Maurice Grieffenhagen who adorned the School with his presence about three times a year, his white spats and black patent shoes gleaming as he silently strode the corridors. It was Crawford and Grieff, as the latter was known, who together found me a studio in the basement, to develop my interest in caricature. As I recall, my first commission came from the playwright James Bridie who asked me to caricature Winston Churchill and other personalities for Glasgow University Magazine. That, together with the now-defunct "Scots Observer", was the start of a long professional career, but one never forgets one's student days.

DR DAVID DONALDSON

GLASGOW IN THE 1930s was a city of vivid style, brilliantly alive, fashionably expensive - something like a blueprint for Chicago. There was a deep self-awareness, and while other cities no doubt felt the same, Glasgow felt it better. I was fifteen years old when I arrived at the School of Art to begin my flight from reality, and with neither bursary, nor educational qualifications, I was not well received. Out of charity they dumped me into something called Commercial Art, an act of kindness I repaid by avoiding all contact with commercial art, though I played tennis a lot and lusted. Two years later, lost and confused, I half-joined the school of Drawing and Painting, and four years after that, finished my apprenticeship - with no degrees and no honours. I was unteachable but I profited from the experience and genius of many people, staff and fellow-students alike. I had found a home for lost dogs.

The School had been designed for its purpose, to teach the principles of our trade, and like Glasgow itself, it was sternly beautiful and practical, scrubbed by a cohort of cleaners, presided over by our janitor Mr Letham, resplendent in a green frock coat and, on special occasions, a green top hat. The staff were superbly talented and properly distant - not yet in thrall to an educational system that demanded their accountability, or so it seemed. There were happy diversions like the annual Christmas Ball, an out-of-season Midsummer Night's Dream which gave us all a chance to be other than ourselves. Some of course continue with the delusion to this day.

Then came the war in 1939 and shrapnel through the windows of the hen run. Students and staff left to join the armed forces, and some were killed. Red Cross ladies took over the ground floor studios, and firewatchers were mustered at ten pence per night, gold nugget time. Thanks to the Germans we became a residential college, with kippers in the refectory for breakfast. Our finest hour. Students on leave found refuge and solace with the firewatching corps, and huge parties were frequent. Then it was over. Home came the majors, captains, lieutenants and rough soldiers, commandos and throat-cutters, to reminisce on campaigns in Norway, Normandy, North Africa; air raids over Berlin, assault-craft on the beaches; shot, shell and fire.

The naval battle of Camperdown was recreated on canvas and presented to the naval command at Rosyth, with Renfrew Street dressed overall for the presentation. Two small pieces of silver mark this event, suitably inscribed. I have one, and the heirs of General William Mathieson, with whom I painted the battle, should have the other.

It is awesome to remember so much talent, and so much understandable arrogance. I came to Glasgow School of Art aged 15 and left aged 65, and by then I had had the privilege of heading the School of Painting. We accomplished much. I owe a great deal to my staff and take this opportunity to thank Geoff Squire, Robert Sinclair-Thomson, Bill Bone, Alix Dick, James Robertson, Sandy Goudie, Leon Morocco, Duncan Shanks, Big John Cunningham and Danny Ferguson who made it all possible. We were the greatest.

....I Don't know why peop mistake me for you... ....I Dont look like either of us and neither Do you

Danny Ferguson's drawing of David Donaldson and Jimmy Robertson.

*'Winter Valley '
by James Robertson 1994.*

Self portrait by Sandy Goudie.

*Opposite: John Cunningham's
'Low Tide Ardnamurchan'.*

CORDELIA OLIVER: GSA AT WAR

STUDENTS OF TODAY may suppose that the 1940's were dull, drab and uninteresting, but this is not so. Shortages of food and clothing, and eventually of art materials, were seen as a challenge to be overcome by ingenuity - dare one say creativity? The School itself was tiny, with fewer than 200 day students in all departments, including the two-year general course. The popular evening school increased the overall numbers considerably overall, and during the war, Miss Alix Dick started the Saturday morning classes for children, with myself as her first assistant.

As the 'phoney war' gave way to the real thing many of the boys disappeared into the services, and some girls too, although as potential teachers, most of us were allowed to finish the diploma course. The School was by no means a nunnery, however, and certainly in the Painting department, the boys on leave would join us in the life class, like homing pigeons. Most of the remaining staff, too, were male.

I have memories of the old refectory where the staff would pass us on their way to what we supposed was decent sustenance while we queued up for deplorable coffee and one digestive biscuit (on exceptional occasions the biscuit might be a Penguin). Hugh Adam Crawford would stride past in the long surgeon's gown he wore habitually for painting, followed by Henry Y Alison, that arrogant little misogynist in his tweed knickerbockers and grizzled, prisoner's haircut. Campbell Mackie of the Design school is remembered as lean, smallish, rust-red of hair and complexion and lacking any perceptible sense of humour; Benno Schotz seemed perennially self-confident, quick to smile - except when angered. There were more male staff than females, then as now, but Miss Dick taught the first-year drawing class along with David Ewart, and Miss McCredie taught embroidery and weaving, encouraging the girls to plunder barbed-wire fences for sheep's wool to be home-spun and dyed.

The technological revolution, like the splitting of the atom, was still in the future. Everything was done by hand, and with the staff necessarily decimated, whole areas of specialised teaching had become impossible. Nonetheless, I remember making lithographs by the time-honoured, back-breaking method, and learning how to throw and raise a pot on the wheel - none of these skills being part of my own diploma course of drawing and painting, for which we had to take an additional two craft subjects. I managed to gain permission to count modelling as a craft subject (Benno Schotz would seem to have made a rare exception in my case) and, in a sense, presaged the present urge to move between the disciplines of painting and sculpture.

Shortages became a spur to creativity: some of us made clothes from non-rationed materials like curtain fabric and parachute silk. I still have a peasant skirt from those days, made of tailor's canvas, boiled and bleached and embellished round the hem with a stencilled approximation of Bakst's design for "L'Après-midi d'un faune". We girls refused to follow the ugly fashions of the day with their short, straight skirts and heavily militarised embellishment. Instead, we opted for simplicity, and must have looked a bit like Augustus

John's Dorelia, carrying our gear around in baskets. Even to wear coloured stockings (we bought nurses' white stockings and dyed them) was to attract curious glances in Sauchiehall Street, but that was something to be relished. Like most art students we enjoyed flouting convention.

Firewatching looms large in the memory of those years, perhaps because our social life tended to revolve around the common-room set aside for firewatchers. That should have been a chore for all students but in the event - perhaps because of differing parental attitudes - some were more willing than others to spend a couple of nights each week (we were paid subsistence of 3/6d, as I remember) to sleep in the School and keep an ear cocked for the air-raid siren. We slept of course in separate buildings, the girls in the Mackintosh, the boys across the street. Many stories could be told of those days, but it is perhaps enough to say that, with a stove for cooking, drink when available, and occasional visits by notable passers-through-Glasgow, those nights were not only sociable but an education in themselves, and many of us were fervent Marxists. Hugh Adam Crawford, then head of Drawing and Painting, and a real power in the School, would bring across from the Art Club any interesting visitor - Duncan Grant, I remember, was one such.

Apart from socialising and discussing art, politics and much else, firewatching also gave us a privilege enjoyed by no student before or since. The whole of the Mackintosh building was necessarily open to us, from the basement to the roof, in the days before the corridors were blocked by mandatory fire doors (and before the awful mosaics were placed in the vestibule). The essence of its magnificent structure was continuing space, forever changing, forever rewarding, but always related to the human scale. I have said nothing yet about the quality of wartime teaching, but I for one enjoyed a visual education from the experience of Mackintosh's building in its structural detail and its spatial totality which must be unique in any art school, anywhere.

The quality of teaching was to be honest fitful (as it no doubt is today). However, in Drawing and Painting, with seven or eight students in each year, we had the benefit of Crawford's full attention, and Crawford was a truly stimulating instructor if you were on his wavelength - to my mind, as good a teacher of art as any in Scotland. Not everyone agreed. When Douglas Percy Bliss (an Edinburgh man), became Director in 1946, he was overheard remarking of the front-runners in the diploma show, "This man is no teacher. The work is all entirely different."

My happiest memories are of a previous Director, W. O. Hutchison, that elegant, but kindly patrician - the only individual who ever looked entirely at home in his RSA cap and gown. In those days we would be given due warning to expect a visit from the Director, and would then tidy up the studio for the moment when Hutchison would arrive in state with Crawford in attendance. Crawford's forte was a general criticism session, with all the easels pushed against one wall and nobody's finer feelings respected - a salutary, but rewarding experience.

The Christmas Ball was held, as now, in the Assembly Hall, with a group of senior students providing the decorations. In 1944 the theme was the Ballets Russes, and my friend Inga Svarc and I covered enormous sheets of paper with images à la Bakst, Goncharova, Larionov, etc. Next day the whole immense undertaking was torn down and thrown into the rubbish bin: the 'art market' of to-day hadn't yet arrived. There was also a 'Friday hop' in the students' common room which boasted a concert grand that had seen better days. The Friday hop, where jitterbugging became the rage for a time, saw many a love affair either begin, or end in tears and recriminations. Plus ça change.

It might be supposed from what has been written about the war years in Glasgow, that the School of Art was peripheral to the 'real' art movements of the day. Not so: the New Art Club revolving around the Ferguson/Morris axis, and the Centre Club in Scott Street co-existed with those of us who felt the need for a full professional training but who were also aware of the wider world. After all, as a schoolgirl in the late 1930s, I had experienced the great exhibition of German Expressionism, the 'Degenerate Art' proscribed by the Nazis, at the McLellan Galleries. It was with that experience behind me that I went up to art school - and in the main that too, was an experience which didn't disappoint me.

Illustration by Alasdair Gray from his book 'Lanark'.

BILL BUCHANAN

It was one of those occasional blistering Glasgow days, in the School Museum where I was completing my application form. Eventually I was summoned along a dark corridor to a large, airy room, and at a long table, in the shadow between two tall windows, sat the august figure of the School's deputy director - Harry Barnes. Despite his formidable presence, in the manner of students everywhere, we were not overly respectful, and were much taken by his southern accent, especially when he described the work we would do during 'our carrairs hair'. We were a mix of mainly West of Scotland weans and returned servicemen, and among us were Alan Fletcher, holding a long painting of a man with a ladder; Bill Crozier, who carried his umbrella crozier-fashion, naturally; Josh MacRae and Jimmie Macgregor on guitars; and Alasdair Gray, whose monologues kept us all in stitches.

In Painting, words counted for little, and in Studio 45 the brushes were regularly taken from our hands and our canvases completed for us. Alas, over the years, I seem to have mislaid that portrait head. I always thought it might be worth something, the work of the now Queen's Limner. Anybody still got theirs?

Twenty-five years on, I returned to the School, and having worked as Fine Art Director at the Scottish Arts Council, with a view over the manicured sward of Charlotte Square and accounts in an Edinburgh restaurant or two, the prospect of the concrete Newbery Tower and refectory food was a little daunting. Scarcely less so was my task to create a School of Fine Art out of the existing departments of Painting, Sculpture and Printmaking. It was both familiar and strange to be back. There were still a few kent faces from my student days, but the School had grown far beyond Renfrew Street, and on a drenching day, Head of Fine Art could be a tough assignment.

A School of Fine Art could not happen overnight, but in time it was established, and even expanded with Environmental Art, Photography and a Master's course. It was a joy to welcome Jack Knox as Head of Painting, David Harding as Head of Environmental Art, and Thomas Joshua Cooper to create and head the completely new area of Fine Art Photography.

Then came a time of what has been described as 'bumpy mince', a period of eighteen months between Directors with the School in serious financial difficulty. As Acting Director, along with the Heads of School and the Secretary, we tunnelled our way through layer upon layer of paperwork, with fresh demands arriving daily. My most vivid recollections of those days are the long hours spent writing in what had once been Newbery's studio. (Will any Director ever paint in that magnificent space again?) I also discovered that Mackintosh's great building creaks and groans of an evening, and I often wondered, as I scuttled through the dark to the front door, how I should greet the shade of Mackintosh were I to find it waiting there?

JOHN MACNEECE

Still naively wearing my school blazer, I matriculated at Glasgow School of Art in 1958, intent on becoming an art teacher, and my first two years were mainly spent learning to draw and paint in the classical style by great teachers like Alix Dick and Robert Sinclair-Thomson, and to sculpt under the patient guidance of Benno Schotz and Paul Zunterstein.

However, it was the charismatic Henry Hellier and the effervescent Maggie Grant who introduced me to the exciting world of interior design, and from then on I was hooked. They taught me what interior design was all about, and form, space, line, colour, texture, pattern became my palette. Planning was everything and function the supreme ruler, as I learned how to employ the raw materials of my chosen profession, and to make them both useful and beautiful.

Nor was it all theory, and Henry and Maggie could always find exciting 'live' projects for us, such as producing design concepts for companies like Timex and Berger Paints, or designing the home of the journalist and future TV personality Magnus Magnusson. With the help and encouragement of my mentors, not only did I find my first job, with architects Keppie Henderson, but I also discovered the romantic world of ship interiors, while still a student, working with MacBrayne's Ferries. This led me, in later years, to design cruise liners for companies like P & O and Cunard, and the School of Art was a watershed experience for me in more ways than one.

While I owe Henry Hellier and Maggie Grant a debt of gratitude, my appreciation would not be complete without acknowledging the powerful influence of Mackintosh himself, through his inspired manipulation of light and shade, bricks and mortar, steel and glass, in what was my spiritual home for five wonderful years.

Amongst all the hours of hard work, bent over drawing-board and work-bench, there was also fun and stimulation from fellow students, like the painter and future playwright John Byrne, the innovative designer and future Director Dugald Cameron, and the shy and gentle Wallace Shaw, who was later to be instrumental in driving the name of Pringle to the forefront of

international fashion. These and many others gave me some of the happiest and most rewarding years imaginable, and I shall always be proud to say I was a graduate of the Glasgow School of Art.

ALEXANDRA J GARDNER

I SPENT twenty-five years – half of my life – at Glasgow School of Art, first as a student, then as a lecturer, between 1963 and 88. To the students of the 1960s the School was a secure base in an insecure world. It was a special place where there was a sense of tradition, a sense of order, a sense of belonging, and an introduction to a privileged world. This was especially true in my case, coming from a working-class background into the cultural melting-pot.

Apart from the joy of working in the Mackintosh Building itself, which is unfortunately no longer the case for many students, I was taught, encouraged and supported by Drummond Bone, Duncan Shanks, Sinclair Thomson and David Donaldson. These men taught me the discipline, sense of imagery and the love of painting and drawing. From Bone I learned the craft of drawing, from Shanks and Thomson new ways of seeing, and from Donaldson the life-long obsession with the reality of painting – not just the idea, but beyond the image. In the days before the tutorial system, he was my tutor. And the teaching of art was not separated from life. When a serious domestic problem arose affecting my studies, he listened and advised. He gave of his time generously and those of us in the Painting School at that time held him in great esteem and affection.

Drawing by Danny Ferguson

In my turn as a teacher, I relied heavily on my experiences as a student, teaching as I had been taught, with enthusiasm and humour. That camaraderie I had experienced as a student continued when I joined the teaching staff, and my colleagues, some of whom had until only recently been my lecturers, became friends and were especially tolerant and supportive of the new girl. I was very fortunate to teach alongside John Cunningham, Dan Ferguson, Jock MacInnes and Stan Bell, and many a time I might have given up but for their support and typically Glaswegian humour: Don't take it so seriously – its only your work!

Like any other institution, the Art School had to develop, to extend its horizons educationally and physically, and changes were forced by political and financial influences. Some of the changes saddened me, others were very exciting. At that time, in the 1970s and early 1980s, First Year studies became a much stronger element, to give students a more personal, direct and thoughtful start to their career. For me it meant working with 'embryonic' designers, as well as fine artists. It was only then I began to appreciate what David Donaldson had meant when he said, "I have learned so much from you students". I think I grew as a painter from this balance of interests, from two-dimensional to three-dimensional, from the discipline of design, to that of fine art.

I suppose the School will go on changing despite, rather than because of those in charge. All of us who have passed through those famous doors keep our own memories and anecdotes. Different periods evoke different names – all characters, like the building itself. It retains its dignity despite fire regulations demanding doors in its long Uffizi-like corridors, studios being taken over for offices, crocodiles of tourists at specified visiting hours and so on. It helped me to survive, and I loved every minute of those twenty-five years... almost.

HANNAH FREW PATERSON

'Red Banner' Pulpit Fall, Hannah Frew Paterson 1984. Gifted by the officers and boys of the 1st Hamilton Company of the Boys Brigade, to mark their centenary year and the 250th anniversary of the Old Parish Church of Hamilton. Commissioned by the Rt. Rev. Hugh R Wyllie, M A.

LONG BEFORE I BECAME A STUDENT, I had made connections with GSA, attending evening classes over a number of years, and while I was employed by J & P. Coats, the thread manufacturers, I was sent to the School for non-diploma classes in Basic Design given by Gordon Huntly, and then Embroidery and Weaving under the tuition of Kathleen Whyte, who encouraged me to apply for entry to the Diploma course.

I was interviewed by Sir Harry Barnes, the then Registrar, who was very kind, but warned me that I would have to work very hard at drawing. This warning cost me many sleepless nights, but thanks to the slightly unorthodox approach of my first tutor, Ted Odling, I eventually relaxed enough to enjoy drawing. I was very fortunate to be enrolled into what was called Section 5, then breaking away from the traditional two-year General Course to develop a more imaginative approach, and we were set a wonderful variety of projects designed to stretch the imagination.

Two years of specialisation in embroidery and weaving then stretched me in other ways, and through Kath Whyte's example, I learned to develop a strong textile appreciation based on a natural love of the surface qualities of all kinds of materials and the endless possibilities of combining thread and fabric. I also had to work extremely hard, since there was a vast amount of practical study demanded in both disciplines, as well as developing design skills in relation to textile applications. It was a period of intense learning which has guided me ever since, both in my own practical work and in my teaching experience. Later, a post-diploma year in Birmingham made me understand just how special GSA is; its wonderful atmosphere sets it apart from all other schools.

Back in 1957, Kath Whyte realised the need for a 'follow-on' for students after graduating, and created the Embroidery Group of Glasgow School of Art. Many graduates, including myself, have benefited immensely from this organisation, enabling friends of like mind to keep in touch and to continue to exhibit and develop their skills. I feel deeply privileged to have been a student at GSA, and to have had many happy years of teaching in the Embroidered and Woven Textiles Department.

LIZ LOCHHEAD

I went to Glasgow School of Art in 1965, at the age of seventeen, into a section called Junior Non-Dip. This was full of people like myself, desperate to get into Art School, some of whom had been turned down for the DA course because their qualifications weren't good enough. (I got a C in Higher Art, I couldn't do a still life in three hours. I'm still slow at everything). Others were there as a sort of finishing school, and did only that one year, parents paying the fees.

It was great – whole days painting with Sandy Goudie and Trevor Makinson and lots of plant and plaster cast drawing with Miss Hansen. I think I also started writing during that year – 'sort of poem things'. They were long and thin with chopped-up lines and I knew they weren't stories, although they had fragments of what I'd now call narrative in them.

During the next four or five years, until 1970 when I got my Diploma, I continued to write. On the side, in secret, and then gradually coming out of the closet. I remember being encouraged by Geoff Squire – very relieved I was producing something he could be generous about, since my lack of confidence as a painter was frustrating his efforts to maintain the fiction I was a talented student – to make my 'thesis' the collection of poems that two years later formed the basis of Memo For Spring, my first book.

I was also helped enormously by the critical acumen of Steve Mulrine, who came to teach in the Liberal Studies Department when I was in my third year. He was very tough on my drafts, making me justify word by word, line by line, and cut and cut and cut. ("If the rhythm's not right, nothing's right – neither the thought, the image, nor the syntax"). This boosted my confidence as a writer – I knew he wouldn't be bothered to do this amount of close textual criticism if he didn't think the work was exciting and alive. I have, I hope, retained much of what he taught me as over the years I do the revisions, redrafts and rewritings which are what constitutes 'writing' anyway.

As well as my education, both sentimental and artistic, what I'm grateful to Glasgow School of Art for is a set of friends and frequent collaborators who are among the most important people in my life to this day.

Harriet Hansen first year drawing tutor, second left, with members of the office staff Mrs Lough, Charlotte Anderson and Miss Ferguson.

Notes on the Inadequacy of a Sketch
at Millport Cathedral, March 1970

Fields strung out so, piecemeal
on a crude felt-tip line
in real life revealed ribs
where the plough had skinned them alive.
My scrawl took the edge off the dyke.
Sure. But omitted to mark how
it held together, the gravity
of the situation (it being
a huddle of rough stone forms in a cold climate),
how it was set to hump across hills, or at what
intervals over which stones exactly
snails had scribbled silver.
I jotted down how fence
squared up to dyke (but nothing of
the wool tufts caught on random barbs),
how it bordered on that
ridiculous scrap of grass
(but failed to record its precise
and peculiarly Scottish green).
I made a sheer façade
of the cruciform cathedral, stated
only that the rectory garden
slanted towards an empty greenhouse
on the graveyard's edge.
For gravestones, I set mere slabs right-
angling to a surface I took at face value.
(I did not explain how at my feet
sprawled a rickle of rabbit bones
ribcage and spine in splinters,
skull intact). I probed no roots.
I did not trace either gravestones'
legends or their moss (it let me read
between the lines the stones' survivals).
I selected what seemed to be essentials.

   Here, where wind and rain
made a scapegoat of a scarecrow, my pen
took it for an easy symbol. But it's plain
setting down in black and white
wasn't enough. Nor underlining
certain subtleties. This sketch became
a simile at best. It's no metaphor.
It says 'under prevailing conditions
smoke from a damp bonfire was
equal in tonal value to the sea'.
So what?

Today on the empty
summer's sand the March rain needled no-one.
(My sketch mentions no rain
neither how wet it was nor how straight
it fell nor that seagulls tried to call a halt
to it). From my quick calligraphy of trees
no real loud rooks catcall the sea's
cold summersalt.

John Byrne's Letter

ROBBIE COLTRANE

I WENT TO ART SCHOOL at a time of great upheaval, but I won't bore you with what has become an over-exposed sense of the era, or say any more than the inevitable, if corny truth that loon pants and cannabis were compulsory and yes, I'm sorry, I was weak, I did inhale. Lots.

I well remember the excitement of walking into the building, its aura of shabby Bohemian gentility exactly as I had fantasised in my neo-Gothic study at school. I imagined Art School as an apprenticeship, where people who had been painting for decades would pass on their technique and knowledge, so that four years later, I would emerge with the tools at my disposal to express all the myriad ideas floating round my imagination.

Yes, it was an idealistic time, don't forget. There were a few teachers like that, of course, but not many. For most, the job was a cosy sinecure, and a way of subsidising long excursions to the pub. I seem to remember only once being told how to actually do anything, and it came like a bolt from the blue. But please don't conclude that I think Art School was a waste of time. Far from it - spending four years in the company of people who are passionate about art, even if only their own, is an invaluable experience, particularly for someone from my educational background, surrounded as I had been by institutional philistinism.

For those of us who went on to do other things, and there were many, to have the idea that creativity was not necessarily a disease, fostered at a formative time in our lives, gave us the strength to carry on through the lean years, and leave us with the question 'Am I good enough?' rather than 'Is this a waste of time?' That security of purpose is worth a thousand times more than any degree or diploma.

As I write this there are twenty letters on my desk - all of them from art students who have been refused grants or who have insufficient grants. Next week there will be twenty more, the week after probably twenty-five. This is where the buck stops - is it possible we can't afford to improve the minds and talents of our young people? More to the point, can we afford not to? I have a nightmare vision of the Art School, gone private, a finishing-school for the jeunesse dorée of Japan, or whichever country is richest in twenty years' time, and the locals having to go out of town, unable to get sufficient grants to do anything more creative than town planning.

Let's celebrate 150 years of Glasgow School of Art by ensuring that it's still there in 150 years' time, as an institution that is totally accessible to anyone who has the talent, and the motivation to do something about it.

MICHAEL HEALEY

I BECAME an art student in 1970, among the first intake to the Boys' Hostel in Hill Street, the place was dominated by ghastly Planning students, who never seemed to sleep, but simply tore the place apart. (They went on to do the same to our inner cities). I had found the School a tough place to get into, and wasn't at all certain it was right for me. Thus, at the end of First Year, a kindly man called Lennox Paterson spent a great deal of time discussing my difficulties. I think he was trying to get me to leave, but that wonderful talk had the completely opposite effect. Something clicked and I never looked back.

The time I spent in Art School was magical. We worked hard at enjoying ourselves in all sorts of ways, and the spirit of the Sixties was still alive. Strong socialism was the order of the day and doing the right thing mattered. Few of the girls wore make-up (apart from thick eye-liner), and the guys did actually say, "Hey, Man!" Platform shoes, ridiculous flares, knee boots, bristling sideburns, anything purple, and thin knitted ties abounded. The students looked wonderful too.

This was also the era of the State Bar. Those who liked folk music, in the great Glasgow tradition, went to the Scotia Bar, where Jerry Rafferty and Billy Connolly played informally, and the Humblebums were the find of the day. The Art School had great dances and concerts where the latest and best appeared. There was the Drama Society and Steve Mulrine's 'Macbeth', and I remember Alex Leckie's famous whole roast pig, piping hot out of the Ceramics kiln, and the crowd that pulled it unceremoniously to pieces.

Activities Week was tremendous. There was David Hockney, and getting to talk to him and 'Mo' at the School Dance afterwards in the Haldane. (I got a signed "Rake's Progress", which my father subsequently sold, when he was broke!) My parents worked overseas at the time and I saw them once a year, usually Christmas. This was no hardship as many other opportunities presented themselves. I simply had to work every summer and usually at Easter. I milked goats in Shovegan, Norway - 200 miles inside the Arctic Circle, pulled pints in a Lake District Inn, did medical illustrations at the Royal Infirmary, and throughout most of Fourth Year, worked nights in the Rubaiyat pub in Byres Road, under the owner 'Monty', who had flown Mosquitoes during the War, and wouldn't allow students in ex-RAF gear on the premises (another fashion of the time).

At the weekends groups of us would go to the Barrows to buy cheap food and clothing. We took photographs and drew, and there was great rivalry in producing huge amounts of extra work, often many times more than we had been briefed.

I remember the staff with genuine fondness, and learned early that I progressed far more under sharp and informed criticism than the utterings of 'nice' people. We were all aware of staff's private work and hunted it out in libraries, shops and galleries. The more they did, the more respect we had for them. They had so much more time in those days to develop their own work, and this created a close bond between staff and students, separated only by experience.

Newspaper advertisement for Robert Wiseman.

Poster series advertising Billy Graham's Campaign, Scotland.

GLASGOW SCHOOL OF ART

*Degree invitation
to the 1988 Show*

When I left Art School for the States, I felt invigorated and confident. Five years later, I was asked to comment on an advertising campaign at J. Walter Thompson's. I told them it had too much "aesthetic dandruff", which is precisely what Kit Grant had said about some of my student typography. I had arrived!

Since those days, I've enjoyed over twenty-five years of association with the School and I'm still learning. Those student days were special, and we can only hope to repay some part of what was invested in us.

Design Center
Ford Motor Company

21175 Oakwood Boulevard
Dearborn, Michigan 48123
Mailing Address:
P.O. Box 2110
Dearborn, Michigan 48123

April 27, 1995

Professor Dugald Cameron
Glasgow School of Art
167 Renfrew Street
Glasgow G3 6RQ Scotland

Dugald,

Enclosed please find a photograph of a luxury car for the year 2000. This vehicle, called *CONTOUR*, has been around the world at all major Auto Shows -- Detroit, New York, Los Angeles, Paris, Frankfurt, Geneva, etc. It was first shown in 1992 , but I feel still strongly represents where I see the automobile as a consumer product going into the next century.

It embodies the principles of a large interior package inside a compact exterior. To maintain luggage space it becomes necessary to make the engine/powertrain as compact as possible. The result here shows a "T" drive transmission which allows a small displacement in-line 8 cylinder engine to be mounted across the car with a drive taken off at right angles between cylinders 4 & 5. It then offers front wheel drive or rear wheel drive or all wheel drive in a very compact unit. The body frame is a composite construction built of aluminum extrusions and modular cast joints. The skin panels are a combination of plastic, low-cost carbon fibre and aluminum.

The vehicle also as a ducted radiator/air flow manageent system and high tech lighting.

The current Fiesta was the last of my Ford of Europe projects, completed in 1986.

Regards,

Tom Scott

Tom Scott, Design Director
Vehicle Centre Two,
Corporate Design, Ford

PETER CAPALDI

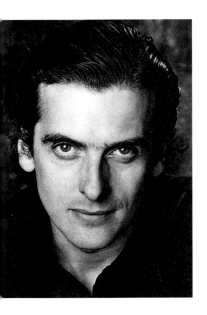

MY FIRST MEMORIES of the Art School are not happy ones. I hated the place. As I'd shown some facility for drawing, my parents decided to enrol me in the Saturday morning children's Art classes. So while other kids were cheering on baggy-tighted superheroes at the ABC Minors or, even better, having a long lie, my poor mother was leading me, with my ten-year-old face tripping me, up that dreaded hill.

On reflection, the place must have been as alien to her as it was to me. We were a family from a tenement in Springburn, so to step into a studio in the Mackintosh building, with walls lined with drawings of what we at St. Teresa's Primary referred to as 'noods' must have made her a wee bit uneasy. In fact, I can remember the expression on her face to this day.

After a number of years of this misery, brightened up only by visits to the School shop where I contracted an unhealthy and lifelong addiction to the texture and smells of art materials, I managed to persuade my parents to forget the idea, and I put the whole thing behind me, having decided to become an actor.

When the time came, however, RADA decided they were not ready for the eye-popping, rubber-limbed and dubiously accented style of acting I had perfected in front of the mirror and gave me a knock-back. So, aided by my patient art teacher Pat Boyle, I put together a folio, went back up the hill, and was accepted as a full-time student. I was there by default but, as sometimes happens, it was the right move and the right place for me. The only skill I had was drawing and I needed to be somewhere where that would be stretched.

That was art school. You could discover ways of seeing, you could begin to form an understanding of aesthetics. Even better, you could wear a big black coat and get a "Lust for Life" crew cut. You could be in a band, you could talk with great authority on matters you knew nothing about, you could explore the hidden delights and dangers of art and adulthood. You weren't at the Uni or the Business College (God forbid) and even the Drama students seemed a bunch of squares. You were at 'the Art School'. And the trick of it was, because nobody on the outside really knew what you did at 'the Art School', it was easy to convince them that at the very least you were an 'artist', and they weren't. Which of course was nonsense.

But there were artists. During my time I had a nodding acquaintance with Peter Howson and Adrian Wiszniewski and now look in awe at the power and beauty of their work. I've stood entranced by the paintings of Stephen Conroy, Ken Currie, Alison Watt and so many other great talents, celebrated and not celebrated, that the place produced.

And I know that what I do now began in what I did and learnt there. The Art School taught me to look at the world and see that there is art in the mundane and obvious, as well as in the exotic. It helped me find my 'eye', and for that I will be eternally grateful.

JANICE KIRKPATRICK

I REMEMBER my mother and father coming to the School with me the first time. All I could see was blackened sandstone stretching along Renfrew Street, there were three dead cats melting in the gutter and I don't recall seeing any Charles Rennie Mackintosh. I suppose I woke up in a labrador and welly-boot-free world, but within weeks I could see Mackintosh and feel part of something vaguely corrupt and terribly enjoyable.

The School of Art was a marvellous city state, like Liechtenstein or Gormenghast, a Mervyn Peake-Twin Peaks parallel world with its own laws, its own feudal system, reproductive system and patented warm-air heating system (complete with wooden paddles). Wagnerian janitors scrabbled about behind panelling and secret doors off stair-landings, rest rooms, life-models' rooms and lower levels where only the blue and the brown-clothed were permitted to go.

I fondly remember Professor Tony Jones's first week as ringmaster. It was Activities Week 1980 and the entire student population was gathered for his opening address in the old livery stables where the sculptors, pot-throwers and George Garson resided. Professor Jones was led on to the stage, blindfolded, and a polypropylene chair placed in front of him. All about the room was a resounding silence. Jim Shields, a First Year student, stood on the chair and gave a speech of welcome, wishing the new Director well whilst dropping his trousers and thrusting his bare backside in Tony's face. I can't see this sort of thing going down too well at Glasgow University, but it expressed the School's almost medieval distrust of power, and its courage to be extreme at a time when the rest of the world was descending into the Thatcherite Dark Ages.

I learned to see at Glasgow. I learned to be liberal, compassionate and a designer. The School gave me the gift of eternal optimism and an unshakable belief in humankind and the value of education. Five and a half years of lawless living galvanised me against the forces of evil gathering outside our hallowed Scottish walls. The place was outrageous, terrifying, excellent and, above all, completely unlike any other.

STEVEN CAMPBELL

MY ARRIVAL at the Art School came after working in a steel mill for five years - an unconventional background for a 25 year-old art student. My first tutor was Dan Ferguson, a man of unusual patience and talent, who helped me to develop in this new world of art. By Christmas, I remember going on holiday and feeling deep regret at leaving, even for a few weeks. The Art School quickly became central to my life, probably because I spent most of my time there, and by second year I had acquired a key to the Printmaking building and a small curious room in a dilapidated part of it. My abiding memory of the Art School is of a community of students, ex-students and lecturers - a world very much of its own with its bars, studios and other students' flats. My only regret is that I can't rejoin the library, as I still allegedly haven't returned a book on Reynolds - not a bad complaint after spending four years there - though my tongue is now firmly in my cheek.

KEN CURRIE

BEING AN ART STUDENT in Scotland in the late 1970s and early 1980s was difficult in that there seemed very little hope beyond art school. Graduates in Fine Art had few real options except secondary-school teaching or applied-arts-based work, such as art therapy, community art and so on. And during my time there, even those glimmers of opportunity were snuffed out by cutbacks introduced by the new Conservative government. There seemed to be a complete myopia about ambition, such limited horizons and so few role models. Scotland was a forgotten provincial backwater and Glasgow a hopelessly blighted city. The idea of becoming a full-time, so-called 'professional' artist was not necessarily discouraged, but was seen as nothing more than a romantic pipe-dream. And in that atmosphere of despondency, some of us felt we had nothing to lose by becoming 'real artists', whatever it took and by whatever means.

To the current generation of students this simple desire may now seem laughable, quaint even. But at the time, it was a truly radical ambition, which has been largely realised and which has created a whole new situation in Glasgow by opening up new possibilities for graduates. I can't honestly say that Glasgow School of Art overtly fostered that ambition, but it was all very much uncharted territory at the time. Now, the School expects a degree of professionalism, self-maturation and discipline that would have been inconceivable only ten years ago. However, it must be said that this new attitude of sobriety and 'career-awareness' has been achieved, arguably, at the expense of a certain militant spirit that made students such a potent political force in the past.

With this in mind, I think the most overwhelming memory I have of my time at Glasgow School of Art is one of conflict - some of it real and some of it no doubt imagined. To students, most issues appeared in stark black-and-white and we felt obliged to take up a confrontational position on virtually everything. I was relatively active in student politics, both as a student rep and with the Socialist Society, and in those early years of Thatcherism we certainly had many battles. The Tories' adherence to monetarism entailed vast cutbacks in public expenditure, not least in education. Here, we saw the gradual erosion of the idea of free, universal education in favour of an archaic elitism that would do little to enhance the future cultural prosperity of either the Glasgow School of Art, or Scotland. And now I think that, perhaps, in spite of all that's been achieved in the last few years, it's still very difficult being an art student in Scotland.

ALISON WATT

IT IS DIFFICULT to compress a lifetime of experiences at Glasgow School of Art into a brief account. I say a lifetime because ever since a visit during early childhood, when the seeds of ambition were sown, it seemed impossible to imagine studying anywhere else. Four years as an undergraduate, followed by a year as a postgraduate, changed my perception of art irrevocably.

I had the advantage of an outstanding tutor in Geoff Squire who made his students aware that drawing informed all aspects of artistic expression. I still remember Geoff in the Life Room producing an exquisite drawing on a discarded scrap of paper, which he then casually pinned to my own overworked life drawing. These recollections surface often as inspiration at moments of despair during my continuing struggle with the human form.

Paradoxically, a jewel of wisdom from another tutor who stated: "Women can't paint because they haven't got the balls for it", provides equal motivation, and Simon Laurie's classic statement to accompany his 1987 degree show also springs to mind: I hope to carry on working and in some way make a living as an artist, and if that fails become a tutor.

The students of Glasgow School of Art will continue to be exposed to such a potent mixture of the inspirational, the inane and the irreverent, often against a background of financial hardship affecting living and working conditions. Despite this, the School creates a highly competitive and challenging environment in which students thrive, producing work of striking originality in every field of individual expression, and Glasgow School of Art will remain an inextricable part of my life.

MARION LOVE: GSA AND EDUCATION

ASK MOST GOOD ART & DESIGN EDUCATIONALISTS what inspires their commitment to their work, and they will reply that it is the privileged opportunity to create the conditions which allow young people to see, question and respond to the world around them. Many Art staff in West of Scotland schools achieved this 'awakening' at the Glasgow School of Art, often through the teaching of one or two charismatic individuals.

In my case it was Robert Sinclair Thomson who, not content with trying to impart skills in drawing and painting, would relay groups in his old Bedford van to Kelvingrove Art Gallery, to experience for themselves the joy in some particular line of tonal drawing. The same van was deployed in taking groups to observe the seasonal colour changes of the Scottish hills, and for some students, brought up in the blackened tenements of the city centre, this was often their first experience of the countryside.

Such commitment inspired many of us in our determination that more young people, especially working class youngsters, should experience this sort of visual education. Why, after all, should the privilege be reserved only for those intending to pursue a visual arts career?

With the medal awarded for her services to art education

During the 1950s and 1960s, tertiary education became increasingly accessible to working class students, whose knowledge of the GSA had often come via dynamic Art teachers returned from the Second World War. Another route was provided in the new residential Summer Art Course at Castle Toward, Argyll, initiated in 1952 by the Corporation of Glasgow. Here some eighty senior pupils could not only spend a fortnight working with experienced Art staff but could also watch visiting artists at work, and attend evening lectures given by them, mainly from the School of Art and including such notable names as William and Mary Armour, Jack Fleming, Geoff Squire, Danny Ferguson and the then Director, Douglas P Bliss.

The School of Art appeared more accessible than many other institutions at that time because of its ongoing programme of Diploma and Fashion Shows

One of the School's best loved tutors, the late Danny Ferguson discussing a painting at Castle Toward.

Student at a Saturday morning class.

which school pupils often attended, though the two-tier education system of junior and senior secondaries then in force militated against this accessibility, and many talented junior secondary pupils were unable to realise their potential at tertiary level.

The 1970s saw the firm establishment of comprehensive education, and new schools with new and very different Art Departments were designed to cope with a broader curriculum. Demand was high for Design School graduates, especially in Printed Textiles, who could explain the mysteries of screen printing to other staff. My own Art Department in Cumbernauld at this time had three painters, two textile designers, two interior designers, one graphic artist and a ceramicist, and all but one had graduated from GSA.

Despite falling school rolls, increased demands on the curriculum by other subjects and diminishing numbers of new Art teachers being trained, the past two decades have been both exciting and innovative. My appointment as Adviser in Art to Glasgow schools in 1979 more or less coincided with the arrival of Professor Tony Jones as new Director of the Glasgow School of Art.

Tony Jones had always shared my "equal opportunities for all" view of education, and it was very clear that there was a new class of youngster requiring positive help. These were young people from very deprived areas, of chronic high unemployment, and often suffering from a severe lack of self-esteem. Many strategies would be devised by the Advisory Service generally, in an attempt to tackle this, since it was not a purely local problem, but the Glasgow School of Art was involved in a number of important initiatives.

One such was the Visual Arts Workshop, for which Professor Jones allocated rent-free space, to accommodate a Saturday morning class of some forty youngsters, mainly from schools in the inner and peripheral areas of the city. With tuition fees, materials and travelling expenses paid for by an Urban Aid Grant, and under the leadership of Tom Chambers, a programme of environmental studies was carried out, using drawing, painting, photography and video. The GSA was an ideal location, not only for urban studies, but for the exhibitions that could be seen within the School and in local galleries. The workshop later moved to link up with the Visual Arts Studio in a nearby school, and eventually closed when art provision became more school-centred.

Pupils who attended the workshop could also benefit from the residential summer course, and steps were taken to ensure this, with increasingly positive input from GSA. Courses were planned with GSA staff in advance, and more areas were developed each year. Hitherto it had been mainly a landscape and painting course, and although those core elements remained, the thrust of the course became more investigative of materials and methods, and more exploratory in content.

GSA staff formed an integral part of the full-time teaching team, participating with equal enthusiasm in the social aspects of the course. Particularly outstanding contributions were made by Jacki Parry, Neil Dallas Brown, Barbara Rae, Alex Leckie and Ken Mitchell, and in the late 1980s, outstanding graduates, beginning to make their name throughout the UK, also took part. Alison Watt, Lesley Banks, Simon Laurie, Craig Mulholland and Ali McCauley (of Timorous Beasties) were an inspiration to course members, who were aware of diminishing opportunities in the Art teaching profession.

To sustain the impetus of the workshop and summer courses, a Visual Arts Studio was also set up in a city centre school, where Sixth Year pupils could meet and work in groups. Initially the Studio ran printmaking classes, but eventually a wide variety of courses were offered as staffing levels improved. Close contact was maintained with GSA First Year staff who visited regularly to give lectures, and when the studio eventually moved to Strathclyde Arts Centre, staff continued their work with artists in residence and designers on an outreach basis to areas beyond the city. It is especially gratifying that artists who benefited from the provision of the 1980's are pleased to return to schools to encourage others. Recent graduates have worked alongside studio staff, course members and children with special educational needs on dynamic projects with Scottish Opera and Scottish Ballet.

Glasgow was of course a huge success as European City of Culture, but that culture, albeit on a smaller scale, remains vibrant in the world of education. The dynamics of 1990 changed attitudes and provision. Doors were opened to artists of all disciplines, and have not closed. Teaching staff have realised the value of people who view the world from a different perspective, and young people enjoy and welcome this different presence in the classroom. As Regional Adviser for Art Initiatives from 1990-93 it was my privilege, along with others, to help open these doors. Successful projects like the placement of art students in schools which began in 1989, organised by Jane Allan of Historical & Critical Studies at GSA, and the Education Department, continues to thrive, and such a scheme can also identify at an early stage that 'committed' teacher.

Whatever the future holds for the visual arts in education in the West of Scotland, the Glasgow School of Art will remain a vital force, providing a major focus for training and development and - almost more importantly - the environment where nascent arts educationalists obtain that initial inspiration to extend the boundaries for their time.

PROFESSOR DUGALD CAMERON

IN JANUARY 1957, having tried out a succession of potential jobs, none of which involved going to art school, I found myself in the Junior Non-Diploma Class. H Jefferson Barnes had seen my efforts, and suggested I might consider Industrial Design. After he told me what it was, I decided that it was indeed for me. And so it has been for over thirty years in many guises, including the most recent, the Directorship of Glasgow School of Art.

Portrait by David Donaldson

The Junior Non-Dip class provided me with a necessary introduction to the the Diploma Course, in which we were taught by the gentle Miss Hansen and the exotic Trevor Makinson. At that time, GSA rejoiced in the art student of legend: Fred Pollock, big, bearded, wild, and eminent; Alan Fletcher, sculptor and practical joker, sadly killed in an accident overseas; Carole Gibbons, dressed from head to foot in black; Alasdair Gray, tales of whose powers as draughtsman served to put the neophyte in his place.

With the luck I have always enjoyed, and the fact that my surname was at the beginning of the alphabet, I joined Section One, Willy Bone's lot. William Drummond Bone was an inspirational teacher who instilled a fierce sense of loyalty in his students, while capturing and directing their diverse talents. To a disbelieving audience, he announced that we might take Sundays off work, but only the mornings, for our devotions. Yet within a few weeks, we were working all the hours given to us, because we wanted to be artists, the greatest thing imaginable!

Later on, Jimmy Goodchild in Industrial Design, and Bob Stewart in Printed Textiles, had a similar influence on those fortunate enough to sit at their feet. Weekly sketchbooks, including mandatory self-portraits, were submitted for detailed criticism. Praise was nectar indeed, damnation precisely that. And we learned. Whenever I draw - and I try to do so every day - I still use the skills Willy Bone taught me.

It was a simpler organisation then: two years General Course, two years specialism; and each General Course section was run by the drawing teacher (the term 'tutor' would have been regarded as pretentious). Drawing was pre-eminent, as it has remained at GSA, and until his sad demise in 1993, Dan Ferguson carried on that great tradition, ably abetted by John Cunningham and Sandy Gardner.

Design, mostly graphic and textile, was under the aegis of the urbane Jack Fleming and Conrad McKenna. Who would have guessed their wartime careers? Jack was torpedoed twice in the Merchant Navy, and the precise Conrad was a Mosquito navigator. Jack Fleming was also the regular MC at that annual event in the GSA calendar, the Fashion Show, usually organised by Textile students. This continues to prosper, though despite the success of its graduates in this area, including the dramatic Pam Hogg, the School has never had a formal fashion course.

Douglas Percy Bliss, Director until 1964, was an entertaining lecturer, and a painter in a rather Pre-Raphaelite manner. His work enjoyed a renaissance just before his death, but his real talents were probably neither exploited nor appreciated at GSA. He invited Joe McCrum from Hornsey to be Head of Design, and together they introduced the subject of industrial design. With McCrum's early departure to the fledgling Scottish Council of Industrial Design, Jimmy Goodchild was given the task of establishing the course, and proved an inspiration to all those he taught - a man who combined the practical skills of the toolmaker, which he had been during the war, with a wide-ranging intellectual curiosity, prepared to cross any boundary. Jimmy Goodchild made us feel that industrial design was the key to the future.

An informal aspect of our education was witnessing, and often participating in, the many practical experiments carried on by 'Jimmy G' and his associate, later Head of First Year, Ted Odling. These ranged from photographing moving trams with the School's half-plate camera (where is it?), to the making of musical instruments whose sounds were usually of an uncontrollably vulgar nature. Fun and games they may have been, but we learned a lot from them. These days we would need the compliance of a wheen of committees before engaging in such adventures.

Among those who created and maintained the traditions and ethos of the School from pre-war days, were David Donaldson and Benno Schotz, who became the Queen's Painter and Limner in Scotland, and Sculptor in Ordinary to the Queen respectively. No one personified the peculiar spirit of GSA more than David, a great teacher and artist, who knew instinctively what was important.

Students of Bob Stewart, Gordon Huntly, Leslie Auld, Kath Whyte, Henry Hellier, Alex Leckie, and the Armours, were fortunate indeed. The painterly tradition of GSA has been carried on by a number of distinguished Scottish

The irrepressible Ted Odling in typical stance by Danny Ferguson.

Gordon Huntly, Alex Leckie, Bob Stewart, George Garson, Kath White, Henry Hellier, David Donaldson, Dugald Cameron as Danny saw them during a Board of Studies meeting.

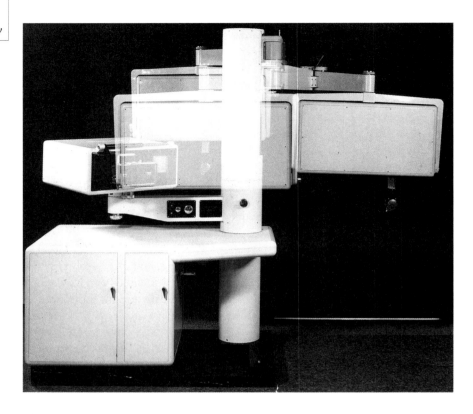

The use of ultrasound for medical diagnosis was pioneered in Glasgow at the Western Infirmary and Yorkhill Maternity Hospital by Professor Ian Donald in association with Tom Brown of Kelvin and Hughes at Hillington. Through Elsa Stevens, Tom's sister-in-law, then a student, I became involved in this enterprise during my diploma year, 1961 and produced the design study for the pre-production machine ordered by a hospital in Lund, Sweden. This machine combined all necessary technical functions with provision for the examiner. 35 years later this country imports this kind of equipment vastly enhanced in capabilities!

painters, including James Robertson and Barbara Rae, and Sandy Gardner, despite severe health problems which caused her to give up teaching, continues the strong academic drawing tradition of the School.

Jimmy Goodchild was invited to join the staff of the Royal College and left GSA in 1962, to return eventually in 1977. Joe McCrum thus came back to the School to take charge of Industrial Design, and I became his part-time assistant. Though this is a traditional means of entry into teaching, it's not wholly ideal, and the novice lecturer does need help. I also enjoyed teaching a form of 3D Studies in the General Course, when a certain James Cosgrove was a mature student, and together we discovered the last dodecahedrons in captivity - living in the Hen Run at GSA!

Joe McCrum had been at the RCA alongside Henry Moore and was a remarkable craftsman in wood and metal, with many enthusiasms, including a classic Rolls-Royce station-wagon of the sort used after the war by farmers and, I recall in the Clydebank of the 1940s, for selling fruit and vegetables round the doors. While writing this piece, I had the pleasure of speaking to him, and at the age of 89 he was still firing on all cylinders. I succeeded Joe in 1970 and enjoyed twelve happy years running first Product Design, and then on Henry Hellier's retirement, what became Furniture, Interior and Product Design, aided by the irrepressible Maggie Grant, and Bob Shaw.

If the academics are at the sharp end of our affairs, they have always been dependent on the support of those described as administrative, secretarial, technical and janitorial staff, who have had their fair share of characters: the dignified Willie Letham, attired in his frock coat and clearly not a man to be trifled with; Davy Currie, Duncan Graham and Bill Black (whose son became an RAF Lightning pilot and recently retired as an Air Vice-Marshal); Charlotte Anderson, in the General Office, in charge of the shekels, both friend and confidante to many a student and staff member who hadn't quite grasped the nature of the financial world.

During Robin Rennie's tenure as Librarian and Liberal Studies tutor, a small group regularly met in the tiny Library office for an intellectual chat and, dare I say, smoke (nowadays a hanging offence). While the redoutable 'Queenie' Rowan had been a State Registered Nurse, visitors who spent any time there were likely to emerge cured in more ways than one. It was there I also met my future wife, and subsequently, in her technical library, our first wee dug!

With the development of Historical & Critical Studies, Stephen Mulrine, the poet and playwright, was given the task of building on the secure foundations already laid by Robin Rennie. He and his colleagues have enjoyed considerable success, but in less serious times, he joined Robin, and Gordon Huntly, as co-authors and producers of some remarkable performances at staff parties, aided and abetted in matters mechanical by Goodchild and Odling, a tradition which has sadly faded. Once seen, who could forget 'Gypsy Flatulengro' or Lennox Paterson in drag? Stephen also directed a number of notable productions for the Drama Society, providing an outlet for the talents of such as Robin MacMillan, now better known as Robbie Coltrane, and encouraged the fledgling poet, Liz Lochhead.

Finally, it is the highest honour possible for one of the School's own graduates to sit in Mackintosh's superb Headmaster's room, or draw in the studio above. Running GSA is a great joy, since nowhere else could one find such an anarchic mix of inspiring, interesting, irritating and creative characters, staff and student alike, who make each day an adventure, in every sense. Along with my colleagues, I will use my best endeavours to ensure that we continue to maintain the Glasgow School of Art as a leading world institution for the teaching and practice of art, design and architecture.

Tailpiece

GSA AND THE CITY OF GLASGOW

THE SCHOOL'S OLD SCRAPBOOKS show just how prominent it was in the life of the City of Glasgow, and although in more recent times it has perhaps been less obviously active, in 1995 it has rebuilt and strengthened many of the bridges which connect it to the City and its institutions, well celebrated in the part it played in Glasgow's successful bid to become City of Architecture and Design within the Arts Council Arts 2000 initiative.

The School has demonstrated the widespread nature of its outreach to the community by displaying its involvement in nursery, primary, and secondary education, and of course by its important role in higher education, together with its longstanding industrial and commercial relationships. The Merchants' House of Glasgow, together with the Trades House, have long supported the School by the provision of valuable prizes and scholarships, and staff and students have been commissioned to produce work for other city institutions, such as the new Caledonian University and the Royal Scottish Academy of Music and Drama.

The Flesher's Goblet,
one of fifteen for each of the Incorporations
of the Trades House of the City of Glasgow
by Roger Millar 1986.

Through the generosity of Lord Forte, the Deacon Convener and fourteen Deacons of the incorporated Trades have each had a ceremonial goblet designed and made by staff and students of the Department of Silversmithing and Jewellery. Under the same auspices, the Lord Provost was provided with a silver jug and traditional tumblers, and the Prince and Princess of Wales Hospice a wall hanging from Embroidered and Woven Textiles. Two recent Chairmen of the School's Governing Board, Bill Leggat-Smith and Harry Abram, both served as Deacon Conveners of the Trades House.

How appropriate then it is for the City, to offer to complete and transfer to the School in 1995, the year of its 150th anniversay, Mackintosh's unrealised competition entry for the House of an Art Lover, a romantic adventure by Glasgow civil engineer, Graham Roxburgh, which lay almost completed in Bellahouston Park - a project intended for the City's celebration of its year as European City of Culture in 1990.

The regeneration of the City of Glasgow and its renewal of confidence in the 1990's is something in which the School has played a significant role, one to be carefully maintained and developed for the future.

Glasgow School of Art, yes, and Glasgow's School of Art.

The silver water jug and whisky tumblers
for the Lord Provost of the City of Glasgow by Eleanor McDougall 1985.

The School

First Year Studies Fine Art.
Third term project, 1994.

Fine Art Photography
David W Hazel 1989.

Fine Art Printmaking John Comer 1994. Etching 'Tricky Nicky Nabokov'.

Fine Art Sculpture Stella Tubia, 1992.

Masters of Fine Art,
Hilary Stirling, 1994

Masters of Fine Art,
Claire Barclay, 1993.
Untitled installation ceramic objects
and lanolin.

Graphic Design student at work

Conceptual Shoes designed by Crawford Bryce (Graphic Design).

Macintosh computers in the Graphic Design Department

*'Absolut Glasgow'
photographed by Charlie
McGeever
(Graphics: Photography).*

*Victorian Sideshow.
Mixed media
Matthew Kerr.
(Graphics: Illustration)*

*Ceramic,
Joy Miller, 1995*

*Ceramic,
Claire Mahoney 1995*

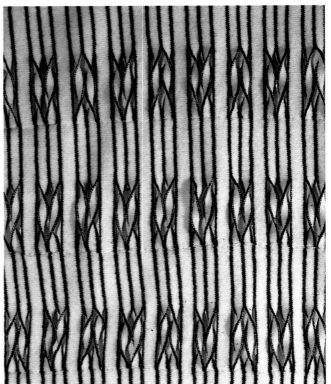

Opposite: top left
Multi layered printed
fabric using
photo imagery.
Karen Ferguson
(Printed and
Knitted Textiles).

top right:
Anne Skeidsroll
(Printed and
Knitted Textiles).

foot:
Printed Textiles

Jane Harris, pleated fabric
for garment and accessories
(Embroidered and
Woven Textiles).

Lee Sowerbutts,
woven wire in
combination with
studded metal
for wall covering

Vivienne Farmer,
Necklace, stainless steel, silver
and fadeite.

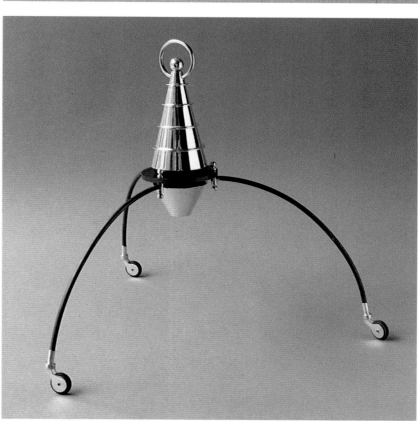

Cara McCrory,
Pepper Mill, silver, steel and
anodised aluminium.

'Purple Longhorn', cafe hot chocolate making machine. William White (Fourth Year Product Design.).

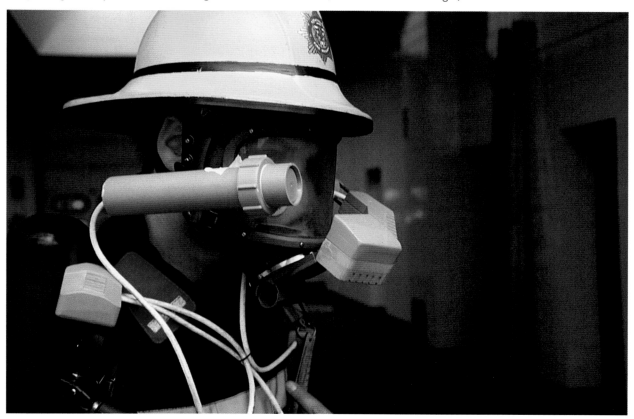

Thermal Imaging Camera Helmet/Chest mounted, Alistair McGown (Product Design).

Bachelor of Engineering. A 'World First' course run in partnership with the Univerrsity of Glasgow.

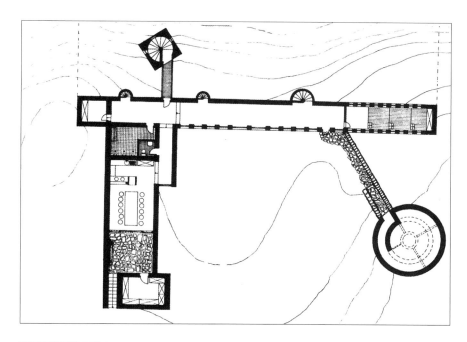

Holy Island (Buddhist Retreat)
Simon Crowder
(First Year Architecture).

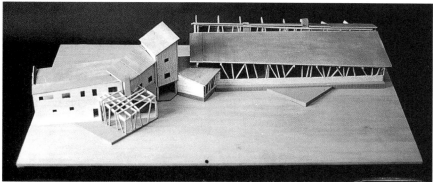

Sculptor's Workshop and House,
Alex Peaker
(Second Year Architecture).

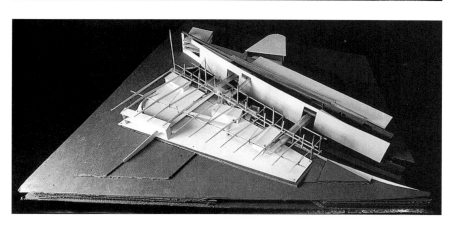

Technology Centre, Adam Knight
(Third Year Architecture).

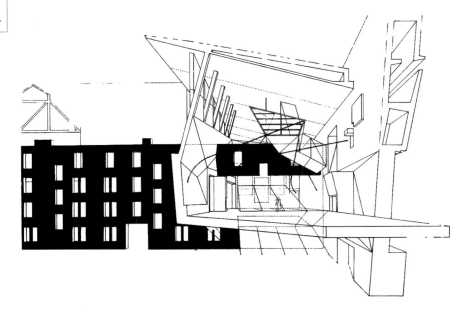

*Environmental Forum
Ian McMillan
(Fourth Year Architecture).*

*Colour Study Urban
Building, Stuart McKnight
(Fifth Year Architecture).*

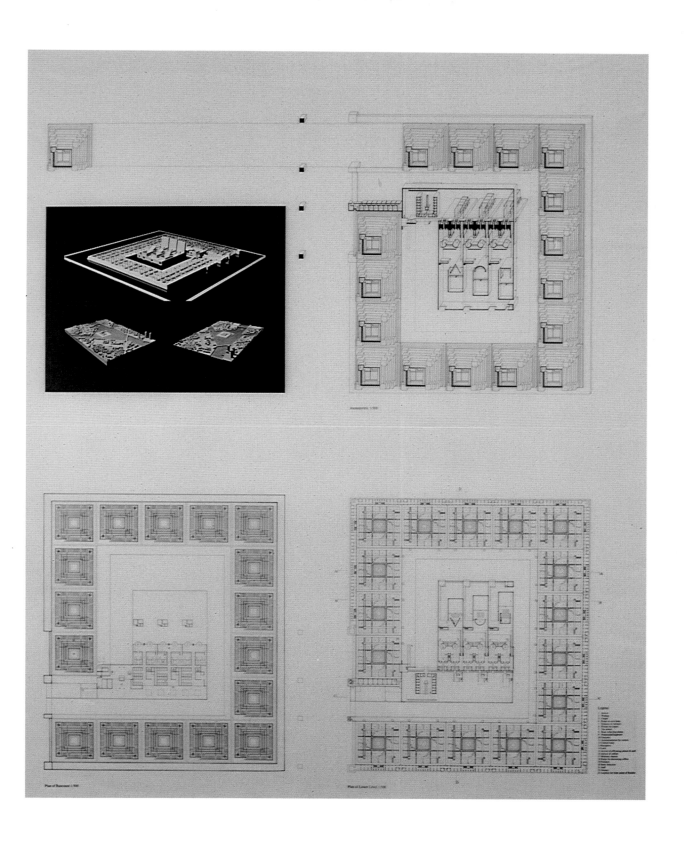

Crematorium Tokyo, Stuart McKnight, Masters Architecture

Historica and Critical Studies in the Mackintosh Lecture Theatre

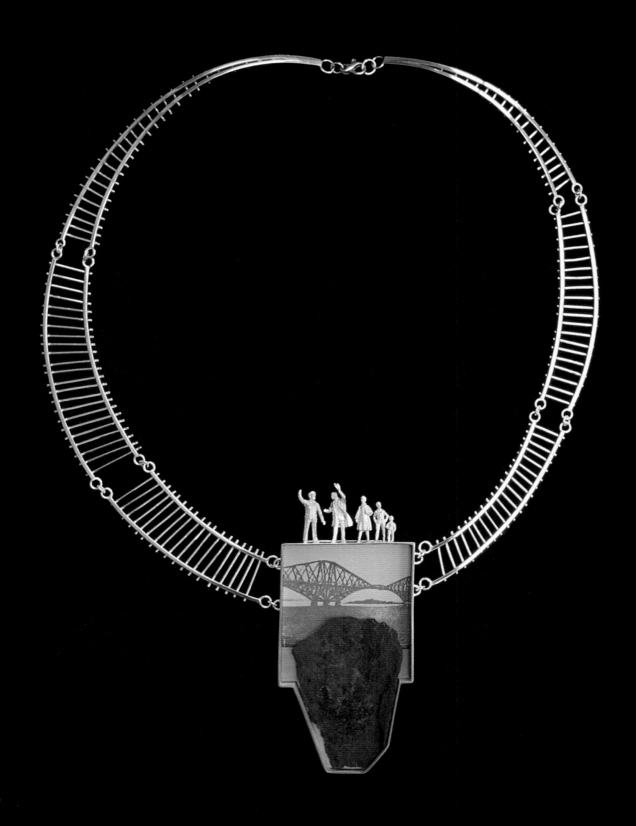

The Staff
at
6th January 1995

Joe	Adams	Product Design
Sam	Ainsley	Master of Fine Art
Ian	Alexander	Architecture
Martin	Allan	Printed & Knitted Textiles
Elise	Allan	Saturday morning
Jane	Allan	Historical & Critical Studies
Alistair	Allport	Graphic Design
Galia	Amsel	Ceramics
Paul	Anderson	Product Design
Robert	Anderson	Library
Alice	Angus	Fine Art
Julie	Annan	Architecture
Ann	Armstrong	Saturday morning Classes
Bruce	Ashwood	Sculpture
Barry	Atherton	First Year Studies
Kerry	Aylin	Graphic Design
Mark	Baines	Architecture
Tony	Barber	Architecture
Helen	Barrett	Environmental Art
Gerry	Barrett	Architecture
Christine	Bates	Secretary
Ronda	Bayley	Graphic Design
Rosemary	Beaton	Painting
Jimmie	Beattie	Embroidered & Woven Textiles
Peter	Beharrell	Historical & Critical Studies
Leslie	Bell	Secretary
Irene	Bell	First Year Studies
David	Bellingham	Photography
Tony	Benn	Painting
Andrew	Bennett	Interior Design
Pete	Bevan	First Year Studies
Jim	Birrell	Painting
George	Birrell	Evening School
Fred	Birse	Product Design
Sean	Black	Printed & Knitted Textiles
John	Blair	Buildings Officer
Alison	Blamire	Architecture
Douglas	Blaney	Finance Office
Richard	Bogan	Audio Visual
Christine	Borland	Sculpture
Cliff	Bowen	Sculpture
Raymond	Boyle	Evening School
Ann	Broadley	Telephonist
William	Brown	Ceramics

Opposite:
Jack Cunningham,
Necklace, 1995 'Rust to Rust'
silver, anodised aluminium,
rusting steel (found object, Forth Bridge)

Irene	Bruce	Finance Office
Moira	Buchanan	First Year Studies
Pavel	Büchler	Head of Fine Art
Alan	Bullas	Photography
David	Buri	Library
Andy	Burke	Product Design Engineering
John	Calcutt	Historical & Critical Studies
John	Calderwood	Ceramics
Dugald	Cameron	Director
Elaine	Campbell	Evening School
Chrisanna	Campbell	Registry
Clare	Cannon	Secretary
Gillian	Carson	First Year Studies
Vivian	Carvalho	Architecture
Jonathan	Cassels	Printmaking
Kathy	Chambers	Exhibitions Co-ordinator
Paul	Clarke	Architecture
Richard	Clarke	Evening School
David	Cochrane	Maintenance
Margaret	Collier	Library
Cathy	Collins	Cleaner
Ashley	Cook	Printmaking
Janice	Cook	Saturday morning Classes
Margaret	Cook	Finance Office
Thomas	Joshua Cooper	Photography
George	Coote	First Year Studies
Paul	Cosgrove	Sculpture
Jimmy	Cosgrove	Deputy Director
Colin	Cowan	Registry
Jacqi	Coyle	Architecture
John	Creed	Silversmithing & Jewellery
Jack	Cunningham	Silversmithing & Jewellery
David	Currie	Embroidered & Woven Textiles
Neil	Dallas Brown	Painting
Tom	Dick	Janitor
Jim	Docherty	Finance Office
Patrick	Dorrian	Evening School
Jack	Dowling	Head Janitor
George	Duff	Sculpture
Maggie	Duff	Library
Jennifer	Dunlop	Photography
Suzanne	Dunscombe	Architecture
Sandra	Falconer	Secretary
David	Falconer	Depute Head Janitor
Ray	Farrell	Head Cleaner
Ann	Ferguson	Printed & Knitted Textiles
Fiona	Ferrie	Finance Office
Ricky	Fildes	Finance Office
Mike	Foley	Assistant Director (Resources)
Cathy	Gale	Graphic Design
Kerry	Gallagher	Interior Design
Jo	Ganter	Printmaking
Julian	Gibb	Design

Kirsty	Gibbs	Evening School
Helen	Gibson	Printmaking
Mark	Gilbert	Evening School
Neil	Gillespie	Architecture
Sharon	Gillespie	Finance Office
Ian	Girdwood	Product Design Engineering
Douglas	Gordon	Master of Fine Art
Mike	Graham	Graphic Design
Ann Clare	Graham	Evening School
Linda	Green	First Year Studies
Stuart	Greig	Night Watchman
Inez	Grierson	Saturday morning
Ian	Grout	Product Design
Charles	Hackett	Printed & Knitted Textiles
Jill	Hammond	Welfare Officer
Dr. Raid	Hanna	Architecture
Jim	Hardie	Painting
David	Harding	Environmental Art
Alison	Harley	First Year Studies
Jim	Harold	Sculpture
Glenn	Harvie	Architecture
Michael	Healey	Head of Design
Chris	Hermansen	Architecture
Ming	Ho	Architecture
Carol	Hodge	Saturday morning
Deborah	Holland	Evening School
Carol	Holmes	Library
John	Holms	Painting
Louise	Hopkins	Adult Day
Jane	Hopkinson	Historical & Critical Studies
Robin	Hume	First Year Studies
Charlie	Hussey	Architecture
Kate	Hutcheson	Archivist
Margo	Jackson	Finance Office
Ian	Johnston	First Year Studies
Frank	Johnston	Janitor
Vaughen	Judge	Photography
Eilidh	Keith	Evening School
Brian	Kelly	First Year Studies
Michael	Kelly	Maintenance
William	Kennedy	First Year Studies
Paul	Keogh	Architecture
Harry	Kerr	Fine Art Photography
Pheona	Kerr	Saturday morning Classes
Louise	Kilmartin	Architecture
Juliet	Kinchin	Historical & Critical Studies
Norman	Kirkham	Adult Day
Janice	Kirkpatrick	Product Design
Jim	Lambert	Master of Fine Art
Craig	Laurie	Architecture
James	Lawson	Architecture
Susan	Lawson	Library
Ivor	Laycock	Printed & Knitted Textiles

Marcus	Lee	Architecture
John	Ligget	Janitor
Alex	Lindsay	Janitor
Alf	Löhr	Environmental Art
Robin	Lorimer	Architecture
Dr. James	Macaulay	Architecture
Willie	MacBeth	Product Design
Charles	MacCallum	Architecture
Alastair	Macdonald	Product Design Engineering
Karen	MacDonald	Evening School
Neil	MacDonald	Adult Day
Colin	MacFarlane	Evening School
Jock	MacInnes	First Year Studies
Maria	MacKellar	Embroidered & Woven Textiles
Maureen	MacKenzie	Adult Day
Stuart	Mackenzie	Painting
Andy	MacMillan	Architecture
Margaret	MacPhail	Embroidered & Woven Textiles
Ken	Macrae	Architecture
Archie	Macrae	Maintenance
Clare	Magnus	Secretary
Jackie	Main	Registry
Mick	Manning	Graphic Design
Helen	Marriott	Silversmithing & Jewellery
Gerry	Mather	Architecture
Jen	Mavor	Architecture
Joe	McAvoy	Evening School
Archie	McCall	Ceramics
Ann	McCormack	Secretary
George	McCreadie	Janitor
Laura	McFarlane	Historical & Critical Studies
Dawnne	McGeachy	Evening School
Graham	McGill	Janitor
Sean	McGlashan	Saturday morning Classes
Peter	McGuiness	First Year Studies
Jim	McInally	Janitor
Ray	McKenzie	Historical & Critical Studies
Henry	McKeown	Architecture
Jane	McLaren	Printed & Knitted Textiles
David	McLaren	Saturday morning Classes
Lyn	McLaughlin	Audio Visual
David	McMillan	Architecture
Norman	McNally	Product Design Engineering
Lynne	McTavish	Secretary
Isi	Metzstein	Architecture
Roger	Millar	Silversmithing & Jewellery
Ken	Mitchell	First Year Studies
Alexander	Moffat	Painting
Kathy	Molloy	Library
Adele	Molony	Library
Jeff	Mongrain	Continuing Education
Ian	Monie	Library
Elaine	Monteith	Library

Catherine	Mooney	Evening School
Neil	Morrison	First Year Studies
Steve	Mulrine	Historical & Critical Studies
Madelyn	Mulrooney	Secretary
Nigel	Munro	Silversmithing & Jewellery
Elizabeth	Munro	Printed & Knitted Textiles
Bill	Murdoch	Architecture
Ann	Murray	Secretary
Jimmie	Murray	Graphic Design
Ian	Murray	Registry
Anthony	Neeson	Saturday morning Classes
Linda	Neeson	Saturday morning.Classes
Billy	Neilson	Architecture
Arlene	Newman	Finance Office
Valerie	Nicolson	Secretary
Jennifer	Nisbet	Secretary
Douglas	Niven	Architecture
Julia	Nouillan	Registry
Stephen	O'Donnell	Evening School
Katherine	O'Higgins	Saturday morning
Lynne	O'Neil	Product Design Engineering
Nicholas	Oddy	Historical & Critical Studies
Bernadette	Ovens	Finance Office
Alexander	Page	Architecture
Roger	Palmer	Fine Art
William	Pandelus	Maintenance
Jacki	Parry	Printmaking
Carol	Paterson	Printed & Knitted Textiles
Adele	Patrick	Historical & Critical Studies
Robert	Paul	Printmaking
Sally	Payne	Embroidered & Woven Textiles
Colin	Pettigrew	Printmaking
Ian	Pickering	Architecture
Chris	Platt	Architecture
Drew	Plunkett	Interior Design
Jean	Pollock	Director's Secretary
Colin	Porteous	Architecture
John	Porter	Architecture
Alan	Prue	Ceramics
Barbara	Rae	Painting
Ian	Ramsay	Saturday morning Classes
George	Rawson	Library
Peter	Reeve	Fine Art
Helen	Richards	Saturday morning Classes
Craig	Richardson	Painting
Julia	Roberts	Painting
Jimmy	Robertson	Painting
Graeme	Robertson	Architecture
Nina	Robertson	Saturday morning Classes
Michael	Roschlau	Printmaking
Fraser	Ross	Graphic Design
Gordon	Ross	Product Design
Wendy	Ross	Secretary

Gillian	Saffrey	Buildings Secretary
Charles	Sandison	Fine Art
Pam	Schenk	School of Core Studies
Jeanette	Scott	Design Secretary
John	Shankie	Fine Art
Dr. Tim	Sharpe	Architecture
Bob	Shaw	Partnership in Practice
Eddie	Shepherd	Maintenance
Derek	Simpson	Architecture
Paul	Simpson	Architecture
Dan	Smith	First Year Studies
Fred	Smith	Architecture
Robert	Smith	Janitor
George	Souter	Janitor
Ann	Spence	Evening School
Gavin	Stamp	Architecture
Andy	Stark	Graphic Design
David	Stark	Maintenance
Catherine	Stevenson	Administrator (Architecture)
Eddie	Stewart	Painting
Janet	Stewart	Cleaner
Sally	Stewart	Architecture
Andrew	Stewart	Saturday morning Classes
Deanne	Stewart	Saturday morning Classes
Ruth	Stirling	Environmental Art
Robert	Strong	Architecture
Pete	Sumsion	First Year Studies
Nikki	Sweeney	Saturday morning Classes
George	Taggart	Evening School
Lindsay	Taylor	Printed & Knitted Textiles
Malcolm	Thwaite	Historical & Critical Studies
John	Tomlinson	Graphic Design
Peter	Trowles	Curator
William	Turnbull	Evening School
Wendy	Turner	Evening School
Ken	Wade	Graphic Design
Maria	Walsh	Secretary
Pete	Watson	Architecture
David	Watt	Printmaking
Crissie	White	Embroidered & Woven Textiles
Ulrike	Wilke	Architecture
John	Wilkins	Painting
Alexa	Wilson	Embroidered & Woven Textiles
Lana	Wilson	Finance Office
Bruce	Wood	Product Design Engineering
Brendan	Woods	Architecture
Sandy	Wright	Architecture
Robert	Wyatt	Adult Day

Class Reps

Susan	Kee	Product Design Engineering Year 1
Matthew	Young	Product Design Engineering Year 1
Gavin	Wright	Product Design Engineering Year 2
Susan	Lamont	Product Design Engineering Year 2
Rosie	Habeshaw	Product Design Engineering Year 3
Michael	Anusas	Product Design Engineering Year 3
Gordon	Hay	Product Design Engineering Year 4
Aileen	Moar	Product Design Engineering Year 4
Craig	Glass	Product Design Year 1
Gregor	Donaldson	Product Design Year 2
Dave	Stovell	Product Design Year 3
Neil	Jardine	Product Design Year 3
Sally	Barton	Product Design Year 4
Louise	Nolan	Ceramics Year 2
Abigail	Black	Ceramics Year 3
Aileen	Neillie	Ceramics Year 4
Claire	Biggs	Interior Design Year 2
Gina	Leith	Interior Design Year 3
Despina	Samara	Interior Design Year 4
Joanna	Levy	Graphic Design Year 2
David	Freer	Graphic Design Year 2
Gaile	Lawlor	Graphic Design Year 3
Debbie	Grice	Graphic Design Year 3
Anne	Hanlon	Graphic Design Year 3
Denise	Baggett	Graphic Design Year 4
Morag	Ekanger	Graphic Photography Year 3
Brian	Hartley	Illustration Year 4
Rebecca	Brown	Embroidered & Woven Textiles Year 2
Miranda	Bradshaw	Embroidered & Woven Textiles Year 2
Katherine	Rae	Embroidered & Woven Textiles Year 3
Melanie	Fowler	Embroidered & Woven Textiles Year 3
Anita	Williamson	Embroidered & Woven Textiles Year 4
Shona	Robinson	Embroidered & Woven Textiles Year 4
Doreen	Gittens	Master of Design
Elaine	Johnston	Printed & Knitted Textiles Year 2
Vanessa	Ball	Printed & Knitted Textiles Year 2
Jenny	Kerwood	Printed & Knitted Textiles Year 3

Frank	Connelly	Printed & Knitted Textiles Year 3
Craig	Jones	Printed & Knitted Textiles Year 4
Frances	McGarrity	Printed & Knitted Textiles Year 4
Patrick	Wilson	Architecture Year 1
Katharyn	Fleisher	Architecture Year 1
Sithabile	Mathe	Architecture Year 2
Craig	Anderson	Architecture Year 2
Tamsen	Mitchell	Architecture Year 3
Chris	Burton	Architecture Year 3
Jamie	Lyndsay	Architecture Year 4
Chris	Milne	Architecture Year 4
Rhona	Morrison	Architecture Year 5
Collette	Burns	Architecture Year 5
Charlotte	Bonini	Architecture Post Grad
Mustafa	Mezughi	Architecture Post Grad
Joanne	Haddock	Environmental Art Year 2
Simon	Polli	Environmental Art Year 2
Deba	Salin	Environmental Art Year 3
Iain	Drummond	Environmental Art Year 3
Zoe	Gadsby	Environmental Art Year 4
Claire	Halleran	Environmental Art Year 4
Ian	Cook	Painting Year 2
Daisy	Richardson	Painting Year 2
Helene	Bohler	Painting Year 3
Paul	Johnstone	Painting Year 3
Ian	Dickinson	Painting Year 4
Katie	Ward	Painting Year 4
Louise	Lockwood	Photography Year 2
Jake	McKinney	Photography Year 2
Paul	Nulty	Photography Year 3
Nina	Larsen	Photography Year 3
Dominie	Clarke	Photography Year 4
David	Cowling	Photography Year 4
Owen	Boyle	Printmaking Year 2
Andrew	Patterson	Printmaking Year 2
Liz	Dew	Printmaking Year 3
Renee	Tibbets	Printmaking Year 3
Pam	Burleigh	Printmaking Year 4
Chris	Barrowman	Printmaking Year 4
Jan	McKechnie	Sculpture Year 2
Dan	Norton	Sculpture Year 3

Aoise	Farren	Sculpture Year 4
Shauna	McMullan	Master of Fine Art Year 1
Angus	Miller	Master of Fine Art Year 1
Jill	Logeteta	Master of Fine Art Year 2
Colin	Stephenson	Master of Fine Art Year 2
Heather	MacDonald	Silversmithing & Jewellery Year 2
Deborah	Rea	Silversmithing & Jewellery Year 2
Linda	Carlin	Silversmithing & Jewellery Year 3
Sarah	Cousar	Silversmithing & Jewellery Year 3
Lisa	Govan	Silversmithing & Jewellery Year 4
Marlene	McKinnie	Silversmithing & Jewellery Year 4
Pia	Conegliano	Environmental Art Year 1
Lucy	Giles	Painting Year 1
Marianne	Greated	Painting Year 1
Mark	Robb	Photography Year 1
William	Rogan	Printmaking Year 1
Craig	Glass	Product Design Year 1
Sonya	Hogg	Silversmithing & Jewellery Year 1
Claire	Gibney	Printed & Knitted Textiles Year 1
Jennifer	Caine	Embroidered & Woven Textiles Year 1
Soni	Alcorn-Hender	Illustration Year 1
Grant	McCaig	Silversmithing & Jewellery Year 1
John	Gigli	Interior Design Year 1
Graeme	Dunnet	Graphic Design Year 1
Sarah	McAleer	Design Course Committee Year 3
Linda	Carlin	Design CourseCommittee Year 3
Lisa	Govan	Design Course Committee Year 4
Marlene	McKinnie	Design Course Committee Year 4
Valerie	Mogan	Design Course Committee Year 2
Mairghread	McLundie	Design CourseCommittee Year 2

Student Council

Robert	Grieve	President
Mia	Messinger	Entertainments Officer
Claire	Clifford	Secretary
Claire	Halleran	Environmental Art Year 4
Iain	Drummond	Environmental Art Year 3
Deba Anna	Salim	Environmental Art Year 3
Simon	Polli	Environmental Art Year 2
Zoe	Gadsby	Environmental Art Year 4
Diane	Sutherland	Silversmithing & Jewellery Year 1
Thomas	Westwood	Architecture Year 2
Mark	Phip	Architecture Year 2
Daniel	Cox	Architecture Year 1
Ian Richard	Cook	Painting Year 2
Daisy	Richardson	Painting Year 2
Helene C	Bohler	Painting Year 3
Jack	Hewart	Ceramics Year 4
Aileen	Neillie	Ceramics Year 4
Anne	Hanlon	Graphic Design Year 3
Deborah	Grice	Graphic Design Year 3
Brian	Hartley	Graphic Design Year 4
David	Freer	Graphic Design Year 2
Denise	Baggett	Graphic Design Year 4
Gaile	Lawlor	Graphic Design Year 3
Michael	McKenna	Printed & Knitted Textiles Year 1
Katherine	Moullin	Printed & Knitted Textiles Year 2
Nicola	Taylor	Product Design Year 1
Jennifer	Gaine	Embroidered & Woven Textiles Year 1
Victoria	Jones	Embroidered & Woven Textiles Year 1
Despina	Samara	Interior Design Year 4
Tassy	Thompson	Sculpture Year 3

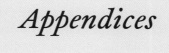

Appendices

APPENDIX A
THE FOULIS ACADEMY
by Robert Brydall in ART IN SCOTLAND (1889)

IN THE SUMMER of 1753 the brothers Robert and Andrew Foulis inaugurated an academy for the study of the Fine Arts, partly in connection with
their business as printers and booksellers... Their father was a maltman named
Faulls, and apprenticed his son Robert to a barber, in which humble capacity
he attracted the attention of Dr Francis Hutchison, Professor of Moral
Philosophy in Glasgow University, and who is supposed to have first suggested
to Robert the idea of starting business as a bookseller and printer. As a higher
education was then more necessary than now for such a business, he attended
some of the classes in the university, although not carrying on his studies so
far as Andrew did, and who for several years taught Greek, Latin, and French.
In furtherance of their object, after visiting the famous collection of books at
Oxford, the brothers went to Paris in 1738.

In the following year they again visited Paris, spending much time in the
public libraries, again collecting a number of Greek and Roman classics,
which they sold in London at a profit. In 1741, Robert began business in
Glasgow as a printer, and in 1742 there appeared the first issues from the press
of the two brothers, followed by their numerous magnificent specimens of
typography, which would almost induce us to believe that printing is one of
the lost arts.

Their academy, which was inaugurated in 1754 was opened in the following
year, in the old University in High Street, the Faculty Hall having been granted the Foulises for exhibition purposes, besides several other apartments for
the use of the students. An incomplete and undated letter of Robert's, in Lord
Buchan's MSS, shows that the projection of the academy was neither a sudden
nor ill-digested scheme. "In the years 1738 and 1739", he writes, "having gone
abroad and resided for several months at each time at Paris, we had frequent
opportunities of conversing with gentlemen of every liberal profession, and to
observe the connection and mutual influence of the arts and sciences upon one
another, and in drawing and modelling on many manufacturers. And 'tis
obvious that whatever nation has the lead in fashion, must previously have
invention in drawing diffused, otherwise they can never rise above copying
their neighbours".

The idea of an art academy such as they contemplated, was from the first by
many people considered a quixotic one, and some of their friends endeavoured
to dissuade them from the enterprise... To quote Robert Foulis's own words,
"There seemed to be a pretty general emulation who should run the scheme
most down." The academy was thus started in the face of very considerable difficulty, as there was little definite and almost no immediate income with which
to meet a not inconsiderable expenditure...

The students wrought in the academy daily at painting, engraving and
making designs from ancient authors for illustrative purposes. On three
evenings in the week they drew from the living model, and on the other three
from the antique, modelling also being practised. While thus employed, the

students who were apprentices received such wages as they might have earned had they followed a more mechanical employment, in addition to which, the great inducement was held out, that such as showed sufficient indications of genius would be sent abroad to study at the expense of the academy.

In the year 1761 an exhibition was held in the open air, in the inner court of the college... The occasion was the coronation of George III, and David Allan, who was then working in the academy, has left a view of the exhibition, in which a copy of Rubens's 'Daniel in the Den of Lions' appears in a lofty and prominent place, literally skied on the wall of the church tower, behind which rises the smoke of a bonfire; the same artist also executed a view of the interior of the academy, of considerable interest...

APPENDIX B

Letter to Lord Meadowbank and the Board of the Trustees' Academy, Edinburgh, by William Dyce and Charles Heath Wilson, 1837

...Unfortunately, the artisans and manufacturers of the country have, for obvious reasons, been unable to keep pace, except to a limited extent, with the advancing taste of the wealthier and more refined classes of the community; and their inability is attended with the most serious results to the manufacturing and commercial interests of the country. Either, on the one hand, the broker and dealer in old furniture usurp the place of the artisan and manufacturer; or, on the other, the imported productions of the Continent, executed under advantages at present unattainable at home, have, from their superior beauty in respect of design, to a great extent injured the sale of the same descriptions of British goods.

The admission of this fact by manufacturers and the heads of commercial houses, which has been most unequivocally made, in evidence before a committee of the House of Commons, we consider as most vitally important, in a country like Great Britain, to the interests of art, and the dissemination of taste. The progress of the principles of fine art can now no longer be looked upon as a matter of individual and private concern. The commercial prosperity of a nation, whose greatness and wealth is dependent on its commerce, has been shewn, by a reason which brought home to the most uncultivated capacity, to be most materially affected by a deficiency in taste...

When we know the great pains taken by foreign governments to afford the fullest advantages to their artisans and manufacturers in the application of art and taste to every department of industry, it ceases to be a matter of surprise that they are so much in advance of us. It is rather to be wondered that we are able to keep pace with them so well as we do.

In France, according to Dr Bowring, there are no fewer than eighty schools of art, expressly for the purpose of teaching the principles of design to manufacturers. "The origin," says he, "of these schools is to be traced to a conviction that the application of the principles of art and science to manufacture, is the best means of improving that manufacture; and there has been a succession of legislative measures, some of them general, some municipal and local, by which these schools of art have been adapted to the wants of peculiar branches of industry..."

APPENDIX C

THE TRAINING OF ARCHITECTURE STUDENTS
Extract from Newbery's Lecture to the Glasgow Philosophical Society (1887)

NAPOLEON is credited with the dictum, "Every soldier carries the bâton of a marshal in his knapsack." He, however, did not wait for the event, but worked for it. The drudgery of marching and counter-marching, and sleeping with the guns, had to be gone through, and gone through in earnest, before the bâton of the marshal was placed in his hands. But he knew its powers, and wielded them the better in the ordering of battalions and the placing of men, for that he had at one time carried the knapsack which figuratively held it. So the architect may command the dull stones of the earth to arrange themselves in ordered masses, and make beauty to live in undying splendour on our walls; may by his proportions lead the thoughts, and by his colours tinge the imagination, of worshippers in a temple, of the earth earthly, so that they may catch a spiritual glimpse of a building not made with hands, and all this by a knowledge and use of powers of the bâton he wields - a piece of pencil.

Now, you can arm a soldier, but you cannot make him fight. You can however show him how, and the providing him with arms is an absolutely indispensable part of this latter proceeding. An architect unable to draw, not with mathematical instruments, which I do not consider the true architect's properties, but with a pencil, is like a soldier starting to battle without the previous provision of offensive and defensive armour. Both are useless for real work...

APPENDIX D

CHARLES RENNIE MACKINTOSH
Extract from an article by D P Bliss in SCOTTISH FIELD 1947

MACKINTOSH WAS NOT A MERE INNOVATOR, a revolutionary, as many must have thought half a century ago: but a traditionalist, as much a traditionalist as his very successful contemporary Sir Robert Lorimer. He seems, said Sir Frank Mears:

> *... To give expression in this building to some inherent quality which distinguishes Scottish art and craftsmanship from that of other countries. Perhaps it is that quality of tallness combined with stability which one finds not only in our old buildings and carved stones but in the clipper ships and great liners of the River Clyde. There is in this building, rising austerely in a cliff-like mass above the froth of Sauchiehall Street, a real affinity with the north face of Linlithgow Palace, or the castles of Hermitage, Borthwick or Huntly...*

This Gothic or Scots Baronial element in Mackintosh's work is in marked difference from its appearances elsewhere, even in the works of Lorimer. For Charles Rennie Mackintosh did not imitate "the styles". It may be said that while both Lorimer and Mackintosh were inspired by the old Scots tradition in building, Lorimer, the pupil of Rowand Anderson, followed it in the letter, and Mackintosh in the spirit.

Mackintosh was not content to build the shell of his structure and to leave the interior furnishing to other minds and hands. In all his buildings (his dwelling-houses, tea-shops, etc) he designed every detail, every piece of furniture, every fitment, every carpet, hat-rack, knife, fork, and spoon, everything down to the last detail. Everything was considered in relation to its setting and in fulfilment of its function. Everything was considered as a unit in a scheme. His fertility of invention was astonishing. Ideas poured from his pencil. He turned all materials to his purpose. A brilliant draughtsman, he proliferated designs which were translated (not always easily) into materials by craftsmen working under his supervision.

Mackintosh's reputation has suffered from his association with Art Nouveau. Actually he was never guilty of the wilder absurdities of the continental phase. There was a taut, vertical quality in all his design which never quite gave way. But his place in history will certainly be that of a master of transition. He bridges the gulf between the art and crafts of Morris and his friends, and the functionalism of Gropius and Le Corbusier. Compared with the English art and craftsmen and the Scottish disciples of Rowand Anderson, he was a functionalist pur sang. Compared with Gropius and the Bauhaus men his work is "literary". He stood at the cross-roads. He belonged to his time and place, but he was a precursor. Like his English counterpart, the late C F A Voysey, he steadily pointed into the future...

APPENDIX E

THE ART STUDENT IN GLASGOW
Extract from an article in "Quiz", August 1893

... She may be an Ayrshire girl, a Dunbartonshire, or a Renfrewshire, but a "term" in Glasgow transforms her into an Art Student.

She begins her career under the wing of "one of Mama's old friends", but in less than a month decides that it is "too far" and forthwith moves into an attic with a concealed bed...

The six-by-four apartment compares unfavourably with her former cosy quarters; but, with a triumphant smile, she dreams of the future, when, her fame on every tongue, people will come to gaze with awe on the four walls that now enclose her...

All this time she is studying Art - and many other branches - at the school.

"You must never work when not in the mood for it," is an unwritten law among students; and as moments of inspiration are scarce, when one is drawing skinny-looking hands and feet, there is time for intellectual conversations regarding religion, politics, and the merits of the respective teachers. It is usually the fault of teachers that pupils in the preparatory are not in the life classes - and our student recalls with regret how talented she was considered at Helensburgh, and wonders how it is that Glasgow is said to be the Art Centre of Scotland. It is a great satisfaction to attend the exhibitions and to criticise the work of her master; and so well does her art "patter" impose on the credulous public, that the managing directors of our Art Galleries are considering the expediency of closing their doors on her and her fellow students, claiming that they spoil the sale of pictures...

Appendix F

THE LADY ART STUDENT

by Harry Furniss (1905)

IN OUR GRANDMOTHERS' TIMES nearly every educated young lady was a student of art. A sort of society conscription existed, by which every lady in her 'teens had to draw, paint, model (in wax), work pictures with the needle, or perish in the attempt; in the same way as they were taught to strum on the piano, whether they had any soul for music or not. Whether these extras were due to the exigencies of the management of the ladies' school, or to the erroneous impression in the minds of early Victorian parents that fine art and music could be as easily taught as dancing and deportment, I cannot say. I only know that we of the present generation do not have to suffer, as the last generation had, by having atrocities inflicted on eye and ear; and being compelled to listen to the inharmonious sounds of the piano or look at the vile contortions, supposed to be the human form divine, mounted and framed on the walls of the drawing-room. Nowadays, when special lessons are given to those who have special abilities, the art student is practically a specialist, and occupies her proper sphere...

Now that the amateur in art has, practically, been brushed on one side, the art students before us are genuine students. As a result we find on the walls of the Royal Academy at Burlington House, pictures by women, as clever as those by men; while below, in the schools, we find women students as clever as men, and far more of them - there's the rub! The narrow clique of narrow-minded artists who govern the Academy, have discovered that women students are quicker and more clever than men, and they have set to work, in every way possible, to drive the female students out of the Academy, by a petty government of tyranny and stupidity that could not be rivalled outside of Russia. There is, however, something to be said in extenuation of the unfair treatment lady students receive; women are supposed not to have the staying power possessed by men. They develop their talent as quickly as do their brothers, they apply themselves to study with far more avidity, a greater proportion of them succeed as students; but, alas! they do not follow up. Once over the pons asinorum of their art they do not take to it with the seriousness of men students. In sporting phraseology the art race is a sealed handicap, and women have been too unfairly placed by judges to care to continue the struggle...

Art should be seriously encouraged among women; for women art students are, to a remarkable extent, more serious students than are the men. Those who, like myself, have been visitors to schools of art, from time to time, are struck with one extraordinary peculiarity that it would be impossible to find in any other occupation: men students - shy, retiring, almost nonentities in ordinary society, are, while at work, the very opposite. They sing solos, join in discordant choruses, throw chalk at each other, break stools, canvas and easels; in fact, turn their studios into pandemoniums. The lady students, on the contrary, are silent, attentive, serious to a painful degree, and the lady art student who, out of the studio may be lively and even self-assertive, is, in the studio, as quiet as a Quakers' meeting...

The red-letter day in the life of the lady art student is when the fond and proud parents sacrifice a slice of their garden on which to erect a studio for the daughter of the house. Here one can see depicted the taste and bent of the student, by the Liberty vases and hangings, the empty ginger jars, Japanese fans, soiled costumes and clean canvases. For the first six months or so, the model knocks regularly at her door, the parents have sat for their portraits, and the cat has been painted, and, if time allows, the cook also. Then comes the first serious commission, perhaps a portrait to be painted in the country. The young lady artist fondly imagines she will return to her studio in a month's time, but the portrait takes longer than she anticipated. There are so many entertainments at the house, picnics, croquet tournaments, and golf, and when the time comes round for the artist to send the portrait to the Academy, she is too busy in arranging her trousseau. For her visit to the country has ended in a commission which has to be ratified in Church, and the studio in the garden is now 'to let'. In short, marriage is the stumbling-block in the successful career, as the Academy knows...

Appendix G

THE ART STUDENT TODAY
Extract from an article by D P Bliss, SCOTTISH FIELD, November 1947

THE ART STUDENT of today is a different man or woman from his pre-war counterpart. This is not at all surprising - after a war and during a crisis. Many students at universities, technical colleges, school of art, music, etc., are resuming their studies after an interval of five or six years. During this time they have brooded quite a lot over the future that faces them and have found this meditation a sobering process. They feel, as the poet says, "chilly and grown old." They have returned to their studies obsessed with the idea of time. To adapt Marvell's lines:

> *Always at their backs they hear*
> *Time's winged chariot hurrying near*
> *And yonder all before them lie*
> *Deserts of vast eternity...*

No need to tell these not so young ex-service students to work and not to waste time. Alas, if anything they now work too hard. Moreover the other students, those fresh from school, take their cue from the older persons, their natural leaders...

The pre-war student (if he had found his vocation) worked hard enough; but he also played hard. He was freer to come and go. He was usually poor but he paid his own way. Nowadays, however, the student nearly always has a bursary or grant of some sort - very few students pay their own way - and, having entered into a bargain with the donors, he honours it by working to the top of his bent. Besides, the way out is not so easy to him as of yore. What used to be an escalator is now a ladder...

In the spacious days before the war much time was spent on revelry. More students had their evening meals in the School Refectory and met together in their Common Room of an evening. Social life had a real intensity and much time and ingenuity was devoted to societies, dramatic, cinematic, and athletic; and to dances...

And of these dances the most important was the Christmas Ball. This costly and elaborate affair pretty well stopped the work of the School for three weeks at the end of every Autumn term. Elaborate decor and recherché costumes were demanded. Food was plentiful and cheap. And the Annual Ball was a great event. Everyone wanted to be there; it was a social occasion. Only too often the very students found themselves excluded, so great was the demand for tickets...

This intense social life is over - at least for the time being. It will revive, but there are as yet few signs of a lusty revival. The students are encouraged to make what use they like of the many advantages at the School for developing an intense social and cultural life of their own. But the impulse must come from within. They themselves must provide the primum mobile.

The old-time Scottish problem of how to live while one is a student is made much easier by generous authorities; but there remains in even more acute form the problem of how to live afterwards. The critical years are the first five after the student leaves the college. In the old days students were less security-minded - they cared less if they got Diplomas or not - they let the future look after itself and went on their Bohemian ways unreflecting. Not so now - with two world wars and the depression of the years between, young people of the Clyde Valley are born to a serious view of life; and Bohemianism is undiscernible at Renfrew Street.

As I believe that the School of Art can and should provide not merely a narrow and technical but a truly liberal education, I am sorry to see students Martha-like and burdened with cares. I should like to see them read more, dispute more, listen more to music, dance more, dress absurdly and enjoy themselves to the full.

We have more students now than ever in the School's history and some of them are very promising. It is a wonderful thing to see how they grapple with their work and how they stride on from stage to stage. I think we are at the beginnings of a tremendous development in the visual arts in Scotland and I feel confident that some of the students with us today will be in the van of the new movement before many years have elapsed...

Acknowledgements

We should like to express our gratitude to the following: Maureen Murray, Jean Pollock
and Maria Walsh for typing the author's manuscript; Kerry Aylin for her book design and computer
expertise and to Lavinia Drew of Scaramouche Promotions Ltd.; Steve Mulrine for all editorial work on the
manuscript; Peter Trowles for help with the illustrative material
To all listed below for the photographs and other illustrations:

T & R Annan & Sons, Glasgow. Scottish National Portrait Gallery. Glasgow Museums & Art Galleries.
The Mitchell Library, Glasgow City Libraries. The Board of Trustees of the Victoria & Albert Museum.
Derby Museums. The Trustees of the National Library of Scotland. Imperial War Museum, London.
The British Architectural Library, RIBA, London. Conway Library, Courtauld Institute of Art, London.
Daily Record, Glasgow. Glasgow School of Art. Dugald Cameron. Sally Hunter Fine Art.
Hugh C S Ferguson. Simon Paterson. Cyril Gerber Fine Art. Danny Ferguson's family.
University Archives, University of Glasgow. Mainstream Publishing. William Hardie Gallery.
Adrian Wiszniewski & The William Hardie Gallery. Ken Currie. Miss M B Brodie. Cordelia Oliver.
Norman McNally. James W Murray. Jimmy Cosgrove. National Maritime Museum, London. Scott Wood.
Lorraine Gilmour. National Gallery of Ireland. The Herald & Evening Times, Glasgow. RIAS Collection.,
Edinburgh. Scottish Record Office, Edinburgh. Angela Flowers Gallery. The Post Office. Jack Cunningham

Whilst every effort has been made to trace the source of all the photographs used in this book,
the publisher would welcome information on any omissions.